AF544691

SEVENTY FACES

Articles of Faith

Books by Norman Lamm

A HEDGE OF ROSES:
Jewish Insights into Marriage and Married Life (1966)

A TREASURY OF TRADITION
Co-edited with Walter S. Wurzburger (1967)

THE ROYAL REACH:
Discourses on the Jewish Tradition and the World Today (1970)

FAITH AND DOUBT:
Studies in Traditional Jewish Thought (1971)

"TORAH LISHMAH"
—Torah for Torah's Sake— in the Works of Rabbi Hayyim of Volozhin and his Contemporaries (Hebrew 1972; English 1989)

THE GOOD SOCIETY:
Jewish Ethics in Action (1974)

TORAH UMADDA:
The Encounter of Religious Learning and Worldly Knowledge in the Jewish Tradition (1990)

HALAKHOT VE'HALIKHOT
(Hebrew)—Jewish Law and the Legacy of Judaism: Essays and Inquiries in Jewish Law (1990)

THE SHEMA:
Spirituality and Law in Judaism (1998)

THE RELIGIOUS THOUGHT OF HASIDISM:
Text and Commentary (1999)

SEVENTY FACES
Articles of Faith (2001)

SEVENTY FACES

Articles of Faith

VOLUME II

BY

NORMAN LAMM

KTAV PUBLISHING HOUSE, INC.
HOBOKEN, NEW JERSEY

Lamm, Norman
Seventy Faces: Articles of Faith Volume 2.
p. cm.
ISBN 0-88125-769-9

Distributed by
Ktav Publishing House, Inc.
900 Jefferson Street
Hoboken, NJ 07030
201-963-9524 FAX 201-963-0102
Email orders@ktav.com
Web www.ktav.com

This book is dedicated to my grandchildren

Tova, Tamar, Ariela, Ahuva Penina
Yonatan, Daniel, Yehuda
Ari, Peninah, Shmuel, Bracha, Devorah
Tova, Bracha, Yael, Shmuel

and my students, too many to mention individually,
for they too are as my children and grandchildren

May the Almighty grant them long and full years in health
and happiness, to live creative lives of Torah and wisdom

I am pleased to acknowledge with gratitude

Debbie and Elliot Gibber

who have graciously sponsored publication of these volumes in memory of their revered father and father-in-law

CHARLES K. GOLDNER ז"ל
(1900–2001)

High principle and commitment to Torah and Israel have characterized his full life on earth and he has been a role model for his beloved children and grandchildren

OF MAKING BOOKS

"And furthermore, my son, be admonished: of making books there is no end"

—Ecclesiastes 12:12

A Hasidic interpretation: Why do people write books? Because they seek to achieve "no end," or immortality.

"By speech first, but far more by writing, and more again by printing, man has been able to put something of himself beyond death. In tradition and in books an integral part of the individual persists, and a part which still works and is active, for it can influence the minds and actions of other individuals in different places and at different times: a row of black marks on a page can move a man to tears, though the bones of him that wrote it are long ago crumbled to dust. In truth, the whole of the progress of civilization is based on this power."

—Julian Huxley, *The Individual in the Animal Kingdom*, 1912

Contents

Volume II

Chapter 6

HALAKHA: JEWISH LAW

Because we live in such tense times, particularly as concerned and committed Jews, the centrifugal tendencies in the community lead to a hardening of positions both within Orthodoxy and among those who stand outside the halakhic tradition. One of the results of this polarization is the erosion of authority in the latter and an equal and opposite reaction within the former. In Orthodoxy, we have witnessed an increase in the authority of spiritual leadership, far more than had been the case in previous years. An unhappy result of this phenomenon is an apparent weakening of creativity in the face of the tendency to accept rabbinical and halakhic authority unquestioningly. The first article in this chapter deals with this issue.

The next two articles deal with aspects of human rights, and the last three with specific items from the vantage of Halakha.

~ 25 ~

THE FUTURE OF CREATIVITY IN JEWISH LAW AND THOUGHT

Creativity requires, as a condition precedent, freedom—both internal and external, both political and spiritual. Where freedom does not prevail, creativity cannot flourish. Authoritarianism is inimical to creativity. At the same time, total freedom, in the sense of a complete absence of discipline, of restraint of any kind, is not an environment that is conducive to creativity. For instance, a sculptor must have the freedom and the right to express his personality, his ideas, his ideals, and his criticism in his art. But if there are no rules, no internal norms, no aesthetic standards which he accepts, no artistic tradition that is the context of his work even only to rebel against it, then there is neither creativity nor art.

True creativity means working out of freedom within certain restricting parameters, whether artistic, legal, moral, or spiritual. Therefore, with regard to Jewish creativity, I shall confine myself to the universe of those who voluntarily accept upon themselves the discipline and restraint of Torah and Halakha. I therefore do not accept such peculiar and misnamed phenomena as "creative services" as illustrations of creativity. They may be aesthetically innovative or pleasing but Jewishly creative they are not. By the same token, I do not accept as examples of halakhic creativity such spurious *heterim* as driving to shul on Shabbat, patrilinealism, "alternative sexual lifestyles"—all of which, incidentally, have been paraded before the public as halakhically justified and as examples of "courageous" halakhic creativity. Such is the latest grotesque "creative adaptation" of Halakha by unrepentant and publicly assertive homosexual Rabbis (or: pulpit pederasts).

What piqued my interest in creativity (in Hebrew: *chiddush*) is a perceived diminished Jewish creativity of the last two centuries, since that incomparable burst of spiritual energy which

---

Adapted from a lecture in June 1992 and published in the Memorial Volume on the Occasion of the Eleventh Yahrzeit of James H. Lehmann.

gave birth to the Hasidic and Musar movements. To see the picture properly, there has unquestionably been some very very fine creativity in Judaism during this period. A few examples: R. Chaim Brisker's revolutionary development of a new halakhic methodology which has conquered the Talmudic world ever since; Rabbi Samson Raphael Hirsch's *Torah Im Derech Eretz;* Rabbis Reines in Lithuania and Revel in America in fostering *Torah Umadda;* Rabbi Meir Shapiro, the founder of Yeshivas Chachmei Lublin, in his novel and creative idea of the *Daf Yomi.* We can go on and on. But somehow one feels that in 200 years more could and should have been done in a creative manner to bolster Torah and Judaism.

This relative aridity or lack of originality or at least sufficient originality was obviously an angry reaction against the 18th century Haskala—the Enlightenment and its attendant Reform movement which, in the name of creativity and the lust for change, wreaked havoc with the traditional Jewish world, religiously and communally. More fundamentally, this withdrawal from creativity was a kind of defensive response to modernity as such. The emerging prominence of the natural sciences along with the acceleration of technology brought with it a growing esteem for creativity and originality and, in many cases, led to the triumphalism of modernity. And with this arrogance of modernity comes the worship or apotheosis of change. There was thus a really legitimate fear that the entire corpus of Torah and the *Mesorah,* the tradition, is imperiled by the demand for change for its own sake—an attitude that underlies so much of modern consciousness.

Consider our contemporary cultural psychology. Our technological society is based on the need for change, the desire for the new. Every year we have to have a new toothpaste, a new-model car, a new kind of computer; even if it serves no valid purpose, it has to be new. At one time, a few years ago, we had moveable shields over the car's headlights. There was no reason for it, but it was new, and the technological imperative is really a quest for what is new. In the academic world, scientific grants and even PhD's in humanities are given for the creation of new ideas—only new ideas, not for remembering or celebrating what others created. We live in a society which worships the new, and not only the new, but the *newest.*

Interestingly, when we meet each other what is the first thing we say?—"How are you?" and "What's new?" Now that says something about all of us. "What's new?"—as if all that is old is passé, it is dated and no longer of interest to me. A great French thinker, Jacques Maritain, referred to this worship of modernity, of the newest, as "chronolatry"—the idolatry of the *chronos*, of time. This is something which is utterly nonsensical as well as dangerous. Someone once said that he who marries the spirit of the age will soon find himself a widower. In religion, the mindless pursuit of novelty, of fads, of the desire to be "with it," is poisonous. Not only does it ignore tradition and history but it despairs of the search for any enduring truth, something which lasts through all the changes and vicissitudes of life.

Trendiness makes for phoniness in religion. This chronolatry, what I like to call *neophilia* (*neo* from "new," *phil* from "love"—the love of the new) evokes an equal and opposite reaction, what might be called, *neophobia*—the fear of the new. With Reform and Haskala and secular Zionism and secularism in the last one or two hundred years championing the new and the revolutionary, we Orthodox naturally tended to the opposite direction—the rejection of all that is new, of all that is *chadash* or *chiddush*. As neophilia became the dogma of the non-religious, so we became neophobic.

From this vantage point, we can appreciate the famous slogan of the great Chatam Sofer, a couple of hundred years ago, which has become the war cry of Hungarian Orthodoxy, *chadash asur min ha-torah*, "All that is new is forbidden by the Torah." Indeed, both his slogan and his policy have dominated much of even non-Hungarian Orthodoxy in our times. However, this repudiation of *chiddush*, of the new and the creative, is limited only to *chiddush be'dat*, the attempt to change religion as Reform tried to change religion. It is not at all meant to reflect on the phenomenon of *chiddush* itself in Halakha because, after all, the Chatam Sofer himself became great not because he said *chadash asur min ha-torah*, but because he was a great *mechadesh*. He was very creative. And he was the one who had the credentials to say that creativity should be limited to *within* Halakha instead of *on* Halakha.

Let us step back for a moment and view our problem against the backdrop of Jewish history and Jewish thought. We begin with a policy against creativity and the insistence upon the preservation and transmission of halakhic knowledge exactly as one received it from his teacher. The protagonists here are two of the greatest names in Jewish history, R. Yochanan ben Zakkai who lived just about 1900 or 2000 years ago, and his great student R. Eliezer ben Hyrkanos, known as R. Eliezer Hagadol, "the great Rabbi Eliezer." We are told about the teacher, R. Yochanan ben Zakkai, that he never said anything that he had not received or heard from his teacher; his student, R. Eliezer ben Hyrkanos, carried on the same policy (*Sukkah* 21a). However, while R. Eliezer clearly is of this opinion, there is real doubt as to whether R. Yochanan ben Zakkai, the master, held this approach.

In the second chapter of *Pirkei Avot,* we read that R. Yochanan ben Zakkai had five great disciples. Two of them were R. Eliezer ben Hyrkanos and R. Elazar ben Arakh. R. Yochanan related his praise of each of his students. Of R. Eliezer ben Hyrkanos, he said that he was a cistern lined with lime which was waterproof so that it never lost a drop. And he praised R. Elazar ben Arakh as a surging well, always giving fresh water. That means that R. Elazar ben Hyrkanos rejected any kind of personal creative activity. He simply was a man who mastered the entire tradition that he received from his teacher in order to transmit it intact to the next generation.

Elazar ben Arakh, however, was the *maayan ha-mitgaber,* the well that always surges new, refreshing water.

A Tanna now tells us that R. Yochanan ben Zakkai, in comparing these two, said that if all of the sages of Israel were on one side of the balance and R. Eliezer ben Hyrkanos was on the other, he would outweigh all of them. According to this Tanna, R. Yochanan ben Zakkai favored carrying on the tradition as it is, without any kind of interference, over creativity.

But Aba Shaul, another Tanna, rejects this position and reverses it. R. Yochanan ben Zakkai said that if all the sages of Israel were on one side of the balance, including Eliezer ben Hyrkanos, and Elazar ben Arakh was on the other, the latter would outweigh them. Therefore, the greater virtue is creativity. So we now have two conflicting traditions in the name of R. Yochanan ben Zakkai. They are diametrically opposed: one favors the retentive memory and accurate transmission, and the other—creativity and originality.

Now this dilemma is compounded—perhaps clarified too—by a fascinating tale told in the famous *Pirkei De'Rav Eliezer*: R. Eliezer comes to visit Jerusalem. There he meets his teacher, R. Yochanan ben Zakkai. The latter is overjoyed to see his student and he says to him, "I'm inviting you to give the *derasha,* to say Torah." He declines to give the *sheiur.* He explains: After all, all my Torah I got from you; is it then appropriate for me to speak in front of you when you are the source of everything that I know and everything that I teach? The teacher would not be deterred and says to him, "You *can* do it." Listen to these words: "You can say Torah more than was given at Sinai." That's a *chiddush!* You may say that you're only a cistern that doesn't lose a drop, but I know that you are exceedingly creative. Get up and say something! R. Yochanan ben Zakkai not only encouraged his student, but he was also a very sensitive man. He knew that R. Eliezer was shy about teaching in the presence of his teacher, so he said to him: you get up and teach and I'll stand outside. And indeed, he got up, went out, stayed at the door of the *Beit Midrash.* The *Pirkei De'Rav Eliezer* reports the following: R. Eliezer sat and lectured. His face shone bright as the sun, and the rays that emanated from his face were as those which shone from the face of Moses. So brilliant was he, so glorious was his visage, that people couldn't tell if it was day or night. When he finished his *sheur,* R. Yochanan came from behind him and kissed him on his head, and said to him: Happy are you, Abraham, Isaac, and Jacob, that such a one issued from your loins. However, in the audience was Rabbi Eliezer's father, Hyrkanos, and he said: [R. Yochanan] should not have said that. Instead, he should have said, "Happy am I that I have such a son."

As far as R. Yochanan ben Zakkai is concerned, this passage clearly supports the Tanna (Abba Shaul) in *Pirkei Avot,* who said that R. Yochanan ben Zakkai favored creativity over simple retentiveness. Perhaps at one point both or either one may have changed his mind. The question is only this—whether R. Eliezer himself, possessed of such enormous creative powers, abandoned his previous conservative approach as a result of this experience, or whether he reverted to his previous idea despite what had happened. Frankly, I find it hard to believe that such a powerful and moving experience in the presence of his teacher and the reaction of both his teacher and his father left him unmoved and untouched.

My own feeling is that indeed during this period of the Tannaim there were two points of view, because that was the period when it was forbidden to write or to publish *Torah She'be'al Peh*. The Oral Law went by word of mouth from teacher to student, and therefore accuracy of transmission and absolutely perfect memory without any change was exceedingly important; otherwise, the whole tradition is corrupted. But after the days of R. Yehuda Hanasi, when it was permitted to write or to publish *Torah She'be'al Peh*, the natural Jewish tendency for creativity came to the fore and, indeed, creativity became a fact of life in the periods of the Amoraim, the Rishonim (the Medieval period), and the Acharonim down to our own day.

Three quick examples: R. Yehoshua of the Talmudic era—there is no such a thing as a school without something new, something creative, emerging from it (*Chagigah* 26). Torah Judaism without creativity is an oxymoron, a contradiction in terms.

The Middle Ages: R. Yehuda Hechasid of Ashkenazic Jewry—One to whom God revealed a new idea, which he considers a true idea, and he does not write it down and publish it even though he can, is in the category of one who, as it were, "steals from God." God gave him the idea not for himself alone, but to share it with his fellow Jews.

In the modern period: the Sephardic scholar, Chida (R. Chaim Yosef David Azoulai) writes: there is a time for every *chiddush* in Torah and therefore, even though we of the later generations are as naught compared to the earlier generations, nevertheless, God left it to us to exercise our own creativity and devise new interpretations.

We turn now to a period of Jewish history where, interestingly, the whole concept of *chiddush* is rediscussed. During the last couple of centuries, the Lithuanian Mitnagdim, the opponents of Hasidism, reopened the issue. Nowhere do we find outright opposition to *chiddush* in the manner attributed in the previous sources, that of R. Yochanan ben Zakkai and R. Eliezer ben Hyrkanos. But we do find amongst Lithuanian *gedolim*, giants of Halakha, a kind of suspiciousness towards creativity even in Halakha itself. Of course, these Lithuanian Mitnagdim were themselves masters of *chiddush*. But they were very circumspect about creativity overdone and originality overvalued.

For instance, the major ideologist of Mitnagdic Jewry and founder of the Yeshiva of Volozhin, R. Hayyim Volozhiner, was very wary about *chiddushim.* His son, R. Yitzchak, in the introduction to his father's *Nefesh Hachayim,* writes that every time R. Hayyim had a *chiddush,* whether in Talmud, Rishonim or *teshuvot,* he was afraid to enjoy it, because he always felt suspicious of himself: Maybe my attempt at being creative is not *la'amitah shel Torah,* part of the search for the truth of Torah. Maybe I'm just trying to be clever and brilliant instead of pursuing the truth. Therefore, he practiced a kind of intellectual masochism and tried to counteract his own arguments in order to make sure that he wasn't simply trying to be clever and original.

So we have here a kind of intellectual asceticism that arose out of a rigorous intellectual honesty. The Netziv (R. Naftali Zvi Yehuda Berlin), later the Rosh Yeshiva of Volozhin, took a similar stance. And the Chazon Ish (R. Abraham Isaiah Karelitz), a leading representative of the Lithuanian schools in our own days, wrote: "We must not propose anything different from what is found in the Gemara. I, by nature, am very wary about any *chiddush* and I believe that, in general, the simple approach is the true one. Therefore, one should not say anything he has not heard from his teacher." Despite his evocation on the tannaitic idea that one should not say anything except what he heard from his teacher, he was really reacting against the method of *pilpul,* or casuistry, not against *chiddush*—because he himself was a great *mechadesh.*

Now, all the people mentioned so far were concerned about creativity in Jewish Law, in Halakha. They did not mention spiritual creativity, the kind we encountered in Hasidism or Musar, at all.

Opposed to this point of view was the Hasidic view. Hasidim were very uncomfortable with this Lithuanian distrust of creativity in Halakha and they demanded spiritual creativity as well. Here we deal with a surprising phenomenon: not merely a defense but a celebration of creativity and *chiddush,* and not only in Halakha but in the nature of Jewish religious experience as well. Thus, the founder of the Ger dynasty, Reb Yitzchak Meir, author of the *Chiddushei Ha-Rim,* said that in every generation new ideas present themselves in interpreting the Torah in accordance with the needs of that generation. And that is what is meant by the Midrash that things that were not even revealed to Moses were revealed to Rabbi Akiva and his colleagues. Why? Because Rabbi Akiva lived in the second century, the time that the *Beit Hamikdash* had been destroyed, the Bar Kochba rebellion had come to grief, when there was a need to have a new blossoming of Torah, a new light of Torah, new interpretations of Torah; greater creativity was needed in the time of Rabbi Akiva even than in the time of Moshe Rabbenu. If that is the case, certainly in our times, says the *Chiddushei Ha-Rim,* when we have so much less than Rabbi Akiva had in his days, we are in even greater need of *chiddushim* and greater luminescence of Torah.

We have here a vigorous defense of the Hasidic emphasis on creativity. Creativity is not only permissible; it is mandatory as a way to greater devoutness and religious experience. If the age is impoverished, then we must not step back and close off the channels of creativity but, on the contrary, reinforce creativity because that is what the generation needs.

Now this enchantment with the new is not unprecedented in the history of Jewish thought. When the Talmud counsels us to have enthusiasm for learning, it says: "Every day the words of Torah must be new in your eyes, as if they had just been given at Sinai." The Zohar is even more emphatic, as well as picturesque. In contemporary terms: just as you don't wear pajamas during the day, and a business suit at night when you go to sleep, so your *shacharit* and your *maariv* and *mincha* must each be different from the other. Every prayer in your lifetime, even if the words are identical, must be utterly new. Each of us must be creative in understanding the words, in putting our own feelings into the words, because *chiddush* is part of *Avodat Hashem.*

This is expanded in later Kabbalah. It reaches its acme in Hasidism with its emphasis on spontaneity and ecstasy. One of the most fertile thinkers in Hasidic history was R. Zadok Hakohen of Lublin, for whom *chiddush* is an expression of human co-creativity with the Almighty. When you create an idea in Torah you join the *Ribbono shel Olam* as the *Yotzer Bereshit,* as the Creator of the world.

In his *Likkutei Maamarim,* he anticipates the Rav (Rabbi J.B. Soloveitchik) in emphasizing the role of *chiddush* as the expression of human participation, along with the Almighty, in the Torah's development: The Sadducees, who took the Torah's words, "the day after the Sabbath," literally, and therefore started the counting of the Omer from the Sunday after Pesach, did so because they believed that the Torah, once given, remained untouchable by man:

> "There is no right for Israel to offer a *chiddush,* but rather to do all as is written and given from Heaven, for only in Heaven is *chiddush* permitted." That is why they held that the celebration of Shavuot is independent of the *Bet Din.*

Whereas the Pharisees held that Torah requires that

> "'if you exert yourself you will attain [find] what you are looking for'" (paraphrase of *Meg.* 6b)—"it is not in Heaven" (Deut. 30:12), but it is in the hands of people, depending on their exertion and industriousness.

In his *Tzidkat Hatzadik* (#227), he avers that *neshama*—the highest of the triadic soul—is characterized by *chiddush,* it is the creative aspect of the human personality. Thus: "This is the power of the *Neshama* that it breathes a new divine spirit into the heart at all times by means of the mind's *chiddushim* of wisdom, telling it to perceive at all times new and vital spirituality."

Elsewhere, he maintains that the *neshama yetera,* the "extra soul" that we each receive on Shabbat, is not the same one returning every week, but a totally new one every Shabbat. Hence, Shabbat is not a comfortably familiar ritual, the spiritual equivalent of a pair of old shoes . . . Rather, it bespeaks spiritual adventurousness, a pioneering drive, a fascination with the unknown and the untried, and readiness to embrace the new as a way to *avodat Hashem.*

What was the rationale of their opponents? The Vilna Gaon, who was the intellectual and spiritual father of the whole school, held that the pursuit of truth and *sevara yesharah* leads you to suspect the specious originality which is pursued for its own sake rather than for the sake of truth. Apparently, his opposition to creativity is purely an insistence upon intellectual honesty and is neither psychological nor ideological.

There is a second element in this fear of *chiddush* and that is the peril presented by Haskala, Reform, secularism, and all of emerging modernity. In the Gaon's case this was compounded by the fear of Hasidism. He held that it too proved that one ought not be overly receptive to novelty and creativity. Then this defensive posture joins with a psychological inertia, a normal resistance to change that is common to most people, and becomes congealed into a kind of conservative mind-set that becomes part of one's whole culture.

However, this critical reassessment of *chiddush* does not translate into an ideology. It was, perhaps, part of the arsenal of traditional Judaism as it confronted a hostile, arrogant, and triumphalist secularism; but it was not absorbed into the warp and woof of Judaism's *Weltanschauung*. At no time was *chiddush* in Torah confused or identified with reformation of Torah, and therefore viewed with hostility or even suspicion. Even the Chatam Sofer cannot be considered the patron of such a view.

And, even if the conservative view of creativity does border on an ideology, never does it turn into the kind of neophobia that puts the brakes on *chiddush* as halakhic creativity. The halakhic enterprise as such remains sacrosanct. Otherwise the Lithuanian giants would never have written and published *chiddushim!*

What is the future of creativity in our Jewish life? On the one hand, there are many encouraging signs of creativity, especially in Halakha. Despite uneven quality, an impressively large number of *sefarim* and journals of Halakha are being published. They are filled with *chiddushim,* both of past generations and of contemporary Roshei Yeshiva and students. The large number of *sefarim* now being published is probably more than was published in the heyday of Polish Jewry. There are today more students in yeshivot and *kollelim* than existed in the days of Eastern Europe in its most fertile period.

At the same time, I think there are some danger signals that we ignore at our own peril. I fear that a kind of neophobic retrenchment may be emerging in our own day—a new animus against originality, a resistance to any intellectual, even halakhic creativity. I most devoutly hope that I am wrong, but I fear that I may just be right—that creativity as such may be looked upon with suspicion and this, in turn, may cripple whatever halakhic creativity does exist in our scholarly community.

I do not have hard evidence. But my concern is aroused because of some anecdotes that have come to my attention. One well-known head of a Yeshiva presented to more senior colleague a number of *halakha le'maaseh* problems—practical problems in Halakha—and sought his approval. The answer came after a month or two: "I've studied the issues and I agree with you that such and such ought to be done, but I'm going to withhold my support because I've never heard my own teacher say it." That absurd humility in a generation some 2,000 years after *Torah she'be'al peh* had been committed to writing!

Compare that attitude to the following statement by Rabbeinu Asher, the *Rosh,* in the Middle Ages in a letter to someone who had said that he can't offer his opinion because the great scholar, R. Yaakov b. Shushan, had already offered an opinion and he was *shalem,* perfect: "This is not a correct argument, for who was greater than Rashi, who enlightened all the Diaspora with his commentaries, yet his own grandchildren, Rabbenu Tam and R. Yitzchak, disagreed with him and contradicted his views; for ours is a Torah of truth, and we must bribe no person [by changing our opinions out of respect to another no matter how great]." Our Torah is a "Torah of truth," not a Torah of authoritarianism. We must never confuse authoritativeness with authoritarianism. A "Torah of truth" requires that we challenge conventional opinions. That is what the *massa u' mattan,* the dialectic of Talmud, is all about. Flattery—excessive respect—for an individual is harmful for Torah.

A man who has published some of the most impressive new editions of the Rishonim has maintained that it took him 20 years to have his new, improved editions accepted in many yeshiva circles. They said: "if the old edition was good enough for my *rebbe,* it's good enough for me." We do not proffer such an argument about making a living; we want to do better than our parents. Why should it not be that way concerning Torah?

I recall some of my own experiences. I offered a colleague an interpretation of a passage in Chumash. He did not disprove it. Yet, he said: I can't accept it. Why not?—"because your interpretation is nowhere mentioned in the literature . . ." I didn't have the proper authoritative pedigree.

I by no means intend to imply that all halakhic creativity is disappearing; not at all. My concern is not with the present but with *emerging tendencies* or almost emerging tendencies. My apprehension is based not only upon anecdotal evidence, but also on the supposition that there are multiple causes for the paralysis of creativity. Sometimes it is fortuitous, pure happenstance. Second, where there is a strong authoritarian environment or bias, creativity is stunted. Third, the reaction against the excesses of novelty, neophilia, and the mindless passion for change give creativity a bad name. There are those who consider—effectively if not openly—that creativity and innovation cannot be contained within the perimeters of Halakha, and sooner or later the pursuit of originality will spill over its legitimate borders and impose itself on Torah itself and operate not within but on Halakha; that *chiddush* in Halakha soon threatens to become a *chiddush* or change of Judaism. I fear that when all other forms of creativity are looked upon askance—not only scientific, psychological, esthetic, and cultural, but even spiritual, on the grounds that any creativity implies change and any change implies a challenge to sacred precedent and authority—then the aversion to creativity must begin to infect the inner life of Halakha as well. As the estimable philosopher, Yogi Berra, used to say, the future ain't what it used to be. If this is what the future holds, then it is not what it used to be in Jewish life.

My question, is: are we beginning to hear a new noise in our Orthodox Jewish world, the noise of mental doors being slammed shut one after the other? Are healthy, vigorous minds being closed tight by their fearful owners? In some circles, anything new is looked upon with dread, and sometimes narrowness is elevated to the level of sacred principle. If this happens, then our whole sacred tradition, our whole intellectual *mesorah* from Sinai down, will be derailed as the very act of *chiddush* is considered suspect. If this lurking apprehension is correct, and I dearly hope that it is not, then we are entering a stage where only memory and repetition will be accepted and respected but all creativity, originality, and innovative thinking will be condemned as dangerous. Should that nightmare come to pass, it will signal the triumph of myopia, of know-nothingism, and reduce Halakha, with its glorious intellectual excitement, to rote questions and answers to be cherished only by intellectual robots. It would confirm every negative stereotype of halakhically observant Jews. This kind of reputation, the result of the paralysis of the halakhic mind, would constitute a massive *Chillul Hashem*. It would be an illegitimate restraint of trade in the coin of intellectual authenticity in the marketplace of halakhic ideas.

Will this happen? I do not think so. May it possibly happen?

Yes. And it is best to be alert to it. The most seminal thinkers of the halakhic tradition firmly rejected such intellectual cowardice and spiritual rigor mortis and we ought to be proud of that.

Thus Rav Kook, first Chief Rabbi of Israel, wrote with deep conviction and passion about the need to "renew and exalt our thought processes and our logic." The specific form of this novelty, he says, "must be felt in all disciplines—in Halakha, in Agada, in all areas of science and ethics, in our conception of life and in our *Weltanschauung.*" One must appreciate the indomitable courage it took for Rav Kook to write these words. He was *the* "establishment man." Yet, he pleaded for creativity and change and movement. He has been mercilessly criticized for these and similar sentiments as if he had been a closet heretic. Still, he persisted against all the viciousness, the sarcasm, the ingratitude directed against him.

The [late] Lubavitcher Rebbe, in a *sicha* published one year ago in the *Algemeiner Journal,* expanded on his plea for all scholars, not only great scholars, to publish their *chiddushim.* I infer that he, too, intuited a kind of fear of *chiddush* even in the realm of Halakha, and that is why he wanted the scholarly among his hasidim to publish.

And, of course, "the Rav" in his famous *Ish ha-Halakha,* elaborates on the *chiddush* activity of man as an act of *imitatio Dei,* of imitating God. God is a *mechadesh be'tuvo be'chol yom tamid maasei bereshit.* He did not perform but one act of creation and thereafter leave the universe to spin along on its own. Every day He renews creation; He recreates. When man elaborates a *chiddush* in Halakha he is performing a Divine act of creativity, he is a partner with God in the creation of the world. This is a vision of man helping to create worlds by virtue of his mastery and creativity in Halakha. Anyone who has heard a *sheiur* of the Rav will know immediately what I refer to and what he meant. This, to my mind, is the authentic voice of Judaism on the question of creativity in Halakha—and life in general.

I hope that my sounding of an alarm does not mark me as a pessimist. Far from it. I believe with all my heart and all my soul that the time is now ripe for authentic Jewish creativity. As so often has happened in Jewish history, when the wells of the spirit seem to have dried up, new sources of spiritual refreshment and renaissance open up magically, as it were, manifesting the wondrous workings of the *hashgacha elyona,* of Divine providence. But in order for this to happen we must, all of us, be prepared for it, at least negatively—by not fearing our own creativity, by not hastening to criticize anyone with a new idea, by opening ourselves up to the infinite possibilities of spiritual as well as national redemption by our infinite and creative God.

I conclude with an illuminating story. My distinguished colleague, Rabbi Aharon Lichtenstein, the Rosh Yeshiva of Har Etzion, as well as Yeshiva University's Gruss Institute, was present when once the Rav, (his father-in-law) gave a *sheiur.* He was scintillating. His *chiddushim* were absolutely brilliant. There was one stranger in the audience who was taken aback at the Rav's intellectual audacity, and said to him, after the lecture, "But Rabbi Soloveitchik, what is your source?"

The Rav answered: "A clear and logical mind."

~ 26 ~

JUDAISM AND HUMAN RIGHTS

New prominence has been given to the problem of human rights on the international scene by President Carter and his administration. As Jews, it behooves us to turn to the sources of the Jewish tradition for illumination on this timely yet timeless question.

To set the issue in proper perspective, it is important to note that Judaism is more concerned with *duties* than *rights*. "What ought I do?" is more fundamental than "What can I lay claim to?" This characterizes all of Jewish law, from marital and domestic law to partnerships, sales, and even torts. At root, the reason is a philosophical perception: man is conceived of not as an autonomous monad elbowing his way through society, but as a responsible individual who must answer for his sojourn on earth.

Nevertheless, the question of rights does come up in almost all areas of interpersonal behavior. While the traditional sources of Judaism are rarely explicit in this respect—Jewish law works from the particular to the general, rather than the other way around—its major thrust in asserting human rights is the protection of society's disadvantaged. The concepts of rights and obligations are grounded in the Biblical conception of man.

A SAMPLING OF how Jewish law expressed its concern for human rights, in a legal manner, includes the following examples.

The condemned criminal had to be executed expeditiously, to avoid the anguish of anticipating death, and was anesthetized before execution (in order, according to the Talmud, to fulfill the commandment, "thou shalt love thy neighbor as thyself!"). In addition, many leading Talmudists were reluctant to enforce the death penalty at all.

From the ADL Bulletin, *September 1977.*

The accused in a criminal trial was not permitted to testify against himself, even if he wished to do so voluntarily. The ban against self-incrimination was a prohibition, not merely a privilege, hence avoiding what during the 1950's McCarthy era came to be known as "Fifth Amendment Communists."

Freedom of thought and speech effectively became rights by virtue of the fact that intellectual activity was regarded as legally non-actionable. Thoughts, no matter how outrageous, were not regarded as matters for the courts. The Torah demands a pure heart and censures deceit and immorality even in the realm of mentation, but one could never be punished for thinking wrong thoughts. Similarly, in almost all cases, speech was regarded as beyond the jurisdiction of the courts (although one would be hard pressed to find antecedents in the Halakhah for some of the more extreme interpretations of the First Amendment).

Slavery was condoned in the Bible, but clearly as a concession. Scriptural legislation severely limited it among Jews. Even though the ownership of non-Jewish slaves by Jews continued into the Middle Ages, it was less prevalent than among other peoples. The Torah's laws kept the treatment of the slave and the relationship between master and slave as humane as possible—so much so, that one could hardly apply the term "slave" at all to such bondsmen. Moreover, the Pharisees, as opposed to the Sadducees, considered the slave a thinking, sentient, autonomous, and hence responsible individual, a judgment that is reflected in the Halakhah.

The dignity and rights of the woman in the marital relationship were of much concern to the Jewish tradition. It is unfortunate that oversimplification and ignorance have led some moderns to a gross misunderstanding of the Talmudic view of woman. The matter is quite complicated and, though not without problems, yields an image of woman to which the contemporary caricature does undeserved violence. As an illustration, Judaism has, since Biblical days, held that conjugal relations are the *rights* of the wife and the *duty* of the husband.

The elderly were assured not only of the rights enjoyed by other age groups, but also of respect, reverence, and support. These were legislated as *duties* imposed upon the young. "Thou shalt honor the hoary head" was applied, by various Talmudic rabbis, to women a well as men, to the ignorant as well as the wise, to gentiles as well as Jews.

Economic well-being was transformed into a right by the Halakhah, which viewed the commandment of *tzedakah* as not merely charity, a voluntary act, but as a mandate upon the community. The courts were empowered to assess all citizens to give their fair share to sustain the poor, the orphan, the widow, the stranger, and other economically disadvantaged.

The laborer's rights to the rewards of his work were enshrined in Jewish law in a manner that stood in bold contrast to the rest of society. The employee was not at the mercy of his employer; more often than not conflicting claims between the two were resolved in favor of the employee. There is considerable literature on the Talmudic views of strikes, unions, and the like.

The artisan and the businessman were protected against unfair competition; the Talmud has a rather sophisticated legal code on this matter, developed and refined in the subsequent responsa literature. Interestingly, teachers were not offered this same protection against competition; the rights of the student to the best education available were asserted as superior to those of the teacher.

An intriguing example of how Jewish law places obligation ahead of rights may be found in the area of privacy. The Talmud discusses the case of two partners who buy a piece of real estate in common. Should they divide the plot, and should either desire to build a fence between the separate properties, both partners must contribute equally to the expenses. It would seem that this is a case of the right to privacy: each of the two may demand that the other share the cost of the partition so as to protect his own privacy. But this is not really the case. Another Talmudic ruling in the same area of the law deals with the following. If the plot is on the incline of a hill and the houses are built so that the roof of the lower house is approximately level with the courtyard of the house on top, then the owner of the lower house must bear the *entire* expense of the fence! Why? Because in Talmudic days, people rarely made use of the roof, whereas a great deal of domestic activity took place in the courtyard. Therefore, even without a fence, the people in the upper house had virtually no opportunity to spy upon their neighbors down below, but the residents of the house on the bottom of the hill had every opportunity to visually trespass on their neighbors above. The Talmud demands that the owner of the lower house pay all expenses because of his *obligation* not to encroach upon his neighbor's privacy. Had the question been merely one of rights, the Halakhah would have ruled that both share equally. Hence, in the first case, where both houses are on the same level, we must infer that the ruling that both share equally in the expense of the fence means that each pays not only to assert his right to his own privacy, but as his duty not to violate the privacy of the other.

Perhaps both these legal concepts of right and of obligation can be traced to the Biblical conception of man in the Genesis story of the creation. Man, the Torah teaches, was created in the Image (*tzellem*) and the Likeness (*demut*) of God.

The Image of God means that man reflects his Maker. This resemblance is, of course, not physical but spiritual. Even as the Creator is the Source of infinite value, so does His human creature possess an irreducible core of dignity. Man, in his essence, images his Creator and, therefore, irrespective of his performance or conduct, whether it be good or evil, wise or foolish, he retains that minimal residue of transcendent value. It is this *tzellem* that endows man with his special dignity and from this flow his enduring human rights.

The concept of *demut* or Likeness goes beyond that. It is to be coupled with the ideal of the Imitation of God. (There is even a verbal similarity pointing to a common etymology in Hebrew: *demut—le'hidamot*.) Man is capable of imitating his Maker, of assimilating the divine attributes of mercy, compassion, generousness, patience, etc. Whence this capacity for such imitation of God's moral character? From the fact that he was created in the Likeness of God. Likeness, therefore, implies Imitation.

The difference between these two similar terms is thus clear: Image is a statement of metaphysical fact. It is a *description* of a state of affairs: every human is created in the divine Image and therefore possesses certain inalienable *rights* which you must respect. Likeness is a *prescription,* it is a goad for you to achieve what in its fullness is unattainable: a Godly character. You must imitate God and His moral norms. This not only calls upon you to respect your neighbor's minimal rights but lays upon you the *obligation* to expand your own *moral character,* to maximize your love for your neighbor, to go beyond what is his minimal due by striving to fulfill your own divine Likeness in your relation with him.

The above is, of course, only a rough and impressionistic survey of the range of Judaism's concern for human rights, its relation to the more important and often supererogatory ideal of duty, and the grounding of both in the twin Biblical concepts of Image and Likeness.

Mankind has a long way to go until it achieves universal human rights. Judaism wants it to go even beyond that, towards the embracing of human obligations.

~ 27 ~

THE TALMUD AND THE TAPES

Now that the highest court in the land is prepared to study the problem of President Nixon's refusal to surrender the famous tapes, it is timely to inquire what Jewish law has to say about this historic confrontation between the executive and the judiciary. Can any wisdom on this issue be gleaned from the Hebrew tradition, one of the main streams that feed into Western culture and civilization?

The Mishnah (the Jewish legal code redacted by Rabbi Judah in Palestine during the early part of the third century) teaches that a king may not judge and may not be brought to trial; others may not testify against him and he may not be made to testify concerning others. The Talmud (the Babylonian commentary and extension of the Mishnah) limits this law to "Israelite kings," i.e. those who were not of Davidic descent. Kings of the House of David, however, are subject to judgment and may be compelled to testify. The Talmud then concludes that fundamentally the law requires that the king should submit to judgment and testimony, but that an exception was made in the case of later Jewish kings ("Israelite kings") because of a historic incident.

In the first century of the common era Jannai was king, and the head of the Sanhedrin (supreme court) was the fearlessly independent Simeon ben Shetach. Now it happened that a servant of the king had been accused of committing murder. According to the law, the master had to be present during the trial of the slave. Jannai obeyed, and presented himself in court. But then Simeon informed Jannai that the law required the master to stand while the trial was in session.

Aware of the sensitivities involved, Simeon hastened to assure the king that "you are not standing before us, but before Him who by His word created the world." Here Jannai drew the line and hurled a challenge at Simeon: "Not when you say so, but only when your colleagues will tell me so." The shrewd monarch

---

Published in SH'MA *November 2, 1973. While this was written concerning the Nixon administration, it bears relevance for certain later administrations as well.*

had made the right move. Simeon turned to his right, and his colleagues "buried their heads in the ground." He looked to his left, and his fellow judges did likewise. Defeated, Simeon was furious and called down the wrath of heaven upon his colleagues who, because of a combination of political calculations and cowardice, had subverted their eminent calling. The text closes with a legend-like flourish: the angel Gabriel came down, smote them on the ground, and they died. Thereafter, Israelite kings were not subject to the jurisdiction of the Sanhedrin.

The limits of power

What the Talmudic sages are teaching us is that in a healthy society the executive is not above the law. The head of state must honor a summons to trial and must offer testimony upon the order of the courts. It is only when the judiciary itself is bankrupt and shows a failure of nerve in its confrontation with the executive head of the government that the "separation of powers" becomes so complete that all interaction between the various branches ceases. With an over-powerful king and an apprehensive and politically motivated judiciary, better abdicate all jurisdiction over the king and attend to other pressing matters, lest the courts be completely destroyed or corrupted.

Scholars agree that the story of this confrontation is factual. Some historians, however, maintain that the actual story took place some thirty years later, with a different cast of characters. Making this change brings the Talmudic tale somewhat into conformity with the report by the historian Josephus. It is important to note the identity of the people involved in the Josephus story, because it adds another element of contemporary relevance. Instead of Simeon, Josephus talks of Sameas (Shemayah) as the head of the Sanhedrin. In place of Jannai, he writes of Hyrkanos. And instead of an anonymous "slave" of the king, the accused is none other than Herod—later to become the detested king—brought up on charges of political assassination. Herod is likewise called *eved,* which in this case means not one who is technically a "slave," but an "advisor" of the king. The opinion of the ancient Jewish Court was, thus, that the king is responsible for the malfeasance of his advisors in the pursuit of their official duties.

Historical analogies should, of course, never be driven too far, and ancient law can at most provide illumination, rarely detailed prescriptions, for complex modern political problems. Yet the sense of the Hebrew legal tradition is clear enough: no one, not even a king, is above the law, and if his advisors commit a crime he is responsible for them. And, as Judge Sirica reminded us in quoting Chief Justice Marshall in his landmark decision against President Jefferson, there is, after all, a difference between an American president and an English king. The argument applies *a fortiori* to our case: if a Davidic king, who was not democratically elected, must submit to the courts, how much more so an American president! (Interesting coincidence: Simeon ben Shetach and John Marshall were both related, respectively, to Jannai and Thomas Jefferson.)

For the good of all concerned

The Talmud is a continuation of the Biblical tradition. Deuteronomy commands the appointment of judges before the crowning of a king. "Judges" ruled in ancient Israel before the rise of the monarchy. This limitation on the political head of the government is not only for the good of the people, but for the good of the king himself: "Thus he will not act arrogantly toward his fellow countrymen or deviate from the commandments to the right or to the left, to the end that he and his decendants may reign long in the midst of Israel" (*Deut.* 17:20).

Will America learn in time what the Bible and the Talmud knew ages ago? If the president is wise, he will obey the courts—if necessary yield the tapes, and "reign long." If he is not, the Congress will have to remind him "not [to] act arrogantly toward his fellow countrymen."

~ 28 ~

IS IT A MITZVAH TO ADMINISTER MEDICAL THERAPY?

When a physician prescribes a course of therapy and treats a patient, does he thereby perform a *mitzvah?*

At first blush, the answer is self-evident. We already know from the Mishna in *Nedarim* 38b that the medical treatment of a patient is considered a *mitzvah.* The Mishna teaches that if someone takes a vow *(neder)* not to bestow any benefit upon his friend, he is permitted to heal him *refuat nefesh* but not *refuat mamon.* The terms are unclear, and the Gemara *(ib., 41b)* explains that *refuat nefesh* means healing the friend's body while *refuat mamon* refers to treating his animals. If you take a vow not to benefit your friend, you may not act as a veterinarian for his livestock, but you may act as a physician for him. Why so? The Rosh and the Ran, citing the Jerusalem Talmud, maintain that human therapy is permissible because *mitzvah ka avid*—in the course of healing a human being you perform a *mitzvah,* and this *mitzvah* overrides the vow. Therefore, despite the *neder,* you are allowed to treat him medically. This does not hold for treating animals, because this does not entail the performance of a *mitzvah.*

What *mitzvah* is it that is performed in the course of treating a patient? The Rambam (Commentary to Mishnayot, *ad loc.)* and the Ran (to *Ned., ad loc.)* identify it as *hashavat avedah,* the return of a lost article to its rightful owner. On the verse *ve'hashevoto lo* ("thou shalt return it to him"—Dt. 22:2), the Sifre comments: *af et atzmo atah meshiv lo*—You must return to him not only what he possesses, but what he *is,* his very self. Hence, if you restore health to one who is dangerously ill, you have "returned" to him his own life, and thus have technically fulfilled the commandment of "Thou shalt return it to him." The Baraita *(B.K. 81b)* notes, concerning this return of self, that *ve'ein lekha hashavat avedah gedolah mi-zu*—there is no greater return of a lost article than the restoration of health that has been lost. Clearly, then, the medical treatment of a patient constitutes a *kiyyum ha-mitzvah*—

This appeared in the Journal of Halacha and Contemporary Society *Fall 1984* that of returning a lost article. (There are even commentaries that conclude therefrom that the prohibition of *lo tukhal le'hitalem*—one may not ignore the lost item but must return it—applies to medical therapy, thus *obligating* the physician to administer treatment to any patient who requests it. See Maharsha to *Sanh. 73a; Ha'amek She'elah* to *She'iltot* 38:a.)

The author of *She'iltot (ibid.)* and Ramban (to Lev. 28:36) identify the *mitzvah* of healing as *ve'chei achikha imakh,* "thy brother shall live with thee" (Lev. 25:36)—and treating one's fellow medically is a way of keeping him alive. Other *Rishonim* (see *Tos. Rid* and *Tos. ha-Rash* to *Ber.* 60a) locate the *mitzvah* in the general rubric of *lo taamod al dam reiakha*—"thou shalt not stand by while thy brother's blood is being shed" (Lev. 19:16). A physician who has the means to revive his fellow man from disease is in the same category as one who knows how to swim and thus must save one who is drowning.

Despite the fact that we have posited three different *mitzvot* to which we can technically ascribe the *mitzvah* of the therapeutic process, our opening question remains a valid question. In order to explain the question more clearly, let us turn to a problem that is raised by a number of *Acharonim.*

In the *Shulchan Arukh* (which codifies only very few laws concerning medicine and physicians), we read the following about medical malpractice: *im ripa bi'reshut bet din,* if a physician licensed by the courts undertook treatment of a patient, and by error caused damage to the patient, then *patur mi-dinei adam ve'chayyav be'dinei shamayim:* he is morally culpable, but the tort is not legally actionable. However, if he unwittingly caused the patient to die, he must go into exile *(Y.D.* 336:1). (This is in keeping with the general law of manslaughter, according to which one is neither executed nor exonerated, but must flee to one of the "cities of refuge" where he must remain until the death of the High Priest.)

Now, the question posed by the *Acharonim* (*Maaseh Rokeiach, Tashbatz,* and others) is this: Why should the Halakha prescribe *galut* (exile) for this case of medical manslaughter? Why not compare it to three other instances in which the manslaughterer goes free, namely, the bailiff who applied excessive force in summoning one to court and so caused his death, and the father and the teacher who caused the son or pupil, respectively, to die by administering excessive punishment? In these cases, Rambam *(Hil. Rotzeiach* 5:5,6) rules that the bailiff, the parent, and the teacher are not condemned to exile, because their misdeeds were perpetrated *be'shaat asot ha-mitzvah,* "in the course of performing a *mitzvah.*" Why does the *Shulchan Arukh* rule that the physician who unintentionally caused a patient's death be treated differently?

The author of *Yad Avraham* (to *Y.D., loc., cit.)* proposes the following solution: In the case of the first three—the bailiff, the father, and the teacher—the manslaughterers are involved in acts of *mitzvah.* They are teaching a child Torah or "wisdom" or a trade, or carrying out the instructions of the court, albeit they are doing it in the wrong way and with disastrous results. However, this does not hold true for the physician. If the doctor lost his patient, then by definition he did not heal him. If there was no healing, there was no *mitzvah.* In other words, the *mitzvah* quality of medical treatment is contingent upon the success of the therapy. If he succeeded in healing the patient, the physician performed a *mitzvah.* If he did not succeed, he accomplished no *mitzvah.* This is in contradistinction to the other three cases which are not result-oriented. This explains why in the three cases mentioned there is no punishment, whereas the physician is condemned to exile. The ruling of the *Shulchan Arukh,* therefore, is not contradicted by the Rambam.

This indeed is the substance of our question: is *Yad Avraham* right, that a course of therapy does not entail a *kiyyum ha-mitzvah* unless it succeeds, or is it to be considered a *mitzvah* irrespective of the results?

In order to elucidate this important point, let us focus on the question of the *Acharonim.* It would seem that their argument with the *Shulchan Arukh* is misaddressed. While it is true that Rambam does not ordain exile as punishment for the first three cases, this decision is not unanimous. Indeed, Ramban *(Torat ha-Adam, Shaar ha-Sakanah)* holds that these three *are* punished by exile. Ramban adds to these three the case of a court-approved abortion in which the mother died. Hence, the halakhic decision of *Shulchan Arukh* requiring exile for medical malpractice, while not according with the opinion of Rambam, does follow the view of Ramban. (See too *Bi'ur ha-Gera* to *Y.D., ad loc.,* and *Or Sameiach, Hil. Rotzeiach* 5:6.)

However, while the *Yad Avraham* strictures may not apply to *Shulchan Arukh,* they seemingly do hold with regard to Rambam himself. Whereas the latter does not say so specifically, he does imply that the physician is exiled. This we infer from Rambam's enumeration of only three cases in which a *mitzvah* was performed and hence no exile is ordained. Thus we may conclude that he considers all other such cases of manslaughter, including the malpracticing physician, as deserving of the punishment of exile. This would lead us to deduce that the Rambam (himself a physician!) did not subscribe to the thesis that medical treatment *per se* constitutes a *mitzvah* but rather that only *successful* therapy can be considered a *kiyyum hamitzvah.*

To summarize: according to both Rambam and Ramban, a physician who unwittingly caused a patient to die is to be penalized with exile. Their controversy concerns the other three cases: the bailiff, the father, and the teacher. Ramban holds that the performance of a *mitzvah* is no excuse, while Rambam disagrees. In addition, they differ with regard to the act of the physician: According to Rambam there is no *kiyyum mitzvah* in the course of treatment, while the Ramban may well hold that medical therapy in itself, successful or not, is to be regarded as an act of *mitzvah.*

Actually, this first controversy (regarding the three cases) between Rambam and Ramban has an earlier source. The Mishna (*Mak.* 8a) discusses the *locus classicus* of manslaughter in the Halakha—the Torah's description of a man who wields an ax, and in the course of lifting the ax it flies off its handle and kills someone. Exile is the prescribed punishment. Abba Saul is cited in the Mishna as declaring that every case of exile for manslaughter must be analogous to the act of chopping a tree: *Mah chativat etzim reshut*—just as the act of chopping a tree is *reshut,* i.e., neither a virtue nor a vice, neither a *mitzvah* nor an *issur,* so every case of manslaughter for which exile is prescribed must arise out of an act that is halakhically indifferent or neutral. However, if it was an act of *mitzvah,* the perpetrator is not condemned to exile. Thus, the Mishna continues, the cases of the father, teacher, and bailiff who used excessive force and killed are excused from exile, because they were involved in acts of *mitzvah.* The Gemara says so clearly; the exemption arises because there was a *kiyyum mitzvah.*

However the Tosefta (*B.K.* 9:3 and *Mak.* 2:5—see *hashmatot* from Ms. versions) says that in all these cases—the three mentioned in the Mishna, plus that of legal abortion in which the mother died and that of the malpracticing physician—all are required to undergo exile. Thus, the Tosefta disagrees with Abba Saul of the Mishna. Therefore, the controversy between Rambam and Ramban turns into a question of whether we follow the Mishna or the Tosefta. Rambam decides in favor of Abba Saul in the Mishna, while Ramban declares for the Tosefta.

It would seem, therefore, that while both Rambam and Ramban hold that the malpracticing physician is exiled, they differ as to whether medical treatment as such constitutes a *kiyyum ha-mitzvah* (Ramban) or not (Rambam). Yet, the matter requires further elucidation and the identification of a source for their respective theories.

The source, I believe, is the famous baraita (*B.K.* 85a, *Ber.* 60a): "In the school of R. Ishmael it was taught: 'he shall cause him to be healed' (Ex. 21:19—in the case of battery and assault the offender must pay for the victim's medical bills); from this (redundancy of the verb *rapo/yerapei*) we learn that the Torah permits the physician to practice his healing arts." Rashi (*B.K., ad loc.*) comments: "and we do not say that the Merciful One made sick, let the Merciful One heal" without human interference. Tosafot (*ib.*, s.v. *she'nitnah)* likewise explains that without this Scriptural dispensation we might prohibit medical treatment on the grounds that it contravenes the divine decree of illness. Most *Rishonim* similarly explain this baraita as negating the presupposition that man must not interfere in the natural process.

I believe that this is also the view of the Rambam. The baraita teaches that it is *permitted* to heal. The verse previously mentioned, "thou shalt return it (the lost article) to him" adds the *requirement* or *mitzvah* to effect a medical cure (see Rambam, Commentary to the Mishnah, *ib.*).

Now, if indeed Rambam assigns medical care to the commandment of return of lost articles, then certain halakhic consequences must flow from this particular rubric. Thus, if the finder takes the article with the intention of returning it to its owner, but for some reason the object disintegrates and the return is never consummated, certainly no *mitzvah* was performed despite the finder's best intentions and efforts. "Thou shalt return it to him" has not been achieved, and hence (on the technical halakhic level, if not on the moral plane), no *mitzvah* was done. Similarly, for Rambam, if the patient died in the course of therapy, the "return of his body" (*hashavat gufo*) to the patient was not accomplished, and the physician cannot be accredited with a *kiyyum mitzvah.*

However, Ramban (in *Torat ha-Adam, Shaar ha-Sakanah)* has a completely different interpretation of this baraita (even though he is not always consistent, neither in *Torat ha-Adam* nor in his Commentary to the Torah). Thus, Ramban (*Torat ha-Adam,* ed. Chavel, p. 41) clearly implies that the Scriptural dispensation to heal is a psychological one:

> "From here we learn that the physician is permitted to practice." The explanation is: lest the physician say, "why do I need all this trouble of (practicing medicine)? Perhaps I will err and thus unwittingly cause someone's death." Therefore the Torah permitted him to practice medicine, and the physician like the judge is *commanded* to practice his profession. The judge too may say, "why do I need all this trouble?" . . . (Yet the Torah rules that) "the judge can rely only upon what his eyes see" (and, having performed to the best of his ability, should have no moral scruples or psychological distress about possible errors in judgment).

While Ramban also maintains the interpretations of the baraita by Rashi and Tosafot (that is, the dispensation to intrude into the natural process by effecting a cure for the malady), his major contribution is the interpretation of *reshut* as permission to enter a situation in which one might take a life unwittingly. Ramban's exegesis requires the assumption that medical treatment per se constitutes a *mitzvah.* Thus, in Ramban's words, the "dispensation" is a *reshut de'mitzvah*—in itself an obligation to heal (in contrast to *Perishah* to *Y.D.* 336:4, who sees here a two-step process: once permission is granted to heal, thereafter the *mitzvah* arises to convert it into an obligation).

Support for this view comes from a Tosafist exegetical work on the Torah, *Moshav Zekenim* (to Ex. 21:19), which quotes Rashi on "he shall surely heal" only to disagree with him:

> We already know from the verse, "thou shalt not stand idly by the blood of thy neighbor" (Lev. 19:16), that if one witnesses his fellow

> drowning or beset by robbers, etc., that he must help him, and we do not say, "The Merciful One made sick, let the Merciful One heal." Rabbi Hayyim interprets (the baraita), "From this we learn that the Torah permits the physician to practice his healing arts," to mean that there should be no (excessive) apprehension lest the patient die because of (the wrong) medication.

Clearly, this supports our understanding of Ramban, and this source too would support the thesis that medical treatment *per se* constitutes a *mitzvah*.

Further support for Ramban may be garnered from the following fascinating Midrash. It is a tale cited in *Midrash Shmuel* (ed. S. Buber):

> R. Ishmael and R. Akiva were once walking in the streets of Jerusalem together with a third person. A sick man met them and said, "Rabbis, tell me how I can be healed." They replied, "Take such and such (potions) until you are healthy." Whereupon their companion said to them, "Who afflicted him with his illness?" They said, "The Holy One, blessed be He." Said he to them, "Then you have intruded in a matter which is none of your concern. (The Holy One) afflicted and you will heal?!" Said they to him, "What is your occupation?" He answered, "I am a farmer, and the scythe is in my hand." They asked, "Who created the soil? Who created the vineyard?" He replied, "The Holy One, blessed be He."
>
> They continued, "And you intrude in a matter which is none of your concern? He created (the soil as is) and you (by working it) eat of its fruits?" "But," he rejoined, "do you not see the scythe in my hand? If not for the fact that I work and plow and turn the earth over and fertilize and prune, nothing would grow." Whereupon they said to him, "Fool! Have you not learned from your occupation that 'man's days are as grass' (Ps. 103:15)? Just as a tree offers nothing if it is not fertilized, pruned, and planted, and if it grows (fruit) but gets no water it dies, so is the (human) body like a tree, the medicine is like the fertilizer, and the physician is the farmer."

It is obvious from this Midrash that R. Ishmael and R. Akiva were not prepared to accept even the hypothesis of the quietistic view, according to which man has no right to interfere in the processes of nature by means of which illness afflicts people. Interestingly, it is the same R. Ishmael in whose school our baraita originated! This would lend further support to our interpretation of Ramban that the baraita's assertion of a Scriptural dispensation was not meant to answer the quietistic hypothesis ("the Merciful One made sick, let the Merciful One heal"), but rather is an assurance offered to calm the apprehensiveness of the physician who is concerned lest his error make his patient worse, by declaring the very process of medical treatment a *mitzvah,* independent of its success or failure.

Having begun this essay by citing views of the *Acharonim,* let us conclude in a similar manner. The law codified in *Shulchan Arukh* that the malpracticing physician must undergo exile is explained by the author of *Arokh ha-Shulchan* differently from the way it was expounded in *Yad Avraham.* The former maintains that this punishment is ordained only when the physician himself knows that he has been negligent, such as not having studied the matter adequately. Otherwise, there is no reason to impose exile upon him. "For if he did study the matter properly, he has committed no sin, for it is a *mitzvah* to practice medicine. The sage once said, 'the physician's mistake is the Creator's intention' . . . Without this element (of neglect), I believe (the physician) is not to be exiled, for he is no worse than the father, teacher, or bailiff—all of whom are exonerated from exile." Clearly, his view is that medical therapy is in itself a *kiyyum ha-mitzvah,* and we need not resort to the solution proposed by the author of *Yad Avraham.*

In summary, the question of whether medical treatment as such constitutes a *mitzvah,* independent of its results, is in dispute from the Tannaitic period—R. Ishmael and R. Akiva, through the Mishna and Tosefta—to the medieval period of Rambam and Ramban, and down to the latest period, that of the *Acharonim,* especially *Yad Avraham* and *Arokh ha-Shulchan.*

~ 29 ~

THE ROLE OF THE BLIND IN THE PERFORMANCE OF THE COMMANDMENTS

In contrast with most of the rest of the ancient world, Judaism exercised enormous compassion for the blind. However, while the Jewish tradition was most generous in providing for care and respect for the blind in the physical, economic, and social realms, what of their spiritual status? In the Halakhah this theme is formulated as: Are the blind obligated to perform the commandments?

The matter is in dispute between the Tannaim R. Judah and R. Meir, the former declaring the unsighted as not obligated and the latter disagreeing. Since the Talmud holds with the view that voluntary performance of the commandments is less worthy than submission to divinely imposed obligation, it is R. Judah who appears to disenfranchise the blind from full participation in religious life.

The key to the understanding of R. Judah's view in a more benign light is the remark of Tosafot that even R. Judah would agree that the blind remain subject to the commandments as Rabbinic edict, in order that the blind feel part of the community, "for if you release him from all the commandments even Rabbinically, he will be like a non-Jew who has no share whatever in the Torah." Based upon this principle, we attempt to broaden the scope of obligation as a way of alleviating the spiritual isolation of the blind.

This is done by invoking the Talmudic principle of *shomeia ke'oneh*, that listening (to a blessing, prayer, etc.) is tantamount to reciting. With regard to the blind, this comes into play with regard to being called to the Torah. One tradition, beginning with ReMA based upon MaHaRiL, permits the blind to be called to the Torah and make the blessing while the reader recites the passage because *shomeia ke'oneh*. An opposing tradition, from R. Joseph Karo

---

A short synopsis of a Sheiur, published by The Jewish Heritage for the Blind in March 1989

through R. Jacob Emden, disagrees and maintains that this Talmudic principle is inapplicable because of the requirement that one actually read *min ha-ketav*, from the script of the Torah scroll. We explain this controversy by distinguishing between two competing interpretations of *shomeia ke'oneh:* whether it implies that listening is tantamount to reciting where, as it were, the words of the reader are borrowed by the listener, or whether it implies surrogacy, i.e. that the listener adopts the identity of the reader. In the former case, the disqualification of not reading *min ha-ketav* remains, and the blind cannot be called to the Torah. In the latter case, the blind man adopts the identity of the reader, who reads from the script; hence, he fully participates in performing the commandment via his surrogate, the reader.

Thus even according to R. Judah (and most authorities decide against him), the unsighted can achieve full membership in the community of the observant by endeavoring, wherever possible, to fulfill their liturgical functions via the legal mechanism of *shomeia ke'oneh.* In so doing, the blind achieve participation as an act of obligation rather than mere voluntary observance, and they thus express their linkage to the covenant of Sinai.

~ 30 ~

ON VISITING THE SICK

In Jewish Law and Thought

It is well known that *bikkur cholim,* visiting the sick, is a "mitzvah," a religious commandment in Judaism. But exactly where does it fit into the rubric of the 613 commandments?

Its technical categorization by Halakhah (Jewish law) is a matter of dispute between two eminent halakhic authorities. One is a great decisor who flourished at the end of the Geonic period and is known as *Baal Halakhot Gedolot,* the author of a historic work by the name of *Halakhot Gedolot* ("the great compilation of laws") and is usually referred to by the acronym *Behag.* The other is the most distinguished name of medieval Sephardic Jewry, R. Moses ben Maimon—Maimonides or the Rambam. Maimonides assigns *bikkur cholim* to the mitzvah of "thou shalt love thy neighbor as thyself," i.e., *bikkur cholim* is but one aspect of the more comprehensive injunction to love one's fellow human beings. His predecessor, Behag, however, holds that *bikkur cholim* is a separate and independent mitzvah, part of the general category of *chesed* or acts of loving kindness.

We can understand Maimonides: *bikkur cholim* obviously belongs with the mitzvah of love of fellow humans. But what of the Behag? If indeed *bikkur cholim* is an aspect of *chesed,* how does one distinguish between *chesed* and that other well-known and oft-discussed Jewish precept, *tzedakah*? If the former means love and concern for humans, is that not identical to the latter—for is not charity given to implement one's feeling of loving concern for the other? And if so, should not *bikkur cholim* be considered an aspect of *tzedakah?*

The answer is given in the Talmud: *Tzedakah* is a mitzvah reserved for the poor as beneficiaries, and it is effected by giving money or anything of monetary value—such as food or clothing—to the poor. *Chesed,* however, is a mitzvah for both the poor

---

This essay appeared as The Meaning of Bikur Cholim *in November 1995, by the Jewish Board of Family and Children's services*

and the rich (yes, the rich too often need love!), and can be performed both with money and with one's body or very self. It is, therefore, far more comprehensive than *tzedakah*. And that is the reason Behag assigns *bikkur cholim* to *chesed*: it is a mitzvah to visit the sick—not only to give material value to them, but the intangible yet far more significant gift of one's presence, one*self*; and the mitzvah applies equally to the poor patient and the rich patient.

NOW THAT WE know the various views on the heading under which *bikkur cholim* belongs, we turn to a more formidable task: an analysis of the mitzvah itself. What are its constituent parts? What must one do in order to fulfill this commandment technically—or, better, properly?

The great halakhic figure and Bible commentator of Spanish Jewry following the time of Maimonides was R. Moses ben Nachman, called Ramban (or Nachmanides). The Ramban identifies three distinct actions as constituting the mitzvah of *bikkur cholim*. They are: to tend to the needs of the patient; to pray for the patient's recovery and well-being; and to give the patient the gift of companionship—literally, "to enable the patient to obtain a restful spirit (*nachat ruach*) with his comrades." The first two are relatively straight forward. To help the patient turn to a better position or offer him/her medicine or water or otherwise nurse him is the fulfillment of the first requirement. Prayer is also simple to understand (but far less observed). Indeed, instead of just offering good wishes, actually *pray* for him. Do not be embarrassed—it is the right and proper thing to do and, if done seriously albeit briefly, the patient will genuinely appreciate it. During World War II it was said that "there are no atheists in foxholes." I believe the same can be said of hospital beds—especially in the intensive care units . . .

LET US THEN concentrate on the third constituent of the mitzvah of *bikkur cholim* according to the Ramban. How does one bring *nachat ruach* to a patient? How do you relieve his or her anxiety, and what does it mean to give the patient the gift of companionship?

The Halakha actually gives us the precise wording of the greeting one should extend to the patient: *Ha-Makom yishlach lekha refuah shelemah be'tokh she'ar cholei yisrael*—"May the Almighty grant you a complete recovery among (or together with) all the sick of Israel." Note that this greeting is almost identical with the classical formal greeting used when consoling the mourner: "May the Almighty console you among (or together with) all the mourners of Zion and Jerusalem." In both cases, the object of our concern is made to feel part of a larger community of sufferers—either patients or mourners. The patient, like the mourner, feels expelled from "normal" society—lonely, misunderstood, rejected, probably guilty, flirting with intimations of his/her own mortality and, mostly, expendable: the world and life go on even while he is incarcerated in his hospital room or in his apartment while "sitting *shiva*." His business and social and professional and even family life manage without him—like a stream of water which parts to accommodate a stone thrown into it and then both sides rejoin each other and roll along merrily without, as it were, another thought about the distraction. Are we that unimportant, that irrelevant? Does the "outside world" really care about us at all? One does not have to be paranoid to be troubled by such feelings of isolation.

It is this feeling of superfluousness or expendability to which the greeting to the patient and the mourner is addressed. We express the hope that he will be *reintegrated* into the routines of life where his place is assured, his virtues appreciated, his contributions important and valued. He is part of a community of sufferers and, therefore, should not feel alone. This is the way we carry out the third of Ramban's trilogy of elements, that of enabling the patient "to obtain a restful spirit (*nachat ruach*) with his comrades."

I would imagine that the best visit and most effective antidote to this feeling of misery—loneliness, helplessness, maybe hopelessness—is that offered by *another* patient. Just as the Halakha demands of the poor man who is a recipient of charity that he himself perform *his* mitzvah of *tzedakah* by giving to another poor person, and just as a mourner is permitted to leave his quarters in order to pay a *shiva* visit to another mourner, so ought a patient, if his physical condition permits it, visit other sick people. Who better than a patient can empathize, understand, and look into the soul of another sufferer? Besides, such a visit may do even more good to the visitor-patient than to the patient being visited . . .

We should emphasize that in acknowledging the "down" feeling of the patient, *bikkur cholim* is directed more at the psychic than the physical condition of the patient—and the two are sometimes quite separate from each other. Thus, allaying the fears or calming the spirits of a depressed person (even if not technically sick) too is a fulfillment of the mitzvah of *bikkur cholim.* Indeed, *every* person suffers from a degree of existential anxiety; it is a universal condition, but one that is severely exacerbated by physical or mental illness.

I recall, in this respect, the powerful poem by D. H. Lawrence—

> I am not a mechanism, an assembly of various sections.
> And it is not because the mechanism is working wrongly
> that I am ill.
> I am ill because of wounds to the soul, to the deep
> emotional self—
> And the wounds to the soul take a long, long time, only
> time can help
> And patience [and a certain difficult repentance.
> Long difficult repentance, realization of life's mistake and
> the freeing oneself
> From the endless repetition of the mistake]
> Which mankind at large has chosen to sanctify.

The poet is not afraid to speak of the presence of guilt—else, why the bold emphasis on repentance?—and to cry out his existential pain at the loss of personhood. This is symptomatic of a universal condition, which is why his words strike such a responsive chord.

THIS LEADS ME to an important etymological point which is quite relevant to our theme and sheds much light on the fundamental nature of *bikkur cholim*. Where does the word *bikkur* come from? It is a word of many meanings—but I have not been able to find any intimation in Biblical Hebrew of the idea of "visit." (This sense of the word may be a modernism; I have also not found the word to mean "visit" in Rabbinic literature.)

What then? I suggest that *bikkur* is related to the word *boker,* which means "morning" or "dawn": When we visit the sick, we must open a window for his depressed spirit, bring in light to his darkened soul, let the dawn and what it symbolizes enter the life of the patient. We must "enable the patient to obtain a restful spirit (*nachat ruach*) with his comrades." That is what, I believe, *bikkur cholim* really means. And it is a challenge worthy of our best and noblest efforts.

There is a well-known verse in the Psalms where this interpretation of the word *bikkur* reveals a new level of meaning. King David exclaims, "One thing I have asked of the Lord, that I will seek after: that I may dwell in the house of the Lord all the days of my life, to behold the pleasantness of the Lord and *le'vaker* in his temple" (Psalms 27:4). If that Hebrew word, from the same root as *bikkur,* is to be translated as "to visit," it is all very confusing: one who wishes to spend his life—"*all* the days of my life"—in the Temple, should not be praying for an occasional visit . . . However, if the word is taken as we have interpreted *bikkur cholim,* it makes eminently good sense: the Psalmist strives to spend his whole life in the Lord's Temple, but what will he do there? If it is only "to behold the pleasantness of the Lord," noble as such a wish may be, it is a bit selfish and self-centered, a sort of spiritual hedonism. But what he really prays for is the ability *le'vaker,* to bring light and dawn and joy into the Temple so that others who worship with him will find their lives transformed and filled with a new light and reason to live.

WE READ IN the book of Genesis (chapter 18) that after Abraham's circumcision at an advanced age, he was sitting at the entrance to his tent in the heat of the day, and the Lord appeared to him. The greatest of all Bible commentators, Rashi, citing the Talmud, tells us that this divine revelation was for the purpose of God performing the mitzvah of *bikkur cholim* by visiting Abraham in his state of recuperation. (In Judaism, God not only *commands* us to act ethically, but He does so Himself and becomes, as it were, a role model for humans.) A verse later we read that three people appeared before Abraham whereupon, despite his indisposition, he ran to make his guests comfortable. Here again we refer to Rashi who again quotes the Talmud: the three "people" were really three angels (or: messengers of God) in human form, and each had a specific mission to perform. One was to inform Sarah that she would, at the age of ninety, become a mother; the second came to heal Abraham; the third to destroy Sodom and Gomorrah. No angel is appointed for two missions; each has one mission and no more.

Now, the question arises: if God entrusted His angels with the three tasks mentioned, especially that of healing of Abraham, why did He not entrust the same angel—or perhaps a special one, in addition to these three—to visit Abraham as an act of *bikkur cholim*? If God is appointing angelic agents for a variety of tasks, why not visiting the sick as well? Why did He have to do that by Himself, as it were?

I believe the answer is this: to bear good news, to heal the sick, to apprise Sarah of her imminent motherhood, to punish the wicked—all of these tasks may be safely relegated to others. Angels prove quite responsible in carrying out such missions. The same would hold true for the first two of Ramban's three elements of *bikkur cholim*—nursing the patient and praying for him. But the third part, that of bringing *boker* or dawn into his life, of letting the sufferer see the light of day and banishing the darkness out of his heart, that *God Himself must do,* if only as a lesson for all mankind. God reserved that for Himself; *bikkur cholim* is too important to leave to others, even to angels. Only He has the capacity—unassignable to another—to demonstrate how to bring joy and light and hope and consolation into the heart of the sufferer. Only after He has shown the way, can humans be entrusted to imitate Him and do likewise.

Only God who knows all—"for the Lord peers into the heart" (I Samuel 16:7)—and humans who have learned from Him the art of understanding and insight and empathy to relate to human suffering, whether physical or emotional or spiritual or existential, with the mission of opening a window in the soul of the sufferer and bringing in morning, the blessing of a new and bright day—only they truly perform the mitzvah of *bikkur cholim*. And only they know the fullness of joy that can come from such a noble deed.

For it is more than angelic. It is divine. And that makes it profoundly human.

Chapter 7

SACRED TIME

The first three entries in this chapter deal with aspects of three "good days" (yamim tovim) or festivals, specifically Rosh Hashanah, Purim, and Passover—days which reflect the concept of sacred time in Judaism.

The fourth concerns the fast of the ninth day of Av, the "black letter" day on the Jewish calendar, commemorating the destruction of the two Temples in Jerusalem—and later national cataclysms. With the restoration of independence to Jews in the State of Israel, do the laws of mourning associated with Tisha Be'Av and the other "minor" fast days retain their legal status?

Ancient custom, integrated into law, ordains that Jewish communities outside the Land of Israel observe an extra day of the Holy Days—thus, two days of Shavuot instead of only one, eight instead of seven days of Passover, nine instead of eight of Sukkot. The rationale for such observance is offered in the next item, "The Holiday of the Exiles."

Finally, the chapter closes with a discussion of the difference between happiness, the biblically and halakhically distinctive element of the "good days," and the contemporary transmutation of happiness into "fun."

~ 31 ~

REPENTANCE BEYOND SIN

The beginning of a new year of learning and living a full Jewish life of mitzvot is a proper occasion to explore the often neglected overlay of meaning of our religious growth in these areas. The following comments are inspired largely by the writings of the founders of the HaBaD school of Hasidism, but they do not necessarily follow them entirely and, indeed, depart from them in certain details.

It is customary to associate *teshuvah* with sin. A person transgresses and he then rues his deed. The proper response is *teshuvah,* repentance. The halakhic analysis of *teshuvah* is highly sophisticated and articulates well with the psychology of the penitent, accompanying him on the various stages of his "return" to his pre-sin state.

However, sin does not exhaust the entire *teshuvah* phenomenon, for were it so, how would we account for the fact that the Talmud and Midrashim recommend *teshuvah* every day of one's life[1] and that the truly righteous are described as those preeminent souls who are in a state described as *kol yamav bi-teshuvah,* spending all their lives in repentance? It is stretching the point to answer that the greater the person the more aware he is even of the most minor infractions. Moreover, the Talmud does posit a category of *tzaddik gamur,* a completely righteous, i.e., sinless, person. Is such a totally blemishless individual to be denied this unique and inspiring mitzvah of *teshuvah*?

The most compelling answer is offered by R. Shneur Zalman of Lyadi, author of the immortal *Tanya* and founder of HaBaD Hasidism.[2] He differentiates between two kinds of repentance which he terms a Lower Repentance (*teshuvah tata'ah*) and a Higher Repentance (*teshuvah ila'ah*). The former is the kind of repentance we are most acquainted with—the confession, contrition, resolution, etc., that follow upon sin. This *teshuvah* may take the form of abjuring evil in any and all its many guises (thus, the

---

From Hamevaser, *the Student Jewish Studies Magazine of Yeshiva University (Vol. XXXVIII, No. 1)*

negative commandments), or that of the active pursuit of the good and the noble and the holy (the positive mitzvot). The choice is as much a function of individual temperament as ideological preference. But both are motivated by the consciousness of moral or spiritual failure.

The Higher Repentance has nothing at all to do with sin or defeat. It is the reaching out for God in an attempt to overcome the human condition of being separate and alienated from Him. Man's soul is the divine "spark" within him, and this *neshamah* strives for *teshuvah,* or, literally, "return" to its Source. In other words, *teshuvah ila'ah* represents a genuinely spiritual yearning, and is unrelated to psychology or disobedience—the realm of *teshuvah tata'ah.* The return, in the former, is not to one's own prior, pristine, pre-sin state, but to one's ontological origin, prior to his very existence separate from his Creator.

Both of these forms of repentance bespeak a high level of spiritual maturity, but the difference in focus results in qualitatively different experiences. Thus, the Higher Repentance is thoroughly rational; the striving to reunite that which once was one. The Lower Repentance, however, is irrational, almost absurd. It seeks to undo the past, declaring that the past transgressions never occurred or have even been transformed into virtues (*zekhuyot*).[3] It is a violation of causality and, indeed, common sense—although without it, we would be condemned to an inflexible, fatalistic, brutish existence. The divine forgiveness which is the shining goal of *teshuvah tata'ah* defies our reason, and the human reaction to such irrational divine pardon is fear or awe, sheer amazement, as we are overwhelmed by the divine indifference to mere reason and His overruling of necessity and causality (*ki imkha ha-selichah lema'an tivarei*).

In the major elaboration of repentance in the Torah, that recorded in *Nitzavim,* both forms of *teshuvah* are mentioned, but there is a clear separation between them. Thus, verses 1–6 apply to *teshuvah tata'ah,* while the following four verses, 7–10, refer to *teshuvah ila'ah.*

R. Shneur Zalman maintains that the Higher Repentance is addressed to God as the Ein-Sof, as the Infinite beyond all relationship, and is achieved through the study of Torah. The Lower Repentance involves an encounter with God in His self-revelation via the Sefirot, the Ten Emanations of His attributes, and proceeds through performance of the mitzvot. This is a most reasonable view, in light of the role of man in both forms of *teshuvah.* In the sin-driven Lower Repentance, a human being strives to reintegrate his personality the wholeness of which has been shattered by sin, and it stands to reason that he should appeal to God in *His* role of personality, i.e., the Ten Sefirot. This reintegration of one's personality is an expression of the psychological dimension of sin and repentance—and this is characteristic of the mitzvot, with their positive and negative modes of conduct both expressing and influencing one's will and emotions. When it comes to the Higher Repentance, however, which is the yearning to rejoin the Source of all being, it is not man's psychic state that moves him but his spiritual fate, his metaphysical and meta-psychological search for his ontological origins. In this stance, therefore, he addresses the Ein-Sof proper, that inner and ineffable essence of Divinity which is beyond personality, beyond the Sefirot, beyond relationship, beyond even divine transcendence itself. This more exalted form of *teshuvah* finds its channel only in the study of Torah, the realm of the "Light of the Ein-Sof."

Which of these two forms of repentance is superior? The question may be irrelevant; both are vital in the development and growth—perhaps very existence—of a religious person. In the *Nitzavim* passage, mentioned above, the progression is from Lower Repentance to Higher Repentance, implying that the latter is the more significant goal for which the former is the necessary precursor. Yet an analysis of the *Aseret Yemei Teshuvah* tends to the reverse conclusion. Thus, Rosh Hashanah hardly speaks of sin at all. Its most cogent and significant message is that of the majesty of God—*malkhuyot*—and the sounding of the Shofar, the symbol of the Sinaitic revelation. The shofar is the wordless cry of the supplicant aching in his spiritual solitude and calling out to his Creator with whom he seeks not reconciliation (for it is not sin that alienates him from the Creator but his very humanity) but reunion, reintegration, the overcoming of the "real" world which creates the distance between Creator and creature, between the divine and the human.[4] Reconciliation after sin is the theme of Yom Kippur, and the whole range of Lower Repentance is evident throughout the day: *vidduy* is recited time and again; the shame and embarrassment attendant upon *chet* is pervasive; the plea for pardon, for *selichah u-mechilah* is repeated again and again. The progression from Rosh Hashanah to Yom Kippur is thus one of *teshuvah ila'ah* to *teshuvah tata'ah,* the opposite direction from that mentioned in *Nitzavim,* and one which, by the same token, would indicate the higher level of *teshuvah tata'ah* over that of *teshuvah ila'ah.*

Perhaps the answer lies in the perspective taken. The Torah is, as it were, the divine point of view: God's anthropology. Here the Higher Repentance is the ultimate desideratum.[5] The cycle of the year, the precedence of Rosh Hashanah to Yom Kippur, reflects the human experience and therefore the human perspective, and so the final goal is *teshuvah tata'ah,* the Lower Repentance, for this more directly affects one's conduct and therefore his daily life. Or, perhaps, the priority of Rosh Hashanah to Yom Kippur, and the different forms of repentance they represent, is meant to instill in us an awareness of the ultimate goal of all our aspirations, indeed all of our lives, before we proceed to the "practical" task of mending what we have broken in the course of our imperfect existence of the past year.

Both of these exalted experiences should be with us, especially during this season of repentance, buttressing our spiritual courage and our determination to master our studies and, even more important, our very selves. May we succeed in these noble endeavors, and may our study of Torah and performance of the mitzvot be enhanced by the consciousness of their respective spiritual achievements, and thus inspire us to higher aspirations in both realms.

May all of us, as we enter the new year, succeed in both endeavors, and may the *Ribbono shel Olam* grant each of us, all our loved ones, all Israel, and all humanity, a year of peace and prosperity, of reconciliation with Him and with each other. And may our ultimate goals be so lofty that we can never fully achieve them—and yet so inspiring that we never despair of so doing.

Notes

1. *Shabbat* 153a; Eccl. R. 9:8; Mid. Psalms 90:16; *Shelah, Be'asarah Maamarot, Maamar* 7 (18).
2. In his *Likkutei Torah to Balak,* 74a.
3. *Yoma* 86b.
4. The wordlessness of the shofar and its superiority to mere speech is much commented upon in Hasidic writings, although the interpreta-

tions are not necessarily those I am suggesting. See R. Shneur Zalman in his commentary to his *Siddur,* p. 242b; and especially R. Menachem Mendel of Lubavitch, *Or ha-Torah,* section on Rosh Hashanah 2:81,82; *Beiurei ha-Zohar* 402:4, and *Derushim le-Rosh Hashanah* 1:374. Cf. the Rav in his *Ish ha-Halakhah,* pp. 57–59.

5. Nevertheless, in the course of one's life experiences, the defect caused by sin must be rectified before the process of Higher Repentance is undertaken. See *Tanya* 1:17.

~ 32 ~

THE MEGILLAH'S DOUBLE VISION

Megillat Esther manifests a remarkable phenomenon of duplication. The repetition of certain things twice seems to crop up all through the work in a manner that begs explanation.

Thus there are two drinking parties, one for the nobility and one for the masses. There are two feasts, one for Vashti and one for Esther. Even more astounding, because it is inherently irrational (for which reason the Sages and Commentaries offer a variety of explanations), there is a repetition of the gathering of the maidens at a beauty contest to choose a queen—even though Esther had already been chosen after the first one. Esther invites the king and Haman twice—even though she could have accused Haman at the first party. The legislation of two days of Purim, one for closed cities and one for open cities, is a distinction which has no parallel elsewhere in the Torah and which defies easy explanation. Mordechai and Esther twice legislate the reading of the Megillah and the attendant *mitzvot* of Purim—even though once would have sufficed.

How shall we explain all this?

Perhaps it is a subtle reaction—but one which most Persian Jews of that time would be sensitive to and understand immediately—against the dominant Persian pagan religion. It has been commented often that Megillat Esther goes out of its way not to emphasize the Jewish religion; thus, there is no explicit mention of the name of God. The references to Him are vague and indirect. This is so, apparently, because the Jews of that era were still in exile, and did not want to upset the local authorities and masses who would not want the Jewish God to be credited with the redemption of Israel and the humiliation of a prominent fellow citizen.

For the same reason, the Megillah included a subtle polemic, sardonic and satiric and even humorous in nature, against the du-

---

From Bein Kotlei Ha-Yeshivah *(Spring 1994), published by the Student Organization of Yeshiva*

alism of ancient Persian religion. By emphasizing the number two in the story of Jewish redemption, they meant to emphasize that the very number that characterizes the Persian religion—the *shetei reshuyot*, or dualism—is the one utilized by the One God of Israel to secure His people's triumph against the Persian tyrant. (Possibly, had the Megillah been composed in a Christian country, all the above events would have happened and been described three times.) Just as the pagan deities of ancient Egypt—the Nile, frogs, etc.—became the instrument of the redemption of Israel (*ki be'davar asher zadu alehem*), so was the dualism of Persia the medium for the salvation of the Jews by the One God.

The tendency to assert the principle of Judaism even under the most unfavorable political and social conditions is thus beautifully expressed in Megillat Esther in this disguised numerical polemic.

~ 33 ~

THE IRONY OF PASSOVER

The Exodus is replete with irony. The pride of Egypt was its fine steeds and its mighty chariots. Yet it was those very sources of Pharaoh's boastfulness that were cast into the surging sea. Thus was the Lord "exalted", *Ki ga'o ga'a* (see *Or ha-chayim* to Ex. *15:1*).

Similarly, as the Midrash puts it, "the Egyptians sinned with water and they were punished with water." It was the sea in which Pharaoh drowned Jewish boys, and into which he had cast even the infant Moses. It was the sea about which Pharaoh boasted that "my river is my own, and I have made it for myself" (Ezekiel *29:3*). And it was that very Nile that turned into blood. The Red Sea that split in order to save the Israelites, and that very body of water which came together again in order to drown the Egyptian hordes and bring Pharaoh himself to a watery grave.

Indeed, the symbol of irony may be found in the paradoxical *halakha* that only those five species of grain which can technically become *chametz*—are qualified to serve as *matza.*

Irony may well be one of the most intriguing and least appreciated themes of Passover.

It is difficult to define "irony" with any precision. Basically, it is the feeling that arises from a sense of contrast or weakness or paradoxical rightness. Irony issues from surprise, from the failure to anticipate the opposite results—results which, upon reflection, indicate a measure of unexpected justice in the world. It is a sudden awareness of the kind of justice that turns on those who fraudulently posture as its greatest advocates, and that undercuts the smug, the certain, and the confident—as, for instance, when we notice a tow-truck in distress at the road-side, a traffic judge caught speeding, or a preacher caught sinning.

Irony is related to humor. Both share the element of surprise at the unexpected turn of events. But the comical is a revelation of the inappropriate, the disjunctive, and the disparate, such as a

---

From the Yeshiva University Haggada *published by the Student Organization of Yeshiva, 1985, ed. Steven F. Cohen and Kenneth Brander*

man in full, formal outfit slipping on the sidewalk and sprawling over it awkwardly. The grotesqueness or disproportion is what causes us to laugh. The ironical too is unexpected, but it is a sudden intuition of proper proportion, of surprising justice, that which turns back and afflicts the one who, despite the greatest pretenses to righteousness, is himself most vulnerable. There are some situations which are on the borderline between the humorous and the ironical; an example would be the remark by a celebrated wit during a mail strike in New York City who advocated giving immediate pay raises to the mailmen, provided they would be sent to them—by mail!

The ironical points to the moral that man must not overreach. Irony results when man's pretenses are punctured, when his arrogance is deflated, when his much-vaunted security turns out to be dust and ashes, when his virtues look seamy, when his achievements prove baseless.

Life itself, irony teaches, rebukes man: It exposes the emptiness of his strength, his virtues, his wisdom. A noted American thinker once wrote, "Irony involves comic absurdities which cease to be altogether absurd when fully understood. Our age is involved in irony because so many dreams of our nation have been so cruelly refuted by history."

So, when astronaut John Glenn successfully returns to earth after a voyage through outer space, only to suffer a serious injury in a household fall—that is ironical and it teaches us something about the tenuousness of the power that we ascribe to ourselves. When the USSR, with its pretense of being "peace-loving", invades a "fraternal" country like Hungary or Czechoslovakia—that is the kind of irony that reveals the underlying hypocrisy of so much of our "ideology." Or, when Yiddishists who used to berate traditional Judaism, now turn to the old-line Yeshivot as the only source for the survival of Yiddish—that is the irony which shows up the emptiness and invalidity of even our benevolent ideologies.

All of Jewish history reveals a divine irony that is active in the affairs of man. Abraham and Sarah, our forebears, had everything people could want—except a child, and they gave up hope of ever having one. Could a man of 100 and a woman of 90 bear a child? "And Sara laughed" *(Ex. 18:12)*, or smiled. In defense of Sarah, one might well argue that it was not a sardonic or skeptical or sarcastic smile, but an ironical one. She saw that her despair itself was a sham, that man does not even have the right to despair in the confidence that his hopelessness is valid!

The eschatological vision of Judaism, that of the Messiah, also abounds in irony: The man who will redeem Israel and raise it to its ancient preeminence is not a man of great wealth and aristocracy, who will come riding in a Rolls-Royce or Cadillac, but "a poor man riding on a mule."

Seen in this light, irony possesses enormous moral significance. To open up oneself to the awareness of irony in history is to acknowledge the limitation of man in the face of God, the ultimate victory of divine justice, and the inscrutable but ubiquitous presence of God in the affairs of mankind. It therefore contains a double teaching: That we must not have too much confidence, and also not too much despair; that we must never be certain—nor must we ever give up. If we forget the ironical, we either abandon hope or turn insufferably arrogant; either way, we lose touch with God's reality.

The Biblical reference to irony is in the expression "the finger of God"—the willful finger of divine irony, puncturing pretenses, and leaving man utterly bewildered. "Then the magicians said unto Pharaoh, 'This was the finger of God'" *(Ex. 8:15)*—a finger which not only directs events and points the way to *geula,* but a finger which also wags under man's nose, which points mockingly at his vain presumptions, which tickles his swollen ego till it explodes in gales of laughter—at his own ridiculous pomposities. "He who dwells in the Heavens will smile, the Lord will laugh at them" (Psalms *2:4*).

In the Haggada we read that when the Torah says, "in great terror" (Dt. *26:8*), this refers to "the revelation of the *Shekhina.*" God is revealed in the moment that man confronts the terror of his own limitations, his own finitude and inadequacy, his own mortality and inevitable death; when he is suddenly startled by his own lack of ultimacy or certitude or security. This is irony—at the very moment he realizes how terribly weak and frighteningly unworthy he is—*be'mora gadol*—at that moment he discovers his greatest blessing and strength and hope and security in God Almighty: the revelation of the *Shekhina.*

The Seder is replete with symbols of irony. The entire Seder is built around children: Various rituals are performed solely so that the children not fall asleep, by arousing their curiosity; the four character types are referred to as four sons or children; it is the child who asks the *Ma Nishtana.* And—it is children specifically whom Pharaoh went out of his way to kill in order to destroy Israel.

Pharaoh is a man who had all the answers. When Moses told him about God, he did not ask anything. Instead, he delivered himself of a tirade: "Who is the Lord that I should listen to His voice?" *(Ex. 5:2)*—and that was not a question, it was a rhetorical explosion proclaiming his own denial. And so, we who relive on the Seder night the triumph against Pharaoh—we are full of questions on this night . . .

Our ancestors did not want to leave Egypt. They wanted to stay there, the land of "the fleshpots of Egypt." They told Moses, whiningly, "We remember the fish . . . the cucumbers and the melons and the leeks and the onions and the garlic" (Nu. *11:5)*—and, so very ironically, we their descendants celebrate our exodus from Egypt and our hard-won freedom not by eating all these vegetables of which they spoke, but with a broken piece of "poor man's bread" and a lump of bitter herbs—and we bless God for it! Throughout their pilgrimage in the desert, our ancestors complained that they did not have enough. And we celebrate our exodus by singing—*dayenu,* enough, enough!

Consider too the commandment of *heseva,* the leaning on the left side when we drink the Four Cups or eat the *matza.* We do so because it is a symbol of aristocracy and freedom. But it has always puzzled me: Why adopt for our Jewish religious purposes a form or posture that was unique to the Romans of 2,000 years ago? Why retain this fossilized Roman custom when we have so many beautiful Jewish customs? The answer, I suggest, is once again: irony. Why is our Seder lacking and incomplete today? Why do we not observe the Passover sacrifice, which was the center of our Seder in the days of our independence? Why *hashata hakha,* are we today in exile? Because the Romans of 2,000 years ago destroyed the Temple. But we shall not allow that destruction to undo us as a people. And so, today we practice that very Roman symbol of freedom, the inclining on the left side. We adopt the Roman posture of leisure—and we thereby celebrate *zekher leMikdash,* remembering everything that occurred in the Temple, while they, the Romans, are no longer in existence!

This indeed is the main intent of the plagues against the gods of Egypt. What the Egyptians trusted most became the source of their travail and woe. The Nile was a deity for Egypt—and it turned into blood. They worshipped the frog, sign of fertility—and God gave them so much fertility that the population explosion amongst the frogs threatened their very lives. The stricken gods of Egypt were an act of the irony by the One God.

We too, in our own lives, can detect—if we are perceptive enough—the workings of divine irony. What are our idols? Science, for one. And so we receive in return—the threat of mass destruction. We worship technology—and we now appreciate how it has interfered with the ecology of our planet. We love machines and prostrate ourselves before them—and they break down before (or just after) the warranty is signed.

We Americans speak so much of love—and we are flooded with pornography. We have identified as "the good life" a life of hedonism—and there is no joy and no happiness to accompany our material pleasures. The State of Israel was founded and given its vision by socialists and "progressives," who adopted the principles of the Left—and now Israel is rejected by both the Old and the New Left.

There is a most remarkable way in which this double teaching of irony, as we have outlined it, is evident in the Talmud. The Talmud *(Berakhot 48b)* tells us that two of the blessings in the *Birkhat haMazon* were composed in different eras. One of them was written by King David and his son Solomon, the other by the Sages of Yavneh, in the period after the destruction of the Temple, specifically after the collapse of the Jewish revolt against Rome and the slaughter of the Jews in Betar. The two blessings are those which speak of God who "rebuilds Jerusalem in His compassion," and of God "Who is good and does good."

One would imagine that David and Solomon, who attained power and security, composed the blessing celebrating divine goodness. Further, they built Jerusalem, and did not have to plead for divine mercy for its upbuilding. Similarly, one would expect that the Sages who witnessed the massacre at Betar would plead with God for compassion and mercy and pity in rebuilding Jerusalem. Instead, the Talmud tells us the reverse: David and Solomon pleaded for divine mercy in building Jerusalem, and the Sages of Yavneh, when the victims of the massacre of Betar were finally brought to burial, referred to God as one who is good and does good because He allowed them to give a decent burial to the victims.

What we are being told is that we must never overlook the religious principle of irony. At a time of national triumph we must not overreach, we must still acknowledge our need for *rachamim*, for divine compassion; otherwise, we risk being undone by divine irony. And at times of national disaster, we must never indulge in despair; thanks to irony, we may yet wrest victory out of defeat, triumph out of disaster, and therefore we must still look to God as *haTov ve'ha-Metiv.*

Passover, then, reminds us never to forget the *etzba Elohim,* that same finger of God first revealed at Egypt and ever since active in the affairs of man—that symbol of divine irony, that which brings down the arrogant Pharaohs of life, and which gives new hope to the downtrodden in the houses of slavery.

It is when we have learned this Passover-teaching of irony and acknowledged this finger of God, that we shall be able to look forward in confidence to the words in the *Birkhat haMazon,* where we place our faith in the Almighty, "to Thy hand, so full and open, so holy and broad, that we may never be embarrassed or shamed."

~ 34 ~

TISHA BE'AV TODAY

Ever since the founding of the State of Israel in May of 1948, there has been considerable discussion in Jewish circles of the necessity and desirability of continuing the observance of the four national fast days (Tisha Be'Av, Tzom Gedaliah, the Seventeenth of Tammuz and the Tenth of Tevet). This is especially true with respect to Tisha Be'Av, a fast which commemorates the destruction of the Temple and the loss of national independence on the ninth day of the month of Av. Why, it has been asked, do we continue to observe this fast day at a time when Israel is again independent?

Shortly after the establishment of the State, its Chief Rabbinate, faced with the problem, refused to abrogate any of the fast days. That ruling, however, did not end the debate. If anything, it gave it added impetus. The atmosphere then was charged with a feeling of apocalyptic fulfillment and of the imminence of the Messianic age, and this found expression in the discussion of the further relevance of the fast days which mourn lost independence. In the summer of 1955, with a good deal of the excitement dissipated, the Israeli weekly *Panim el Panim,* a splendid journal which has since unfortunately ceased to exist, published a symposium on the problem. The consensus was unanimously against the abrogation of Tisha Be'Av, but there was one well- documented opinion arguing for the discontinuance of the other three fasts on halakhic grounds. At times the situation became wryly amusing. People who never even dreamt of observing the day, let alone actually fast, turned into passionate polemicists arguing either for or against continued observance.

Nevertheless, the problem remains a real one, for it may reflect the deeper and more basic questions of the effect of the creation of the State of Israel on Jewish religious consciousness in general. Yet there are halakhic grounds for dealing with the issue from which we can derive a genuine Jewish point of view. The starting point for any valid delineation of a halakhic approach to the problem is the Talmudic discourse in Tractate *Rosh Hashanah,* 18b:

From Jewish Life *(July–August 1956)*

> Rabbi Hanah ben Bizna said in the name of Rabbi Simeon the Saint: What is the meaning of the verse, "Thus saith the Lord of Hosts: the fast of the fourth month and the fast of the fifth and the fast of the seventh and the fast of the tenth shall be to the house of Judah days of joy and gladness?" (Zechariah, 8:19.) The prophet calls these days both days of fasting and days of joy, signifying that when there is peace they shall be for joy and gladness, but if there is no peace, they shall be fast days. Rabbi Papa explained: when there is peace, they shall be for joy and gladness; if there is persecution (lit. "decrees of the government") they shall be fast days; if there is no persecution but not yet peace, then those who desire may fast and those who desire need not fast. If that is the case, is Tisha Be'Av also optional? Rabbi Papa replied: Tisha Be'Av is in a different category, because several misfortunes happened on it, as a Master has said: on Tisha Be'Av the Temple was destroyed both the first and second time, and Betar was captured (in the war of Bar Kochba), and the city of Jerusalem was ploughed.

In line with the later authorities, we accept the interpretation of R. Papa who leaves us a third alternative: that of no peace and no persecution when the fast is optional.

The crucial words in the text are the words "when there is peace." Just what determines whether a state of peace exists or not? Rashi defines it as a condition of national independence—when Israel is not under the domination of non-Jews. Accordingly, contemporary circumstances would call for converting the four fast days into national holidays!

However, most of the authoritative commentators maintain a more restrictive definition of the concept of "when there is peace." R. Chananel, Nachmanides, R. Zadok Ha-kohen, even Rashi himself by implication, and others define "peace" exclusively in terms of the existence of the Temple in Jerusalem. Thus, if there is a Temple, these days are holidays. If there is no Temple, and there are persecutions, they are mandatory fasts; if there are no persecutions, they are optional (except for Tisha Be'Av). This opinion would bind us, in the context of present day conditions, to continue the observance of the fast days in toto.*

**In 1956, when this article was published, Jews were being persecuted behind the Iron Curtain.*

THE TALMUD ITSELF seems to confirm this opinion. After the passage quoted above, the Talmud records the statement of two sages that "the All-Merciful made (the four fasts mentioned by Zechariah) dependent on the existence of the Temple." As an added point, Nachmanides and R. Jacob ben Asher (*Tur Or. Chayyim* 550) define "if there is no persecution" to refer to every place, not only to the Land of Israel. Considering present conditions of *world* Jewry, this definition does not permit abrogation of any of the fasts.

There is, in addition, a third opinion which synthesizes the two mentioned above. Maimonides maintains that during the Second Commonwealth the fasts other than Tisha Be'Av were optional. Historically, the Second Commonwealth saw the existence of the Second Temple, but national independence, which is Rashi's definition of "peace," was not achieved. Seemingly, Maimonides requires both national and religious conditions (Temple and independence) for discontinuance of the fasts and their transformation into "days of joy and gladness."

Concerning contemporary observance of three of the four fasts, therefore, the weight of authority is against abrogation, with a difference of opinion as to whether they are to remain optional or mandatory. But we face a different situation with regard to Tisha Be'Av. The Talmudic dictum quoted above, that Tisha Be'Av is in a different category because of the multiplicity of national misfortunes associated with that day, takes the issue out of halakhic debate. Nothing less than the most radical change in the world-wide Jewish situation, both political and religious, can transform the character of that day from one of grief to joy, from fast to feast. Until that redemptive era arrives, the Tisha Be'Av observance cannot be altered.

TECHNICAL HALAKHIC CONSIDERATIONS aside, what is the relevance of Tisha Be'Av to the contemporary Jew, who lives in the days of the "Third Commonwealth?" Is this fast only the anniversary of an ancient calamity which is no longer real to the twentieth-century Jew?

Let us dispose at once of the word "only" in that last sentence. We do not need a Martin Buber to tell us that "in Israel, all religion is history," or an Abraham Heschel to remind us that "Judaism is a religion of time." It is a manifest truth, demonstrated in the ordinary, daily life of the observant Jew. God encounters man in time, and therefore the recapturing and the reliving of the historical moment is a religious imperative and a spiritual experience. The Jews in the Warsaw Ghetto observing Pesach relived the historic liberation in the very shadow of death. The re-experiencing of *churban,* of destruction, should be no less meaningful to American Jews. It is perhaps just as important a function of the religio-historical observance to startle man into the realization that his "security" frequently rests on the gossamer threads of his imagination, as it is to hold out for him the eternal promise of hope and redemption. National fast days are affected by contemporary circumstances more than are other history-oriented rituals or observances. That is precisely what the Talmud meant when it qualified the necessity for continuing the fasts with the conditions "when there is peace" or "if there is persecution."

Obviously then, the fasts are to be more than recollections of specific *events* in history. Rather, the particular national catastrophe is being commemorated not as an isolated incident per se, but as the initiation of an entire historic *process.* Thus, if currently the national condition is unfavorable ("when there is no peace"), then the contemporary situation is understood as a continuation of the not yet complete tragic process initiated by the particular traumatic event. Hence the fasting is the expression of grief for an extended, cumulative national misfortune which is still observable at the present. Whereas if the contemporary situation is favorable, "peaceful," then the process initiated by one of the four specific historical tragedies is regarded as having been completed, and hence there is no call for grief. On the contrary, there is cause for rejoicing, for the process begun by those events is now, hopefully, ended forever.

Understood in this light, the three differing interpretations, previously mentioned, of "when there is peace" are basically three world views on Jewish history in general and three different appreciations of our contemporary status, depending on the relative evaluation of the two great tragedies of our exile: the loss of national independence and the loss of religious centrality and piety. A number of current ideological trends in Jewish life can trace their germinal thoughts to this halakhic controversy.

"Churban Europa"

Practically, the continued observance of Tisha Be'Av must concern itself with the two great historical events of modern times as well as with past history. These two are: *Churban Europa* (the Holocaust of European Jewry) and the founding of *Medinat Israel*. How are these to be dealt with in the present observance of this fast day?

In view of what has been noted above, it is only to be expected that the liturgy of those days and the meaningfulness of the fast itself will refer to subsequent misfortunes in the chain of national woe as well as to the precipitating catastrophe itself. Indeed, such is the case. In the Talmudic passage we cited at the beginning of this essay, a number of separate tragedies are recorded as being associated with Tisha Be'Av. In the liturgy of Tisha Be'Av, the *kinot*, a larger number of such disasters is mentioned, including the burning of the Talmud, the expulsion from Spain, the Crusades and, of course, the celebrated martyrology *Arzei Ha-levanon*.

There is no reason, therefore, not to include *Churban Europa*, which far dwarfs all its predecessors in magnitude and sheer horror, in this woeful list of historical events connected with Tisha Be'Av. First, it should be recalled, as Rabbi Mordechai Cohen pointed out in the July 27, 1955 issue of *Panim el Panim*, that the important dates of a great number of modern disasters did indeed begin on the ninth of Av. We need only mention the outbreak of World War I in 1914 and Hitler's first extermination order against Polish Jewry on July 27, 1942, both of which fell on the ninth day of the Hebrew month of Av. Second, and even more important, the Talmud itself maintains that it is not necessary to insist on the exact calendar day of the inclusion of an event to be mourned on a previously fixed national fast day, and that even the disasters related in the Talmudic passage mentioned above occurred on *or about* the ninth of Av. The principle is laid down by the Rabbis that happy events are celebrated on days already reserved for festivity, and sad events are mourned on days previously fixed for mourning.

HOW SHOULD *Churban Europa* be commemorated on Tisha Be'Av? There have been many suggestions. Some recommend reciting appropriate selections from modern Hebrew poets as part of the liturgy. Others reject this idea on grounds of impropriety: it is wrong to use the literary creations of men of questionable piety for liturgical purposes—and the traditional fast days, national in character though they are, cannot be divested of their essential religious nature and expression.

Most people deplore the generation that has witnessed such unprecedented havoc and has not produced one *kinah,* one elegy to commemorate it; or, if it is not "the generation," then it is "the Rabbis" who are blamed for this literary sterility. I believe, however, that both responses fail to take into consideration the very basic fact that no poet or liturgical genius could conceivably do justice to the unimaginable horror to which we have been witness. Certainly our generation is too close to it to assimilate and then express the enormity of the destruction. The Prophet exerted all his eloquence to lament the destruction of the Temple and the ploughing of the Eternal City. The medieval liturgist did the same for the havoc wreaked on Jewish communities in France and Germany. The greatest modern Hebrew poet, Chaim Nachman Bialik, stirred to the core of his soul by the horrors of a "modern" pogrom, produced his angry elegy, *Be'ir Haharegah.*

But can we expect any human being to express in *words* the torture and murder of over six million Jews? Can even the greatest conceivable poetic genius do justice to the residue of misery left with the survivors? To suggest that would be to overrate the human capacity for expression and to underrate the inhuman suffering of *Churban Europa.* Any attempt to designate a particular poem or selection of them as authoritative "kinot" for the Holocaust would be, I submit, not only a fantastic understatement, but a desecration of the memory of the martyrs. The horror simply surpasses the limits of human comprehension or communication. Perhaps the passage of time will permit the effort of literary expression of our unprecedented national cataclysm. Maybe later, but not yet.

Precedents for Silence

Yet there is sufficient historical precedent in Judaism for *silence* as an expression of grief. The two sons of Aaron, High Priest of Israel were killed. *And Aaron held his peace.* Ezekiel was told that his wife would die and he was commanded, *Sigh in silence.* Job was sorely stricken, and his three friends came to commiserate with him and console him. *So they sat down with him upon the ground seven days and seven nights, and none spoke a word to him; for they saw that his grief was very great.* The Talmud, in keeping with this tradition, forbids the mourner to greet a visitor, even to study Torah. This is not the place to confirm the psychological soundness of this ancient Jewish custom, but it should be mentioned that there *are* excellent psychological grounds for such an attitude, especially where it relates to mourning for a national cataclysm.

What I am suggesting is not a day of absolute silence. I mean, rather, that in place of creating new forms of lamentations to bemoan *Churban Europa,* which are bound to prove embarrassingly inadequate, we refrain from explicit mention of the Holocaust for the reasons given above and find an outlet, instead, in our subjective reading of the words of the Book of Lamentations traditionally recited on Tisha Be'Av. Can not almost any verse from Jeremiah's superb elegy serve better than anything we could compose to bewail *Churban Europa* as well as *Churban Habayit?* Are not the words of Lamentations true of European Jewry even as they were of Jewry in ancient Eretz Israel?—

They that are slain by the sword are better
Than they that are slain with hunger

Are not the following words appropriate for the victims of Nazi persecution?—

See, O Lord, and consider
To whom thou hast done thus! . . .
Thou hast slain them in the day of Thine anger;
Thou hast slaughtered them unsparingly.

Can not we who have survived cry out in the anguish that comes from personal knowledge and experience?—

I am the man that hath seen affliction
By the rod of His wrath.
He hath led me and caused me to walk
In darkness and not in light . . .
He hath filled me with bitterness
He hath sated me with wormwood . . .
Terror and the pit are come upon us,
Desolation and destruction.
Mine eye runneth down with rivers of water,
For the breach of the daughters of my people.

I am not merely recommending a new exegesis, submitting a novel method of interpretation. I am convinced that every pious Jew who has recited these verses from his tear-drenched prayer-book, since the first news of the Holocaust came to our attention, has had these very subjective thoughts in mind. He has poured out his grief for the extermination of European Jewry in the very same words in which Jeremiah lamented that of Jewry of another day. This is not a plan that must be imposed from without; it is something which is already practiced, for it comes naturally from within. And what is to prevent our Day Schools and Talmud Torahs from teaching Lamentations in just such a manner; teaching meanwhile that the wisdom of Israel is eternal and not restricted to local events and places? Has it not been a time-honored custom of Jewish thinkers to find, in the ancient texts, hints of great events of national importance that occured *subsequent* to the writings of these texts? Is there any reason why our generation cannot continue this creative homiletic process in the framework of the grand Midrashic tradition?

Medinat Israel

Let us now turn to the effect of the creation of the State of Israel on the observance of Tisha Be'Av. Having established that the creation of an independent state cannot result in the abrogation of Tisha Be'Av at the present time, it does not necessarily follow that it deserves no recognition whatever in our religious observance of the day. While we shall not endeavor to propose any specific plan or program, let us least demonstrate the possibility of according some kind of due recognition to this "beginning of the redemption."

The Halakhah deals with the introduction of a festive element in this mournful day on two levels. The first involves a completely extraneous occasion of joyousness which ordinarily would be observed on this day. This is the matter of the circumcision of a child on Tisha Be'Av. If the eighth day falls on Tisha Be'Av proper, then the father, who is the chief celebrant, may not break the fast, but is relieved of certain of the minor requirements imposed by Tisha Be'Av, "because a circumcision should be performed in joyousness." If, however, the eighth day falls on a Sunday which is the tenth day of the month of Av, but which is being observed as Tisha Be'Av (because fasting is forbidden on the Sabbath and hence must be postponed one day), then the father may break the fast after the ceremony, "because this is his holiday."

Thus, while an independent occasion of festivity may modify some of the minor laws of Tisha Be'Av, it cannot eliminate the major expressions characteristic of the observance. Nevertheless, we have here some indication of how the modern independence of Israel can be recognized in the observance of Tisha Be'Av. And although the case of the festivity of circumcision is different because its timing requires it to be observed only on this day, still, as we shall see shortly, the celebration of *Medinat Israel* may also be regarded as peculiar to Tisha Be'Av.

Festive Aspects

The second level on which the Halakhah deals with *simchah* (joy) on Tisha Be'Av concerns not external elements but a festive note which is inherent in the character of the day itself. An ancient tradition maintains that on the day the Temple was destroyed, the Messiah was born. This fusion of the elements of hope and mourning (never despair) was read into a verse in Lamentations itself: *He hath called a solemn assembly against me.* The word which is here translated as "solemn assembly" is, in the Hebrew, *mo'ed,* which usually denotes a holiday. Hence, it was homiletically established that Tisha Be'Av itself has a festive aspect. The Halakhah, too, recognized this discordant element of cheer which tradition—perhaps the innate national hope and will to live—had imposed on Tisha Be'Av. Thus, it declared that the daily penitential and other such solemn prayers which are not recited on festive occasions are to be omitted from the Tisha Be'Av liturgy, because the day has the character of *mo'ed.*

An interesting application of this principle is recorded by the Sephardic Rabbi Chaim David Azulai who writes (*Birkhei Yosef*) that he read of a decision concerning Italian Jewish women who were evidently lax in their observance of some of the minor laws of Tisha Be'Av. The author advised the rabbis not to interfere with the practice of these women of "weak faith" since Tisha Be'Av includes the festive nature of hope for redemption, and it is better to "strengthen their hands that they may retain that faith in the redemption, that they shall not—heaven forbid—despair."

This antithetical character of a fast which is partly festival, and a mourning for exile which contains the promise of redemption, is echoed in the liturgy of the day as well. The Lamentations themselves are elegies interspersed, here and there, with unsupressed outbursts of hope. The rays of redemption pierce the gloom every now and then. Even Isaiah's dire prophecies, read as the Haftorah on the Sabbath preceding Tisha Be'Av, reveal this dual, paradoxical nature, and they are followed by the "prophecies of consolation" on the seven Sabbaths following.

Hence, the recognition of *Medinat Israel* as at least "the beginning of redemption" is quite appropriate to Tisha Be'Av itself. This recognition need not be expressed by subtracting from the main Tisha Be'Av observance. Instead, some method might be found for introducing a special service of thanksgiving in the afternoon of the day, or perhaps, as has been suggested, the night after Tisha Be'Av. The exact nature of this service, or whatever character the commemoration will take, is something which will have to be determined by authoritative Rabbinic bodies, preferably the Chief Rabbinate of the State of Israel.

Thus, a valid Orthodox view on the question of continued observance of the national fast days, based on halakhic grounds, sees no need of discarding them because of contemporary developments. It sees, rather, in the great historic events of the last two decades, an opportunity for deepening our experience of these days, an occasion for discovering new avenues of expression of the entire gamut of our national experiences within rather than without the framework of the hallowed traditions of Israel. By blending these historic events into the grand stream of Jewish religious life, we will find an opportunity for giving new dimensions to our near-emasculated religious consciousness.

~ 35 ~

HOLIDAY OF THE EXILES

The "extra day" added to each major festival observed by Jews in the Diaspora has been a subject of discussion for over a century. Reform Jews have banished these days altogether from their religious calendar. Some Conservative leaders have tended toward abolition, though most Conservative synagogues still observe the extra days.

Orthodox Jews are increasingly called upon to explain the discrepancy between the holy days we observe and the festivals as prescribed in the Torah. We observe one extra day each at the beginning and at the end of Passover and Sukkot as well as an extra day of Rosh Hashanah and of Shavuot. Except in the case of Rosh Hashanah, which is observed for two days in Israel as well, all the extra days are observed only in the Diaspora. Hence, they are called *Yom Tov Sheni Shel Galuyot,* the "Second Holiday of the Exiles."

How did this practice originate? Since a complete halakhic and historical answer would require a full volume, a simplified explanation must suffice here.

THE JEWISH CALENDAR is based upon the moon (with built-in corrections for accommodation to the solar year). Before the exile which followed the destruction of the Temple and the widespread use of a fixed calendar, the new month was determined by visual observation. Some lunar months are twenty-nine days, others thirty, depending on when the new moon is first sighted. In the old days, the Sanhedrin in Jerusalem would officially declare the new month begun only after hearing from witnesses who had actually seen the new moon. This decree was called *Kiddush Ha-chodesh,* sanctification of the month.

As soon as the Sanhedrin thus sanctified the month, messen-

This article appeared in Jewish Heritage *(Spring 1966)*

gers would be sent to all Jewish communities, informing them which day had been declared *Rosh Chodesh,* and hence when all holidays of that month would fall. While the Jewish communities of the Holy Land received the news quickly, communities in the far-flung Diaspora often experienced a long wait. Sometimes, the holy days of that month would come to pass before the messengers had even arrived. Hence, there was always doubt about one day: the Talmud calls it the *sefeka de'yoma.*

This is why the Diaspora communities would observe each holiday for two days—just to make sure that they had observed the proper one. Even after the calendar was formalized, based on a sound mathematical foundation predicting precisely the new moon centuries in advance, Jews in the Diaspora maintained the tradition of two days. So universal had this practice become that the rabbis then pronounced the "Holiday of the Exiles" (*Yom Tov Sheni Shel Galuyot*) as formally binding on all the Diaspora. The only ones to reject them were the medieval Karaites and, in our own day, Reform Judaism.

Orthodox Jews remain loyal to this tradition, and have not deviated from the age-old acceptance of the sanctity of the "Holiday of the Exiles." The codes, from Maimonides to the *Shulchan Arukh* down to our own day, are unanimous in declaring the "second days" an integral part of Judaism in the Diaspora. No authority, not even a reconstituted Sanhedrin—according to the structure of Jewish law—could abolish their observance. Traditional Jews maintain this practice because of their commitment to Jewish law, despite the facts that we now have a scientifically correct calendar, that we can accurately predict the appearance of the new moon, and that our communications are almost instantaneous. Abolition of the "second days" will not increase observance of the "first days" any more than the abandonment of Hebrew by Reform enhanced its followers' practice of regular prayer.

IN ADDITION TO Halakha, there are spiritual values that inhere in these "second days." First, our observance of the "Holiday of the Exiles" evinces a respect for *minhag,* Jewish custom or tradition. The question had already been asked in Talmudic times by the Sages of Babylon as to why the two days had to be observed since the calendar was already known with precision. The Sages of Palestine sent back the answer: "Be careful to observe the customs your ancestors transmitted to you" (*Betzah* 4b). According to the Geonim, the custom originated as far back as the days of the Prophets.

In Jewish life observance is an expression either of *din,* law, or *minhag,* custom. *Din* and *minhag* differ essentially in this respect: *din* issues from without, *minhag* from within. *Din* is what God reveals. *Minhag* is Israel groping for God—the expression of the collective religious will of the people of Israel. While *din* tells us what Jews should be, *minhag* tells us what they already are. *Minhag* is the mirror of the Jew's life and, like the reflector of a telescope, it focuses into one point all the various strains and tendencies of the Jewish heart and soul.

What matters is not that we now have telephone, telegraph, satellite communications and that we no longer are beset by doubts over the correct day of the month. What matters is that Jews observed these days for centuries—even when they knew the right day with certainty—and this observance expresses the collective inner spirit of our people. The late Rav Kook maintained that when we observe a *din,* a law, it is essentially an expression of our love of God. When, however, we observe a *minhag,* a custom, it is a profound reflection of our love of Israel. Hence, when we observe the "Holiday of the Exiles," we proclaim that we are not only children of God but also brothers to our fellow Jews in all ages.

Even more than *minhag,* however, the "Holiday of the Exiles" is today part of rabbinic law. The Sages, approving the widespread observance of this tradition, declared it mandatory. Judaism is more than folkways, more than dogmatic faith, religious experience, study of Torah, and even more than the sum total of its commandments. Judaism is primarily the authority of the Rabbis in interpreting the Bible. The Jewish faith cherishes the Oral Law equally with the Written Law, and accepts Scripture only according to the authoritative interpretation of the Sages. The Torah itself commands us to obey the duly constituted religious authorities of each age. What distinguishes Judaism from various forms of fundamentalism is our acceptance of rabbinic interpretation and legislation. There is no single *mitzvah,* no single Jewish religious institution, that is not rabbinically defined.

So it is with the "Holiday of the Exiles": it is not only a custom, but an irrevocable rabbinic ordinance. These "second days" are of sufficient importance for us to refrain from laying *tefillin,* even though, insofar as the calendar is concerned, they are really weekdays. Similarly, we recite the holiday *Kiddush* and prayers, although normally an unnecessary or irrelevant blessing is considered a violation of the third commandment. The second day of *Yom Tov* is as precious as the first; we observe both equally (with the exception of certain emergency situations which the Rabbis exempted).

Finally, our observance of the Holiday of the Exiles reminds Jews that we are in exile. Israelis do not need to observe these days because they are in Zion. R. Moses Sofer (*Derashot Chatam Sofer* to *Bo*) declared that these days will be observed in the Diaspora forever, if only in remembrance of our bitter two thousand-year-old *galut,* just as we still observe tokens of our earlier exiles in Egypt and Babylon. Exile, in the Jewish view, is not necessarily defined as loss of freedom or the state of being subject to overt persecution; it is not primarily a political concept or an economic state, but a spiritual and psychological condition. In ancient days, even Jews in the Diaspora who enjoyed a large measure of autonomy never doubted that they were anything but exiles; whereas Jews in Palestine, even under a brutal foreign yoke, never considered themselves exiles.

From this point of view, the Holiday of the Exiles is more important for the modern Diaspora Jew than it was for his parents and grandparents in Russia, Germany, Poland, Hungary. They knew they were in exile; they needed no reminder. But we who have made such great political and economic strides and who enjoy such a marvelous measure of freedom need a Holiday of the Exiles to remind us of our spiritual *galut.* This is probably what the great kabbalist Rabbi Moses Cordovero meant when he said that every holiday is, in essence, a channel for transmitting holiness to the Jews.

Every festival is a specific means for Israel to attain a higher degree of sanctity. Exile, with its threat to the spiritual vitality of Jews, requires twice the number of days. The assimilatory tendencies that threaten our existence as Jews in the Diaspora can be countered not by less, but by more *kedushah.*

~ 36 ~

HAPPINESS AND FUN

When the Founding Fathers of America wrote the Declaration of Independence, they included one new phrase which was to have wide repercussions later in the history of this country. That phrase is, "the pursuit of happiness."

The idea of happiness is, of course, nothing new. Americans did not invent it. It has been known in a hundred languages and experienced universally for millennia. Our own Torah dedicates three entire sections as *parashat moadim,* the description of the major holidays on which we are commanded *ve'samachta be'chagekha,* "thou shalt be happy in thy festivals." What was new in the formulation of the Founding Fathers was the emphasis on happiness as something to pursue.

Serious thinkers have not always looked with favor on this phrase. Not that there is anything wrong with being happy—their outlook is not jaundiced—but they have two reservations: first, is happiness really to be the highest goal of man? Is it subordinate to or more important than, let us say, the idea of duty, or respect for others, or faithfulness, or honor? And second, can happiness really be acquired by pursuing it? Is it not really a rather elusive prize which you can win only indirectly by living in a certain way, and not by a direct chase?

But all these debates are really academic. Today we accept happiness as surpassingly important; for many it is the highest value that life has to offer. And we no longer ask questions about the wisdom of pursuing it in order to attain it. We do not simply pursue it; we are relentless, fanatical, single-minded in our hot chase of happiness. Also, we have changed the word "happiness" to "fun," and with it has come a change in the content of our aspirations. Happiness, at least, implies an ordered, harmonious way of life which offers deep satisfactions. Fun is nothing of the sort. It is escape, pure and simple. It is a matter of losing yourself consciously in a world where all tensions are released

---

"The Pursuit of Fun" appeared in Jewish Life *under that title in the late 1950's*

and inhibitions loosened. And the pursuit of fun has become America's chief avocation.

IN ESSENCE, THERE is nothing wrong with occasionally having fun, provided it is decent, clean, controlled, and harmless. There is no mitzvah to be a humorless bore. Some diversion or escape is always necessary and welcome. My concern is, however, with that great number of Americans—and American Jews—who have unconsciously transformed fun from entertainment to *Weltanschauung,* from casual distraction to consuming passion, from occasional release to total immersion in escape from the challenges to which life summons us. Perhaps life in this complicated, dangerous world is too deadly serious for most people; but that is an explanation, not an excuse for avoiding its problems.

Consider how the original concept of "the pursuit of happiness" has degenerated into the "fun for all" disease that affects every part of our society. At Cape Canaveral not long ago a human being was shot into space. Fortunately he returned safely; God was good to him, his wife and children, and the injured prestige of his country. The days and hours before the firing were tense ones. They should have been, as they were for many, a time for prayer, and the sobriety that comes from knowing that a man's life is at stake. Yet one reporter told of the carryings-on at the entertainment spots surrounding the missile area: large crowds overflowing, drinking, joking, and dancing in anticipation of the firing. Commander Shepard hovers between immortality and deadly failure—and Cape Canaveral turns into a carnival. A man faces the terrible loneliness of outer space, and his fellow men clutter up whatever inner space they possess with embarrassing nonsense.

Here is a second example. A certain Jew who lives in the South has made a great success as a humorist by drawing upon immigrant Jewish experience on the Lower East Side. He has painted funny verbal pictures with "Only in America," and admonished us to "Enjoy, Enjoy." Some of us may like his brand of humor, others may not. That is irrelevant. But what does one say in response to a supposedly funny piece in which he writes a kindly, good-humored description of a Jewish girl taking her vows as a

Roman Catholic nun? When a prominent Yiddish writer took him to task for it, Harry Golden insulted his critic and replied that he takes such conversions in stride—with gentility, kindliness, and a sense of humor! Is this not carrying the idolatry of fun a bit too far? Jews know that on occasions of this sort you tear *keriah* and sit *shivah*—and the apostle of good humor has fun!

THE WORD "fun," according to Webster, comes from the Middle English *fonnen,* which means: to be foolish, to fool someone. Too much concentration on "having fun" is indeed the epitome of foolishness. And if you spend your life in that nervous, anxious, guilt-laden pursuit of fun, then you fool no one but yourself. No, this is not happiness. And it certainly is not *simchah.*

I recently chanced upon something known as "Chase's Calendar of Annual Events," which is a compendium of eight hundred occasions of celebration, fun, and festivity observed in the United States. We are, a reading of this book reveals, a holiday-ridden people. There is scarcely a single day in the year when some citizens in some part of this great country will not be celebrating something or other. We have every conceivable kind of holiday, from weeks dedicated to the peanut and girl scouts to months celebrating children's art, from extolling the egg to days hailing mothers, fathers-in-law, buzzards, and bachelors. For everything there is a parade and the occasion for some group just "to have fun." Amazing: a complete *luach* dedicated to the principle that every day is a time for fun! And yet, no one will disagree, there is not a day that passes but what more and more people become more and more miserable. Fun is, evidently, a failure.

OUR OWN JEWISH calendar is one that presents us with a number of *chagim u'moadim,* holidays and festivals. They are days of happiness, of *simchah.* Do our *chagim u'moadim* bear any resemblance to the fun-fare that we have been describing? Assuredly not—yet sometimes it seems that we have so assimilated to the fun-culture of contemporary America, that we have failed to appreciate the vast abyss that separates them. That is why only a few years ago one of our "defense organizations" published a book purporting to acquaint our non-Jewish neighbors with the essentials of Jewish belief and practice. Although a fairly good book, a remarkable picture emerges from it: Jewish life is a merry-go-round of joy upon joy, a breathless round of celebrations, all smiling faces and wine-drinking and feasting. Rosh Hashanah and Yom Kippur are primarily happy times filled with laughter and fun. Even Tisha Be'Av "has lost much of its tragic overtones." The Jews, we are told, "are overjoyed that freedom is flourishing in so many parts of the world." Of course, the remnants of Eichmann's victims and the Jews in Morocco and behind the Iron Curtain are not aware of this—but then, they do not appreciate that the Jewish calendar is like the unofficial American calendar, and that both are dedicated to the proposition that the pursuit of fun is the noblest goal of man created in the image of God.

Real *simchah* is, of course, nothing of the sort. True joy, in the Jewish sense, is not an escape from life but an intensification of its loftiest features. *Simchah* is the elevation of man, the enhancement of his spirit that comes with the realization that he stands in the presence of God—that he is not alone on the face of the earth. That is why *simchah* is the special characteristic of the three pilgrim festivals, the *shalosh regalim*, for then the Israelite would ascend to the Temple to "be seen before the Lord." To enjoy the companionship of God and His gifts—that is the gist of happiness. *Simchah* does not come from avoiding the knowledge that there is evil in the world, from blinding oneself to the enormous threats of pain and death. It comes from an appreciation that in this kind of world, despite evil and sickness and suffering, there *is* a God Who watches over us, that we *do* have the opportunity to vanquish evil, that there *is* a vibrant, active principle of holiness and purity and goodness. We do not use the historical origin of our holidays as an excuse just to pursue happiness or have fun. The holidays are themselves expressions of joy when man faces the world with open eyes and open heart, and each holiday has its own character and its own joyousness.

IT WOULD BE too much to try to exhaust the meaning of each of the *yamim tovim*. A Jewish holiday is like a human personality: it has a thousand different facets, each more intriguing and fascinating than the next. Let us, rather, examine only one facet of each as a source of *simchah,* as interpreted by the Hasidic sage and saint, the author of *Sefat Emet.* He points out that in *Vayikra* (Leviticus) the *parashat Moadim* follows immediately upon the mitzvah of *Kiddush Hashem,* the sanctification of God's Name. "And I shall be sanctified amongst the Children of Israel," was interpreted by our Rabbis to mean that a Jew must submit to martyrdom rather than violate any of the three major sins known to Judaism: idolatry, unchastity, and murder. The three major festivals of Pesach, Shavuot, and Sukkot, the *Sefat Emet* maintains, come to preserve and enhance each of these three principles for which we must be ready to give our lives in *Kiddush Hashem.*

A man must give up his life if ordered to take the life of another, for homicide is an unforgivable sin. The positive principle is celebrated in Pesach when we recall that God took us out of the land of slaves where life was cheap and man worthless, where babies were tossed into the Nile. Pesach fills us with joy as we appreciate the transcendent value of life in a world where people usually speak of the destruction of millions of people in the impersonal terms of cold statistics. We do not just "have fun"; we are instead suffused with happiness that life was granted to us, and that we are entrusted with its safe-keeping.

The principles of morality or chastity must not be violated even under pain of death, for so is God made holy in Israel. And the festival of Sukkot reaffirms that concept by emphasizing the importance of the home. For an immoral act is in essence an offense against the family. In the presence of immorality husband and wife can have no love for each other; children and parents at worst do not know each other, and at best despise each other. Sukkot is the time we remember how our God took us out of Egypt with its lust and fleshpots, its incest, its sexual degeneracy, and led us through the desert in order that for forty years we learn to dwell in *sukkot,* each family protecting the wholeness of its home and its sacred integrity. On Sukkot we are joyous that every Jewish family can hold aloft the banner of *tzeniut,* that we can learn to respect the personality of another human being and not treat another as merely an animate object of our desire. We are happy that we can preserve the family and home even in a world filled with *giluy arayot,* a world where obscenity more and more becomes legally accepted and morally respected, where degeneracy receives the sanction of literature and the blessing of art, and where home after home falls apart.

FINALLY, AND PERHAPS most important, a Jew must perform *Kiddush Hashem* and relinquish his or her life rather than submit to idolatry. Shavuot, which commemorates the giving of Torah at Sinai, affirms the Jewish appreciation of Divinity itself. We are happy that in a civilization that has silenced the voice of God by denying that He is concerned with man, and set up the idols of power and money and science instead, we Jews are the recipients of His Torah and can to this day partake in the supernatural experience of Revelation by studying the Torah. When we study Torah we know that God is not silent, that He speaks through its pages, that He has let us know how to live without loneliness, without despair, without emptiness. What a source of joy!

Here, then, is an example of how Jewish joy differs from secular "fun," of how the Jewish calendar, based upon *simchah,* is different from the ordinary calendar. Unlike fun, which is a form of escape by being blind to life's dangers and evils, Judaism's *moadim* provide *simchah* by a direct confrontation with them. Unlike fun which is amoral, and often immoral, *simchah* is eminently moral and ethical and spiritual. It shows you the face of a world which tolerates murder and genocide and tells you to revere life: the ethics of *simchah.* It reveals to you a society corrupt with unchastity and commands you to respect the integrity of every home and family: the morality of *simchah.* It bares before you a civilization that has largely forgotten God and reminds you of His ever-loving presence: the spirituality of *simchah.*

Ashrenu, mah tov chelkenu, u'mah na'im goralenu, u'mah yafah yerushatenu. "Happy are we!—for how good is our destiny, how pleasant our lot, how beautiful our heritage!"

Chapter 8

THE RABBINATE

The rabbinate continues as a calling, but as a profession it is in the midst of constant change. The first article speaks in general of the challenges to the rabbinate in our contemporary period, and the second focuses on one important aspect of the profession, namely, the sermon—both as a form of communicating the teachings of Judaism and as an art form in its own right.

The next six entries consist of addresses I delivered at what have now become the quadrennial commencement exercises of the granting of Semikhah (ordination) at the Rabbi Isaac Elchanan Theological Seminary, the affiliate of Yeshiva University. They spell out my attitudes concerning the rabbinate and spiritual leadership in general over the course of thirteen years.

The last item is a talk I gave at the Centennial of the Seminary, one that was rather widely misquoted by those whose polemical interests were best served by such distortion. Let the reader judge!

~ 37 ~

THE CHALLENGES OF THE MODERN RABBINATE

The Rabbinate today has fallen upon hard times. In the last year or two, there have appeared a number of articles announcing the imminent demise of the Rabbinate, one of the greatest of Jewish religious institutions. Its functions have been taken over, one by one, by others—the *Rashei Yeshivah* and the professors, the fundraisers and the social workers—and the Rabbi has become a vestigial functionary, a charming anachronism. Sooner or later, the community will manage very well without him, perhaps devising some other functionary to preside over synagogue services.

Now, I do not wish to address myself specifically to this question of the future of the Rabbinate. "I am neither a prophet, nor the son of a prophet." Besides, the Talmud makes some unflattering remarks about those who pretend to the mantle of the seer. Furthermore, our loyalty to Torah unquestionably transcends our loyalty to the Rabbinate, and if Judaism can get along without professional Rabbis in the future—as it has in the past—so be it. I may be sad at such morbid prospects, but not crushed.

However, I honestly do not believe the grim prognosis. As Mark Twain once said, upon reading an announcement of his death in the morning newspapers, "I have read my obituary and believe it is much exaggerated."

It is, of course, true that the Rabbinate is in trouble—and it is in greater trouble in Israel than in the English-speaking countries (although I shall confine my remarks to our communities in the Diaspora). I believe we have slipped into a rut, but we are not lost. We are in many ways stricken, but not irreversibly. I submit that we still can recapture our commanding role as spiritual leaders and effective guides if we bestir ourselves—before it is too late. The verse *mipnei sevah takum* ("before a hoary head shalt thou rise"—Lev. 19:32), is interpreted by the Zohar temporally

---

Adapted from an address at the Anglo-Jewish Preachers Conference held in Manchester, England, in May 1968 and published by the Conference

rather than spatially: "before" implies a chronological priority, as if to say, "before you grow old, rise!"

There is still time for the Rabbinate to rediscover the sources of its inspiration and to rise to the summons of history, before it becomes encrusted with and disheartened by its diminishing authority and scope. Perhaps, in face of this trivialisation, our greatest challenge is precisely to rediscover our real, genuine challenges. Merely to identify them correctly is, in part, the beginning of an authentic response, even as the Neo-Kantians taught that the right question is half the answer. Permit me, therefore, to point to what I believe are *some* of our major challenges, and in some of these cases to adumbrate what I feel ought to be the direction of our responses.

The first of these challenges is that posed by the existence and success of the State of Israel. Israel represents one of those major turning points in Jewish history, the consequences and ramifications of which take generations to measure. In addition to the obvious salutary effects of the founding and survival of the State, which require no elaboration before an audience of this kind, its emergence has given rise to as many new problems as it has solved old ones. To put it bluntly, it has called into question our very existence as autonomous and self-perpetuating Jewish communities in the *Golah*. It does this in two ways, one more immediate and the other more theoretical.

Practically, it has—paradoxically!—accelerated assimilation in some circles. Before 1948, there were many marginal Jews who stubbornly retained their Jewish identity and affiliation because they felt a personal responsibility to the Jewish heritage and people, and did not want to be guilty of contributing to its disappearance. With the State emerging as the guarantor of the Jewish future, many of these peripheral Jews no longer accept such an obligation, and have no qualms about gently and softly sliding into the gaping void of eternal oblivion. I do not believe there is anything we can do, in a direct way, to counter this rather unconscious argument. It tells us that we can no longer appeal to the Jewish instinct for survival, but that we must address ourselves to the strictly religious yearnings, inchoate though they be, of as yet uncommitted Jews.

The second effect of this historic watershed is theoretical, but no less urgent. It constitutes a reproach to our very determination to survive as Jewish communities outside of Israel. I do not want to get into the maze of dialectics of affirmation or negation of the Golah. Such debates are fascinating, troubling, but often inconclusive. We do know, on the one hand, that we *ought* to go on Aliyah and encourage others to do so; that is part of our Torah commitment. But we know just as well, on the other hand, that barring any unforeseen events, the great majority will not go. Hence our duty is to go and to inspire others to go on Aliyah—and at the same time to build a firm and stable and enduring Jewish life here and in the United States and elsewhere. Intellectually, this means picking our way through a minefield of ambivalences. Practically, we must devise a plan whereby at least one member of every family will be encouraged to go. But no matter what the specific solution, it is a problem that cannot and must not be avoided.

The second challenge is the *communal* one. Three elements are discernable here. Let us enumerate them in ascending order of importance.

First is the question of co-existence with non-Orthodox religious groups within the Jewish community. The problem is ubiquitous and sufficiently well known for us to dispense with any descriptions. We in the United States face an almost identical situation, *mutatis mutandis.* For myself, I accept neither extreme. I do *not* believe that all differences are confined to the liturgy and that communally we must accept each other's convictions as equally legitimate. If we are indeed Orthodox, then we have commitments that we cannot in good conscience compromise in the name of sportsmanship or good fellowship or even unity. To ask us to recognize as a bona fide Rabbi one who is lacking in acceptance of Halakhah or in the requisite knowledge of Torah, is to ask us to abandon our own principles. It may lay us open to the charge of having closed minds, but I always recall Prof. Lionel Trilling's remark that some people are so open-minded that their brains fall out.

At the same time I refuse, without cogent reason, to read anyone out of the Jewish community. We have suffered so much by the decimation we experienced in the Holocaust, by increasing intermarriage and assimilation combined with a decreasing birth rate, that we can ill afford the luxury of denying the identification of Jewishness to those who desire it. To take a "hard line" means not only to lose those who currently consider themselves officially non-Orthodox, but to abandon their children and the masses of undecided onlookers, including so many of our own people, who can only be discouraged and repelled by an inflexibility they do not comprehend and therefore consider Neanderthal.

We are challenged, therefore, to develop a theory of Jewish communal relations according to Halakhah—and I believe this can be done if we are straightforward and fearless—and to apply it practically in steering through this dilemma on a safe course.

The way we have managed it so far in America, for better or for worse, is to distinguish between *kelapei penim* and *kelapei chutz*. Internal matters of the community, those relating to religious observance and halakhic authority, are reserved by us for those who accept the sovereignty of Torah. All other matters, dealing with external relations, be they Israel or the general society or government, are considered as properly requiring our full cooperation with all interested Jews. It is the middle ground where the difficult questions arise and which most tax our wisdom, our tact, and our prudence as we juggle the often contradictory values of religious purism and mutual respect.

But this leads to the second element of our communal challenge. Before we confront the dilemma of the Orthodox community in its relations with others, we must manage to hold our own *kehillah* together and prevent it from flying apart by the centrifugal forces tearing at it precisely because of the question of relations with the non-Orthodox. Here too we face a thorny challenge, and one that may well be more fateful than the first, which I feel is often exaggerated and inflated by empty and acrimonious polemics. We have got to learn to retain the sense of fraternity amongst *all* segments of the Orthodox community. The segregationists must not imagine that they can keep on reading out of Orthodoxy anyone whose communal philosophy is somewhat to the left of their own. Ultimately the circle of the acceptable becomes narrower and narrower, until it disappears; it is much like peeling an onion until you discover that you have nothing at all left. *Benei Torah* are a *community*—and must never become a mere sect. At the same time, the more liberal, integrationist, elements must recognize that in the Hasidic and Yeshiva communities we have invaluable resources of learning and passion that we renounce only at the risk of our own disintegration,

Heaven forfend. As Rabbis, it is up to us to contribute to the equipoise and tranquility of the community.

But both of these questions are as nothing as compared with the single most urgent issue of all: adequate Jewish education, both quantitatively and qualitatively. Unless a community can successfully build Day Schools where its children, both boys and girls, will receive a thorough Jewish education up to the university level, it cannot expect to survive; nay, it has no right to expect to endure.

American Jewry was a dying community until the Day School movement breathed new life into it. It provided us with a reservoir of *baalei-batim,* of potential Rabbis and religious functionaries, of those who at least will know what they are rejecting—and what they may some day return to. To our chagrin, I admit that it was not primarily Rabbis who initiated the Day School movement. But once it was under way, pulpit Rabbis encouraged it in all ways: educational guidance, recruitment, and fund-raising. Every self-respecting Rabbinical student knows that his first duty in coming to a new position is to build a Day School. He may try and fail—but it is nobler to try and fail than to fail to try.

The third main challenge is the *institutional* one. Because I am unacquainted with the structure and nature of the typical Anglo-Jewish synagogue, I must confine my remarks to the American Orthodox synagogue and assume that my observations will be of interest if not of relevance to you.

The synagogue in the U.S.A. is becoming progressively more secularised. Not only the Conservative and Reform temple, but even our own Orthodox synagogues have been affected. No longer is the "shul" only a place of prayer or study. It is also the social center of the Jewish community, particularly in the suburbs and provinces. The social hall has encroached on the sanctuary. People join a synagogue for a variety of reasons, but not necessarily for purely religious ones. There are clubs, parties, balls, and discounts for members' Bar Mitzvahs.

Now that is not all bad; not at all. I would rather have Jews congregate about the synagogue than in places completely devoid of Jewish associations. However, it often becomes questionable which aspect is more important and which influence prevails. And then we are in trouble.

I am reminded of the words of Joel (ii, 17): "Between the court

[hall] and the altar let the priests, ministers of the Lord, weep; and let them say, 'Spare Thy people, O Lord . . . why should the [other] nations say, Where is their God?" We, the *Kohanim* of our synagogues, often weep out of sheer frustration. We and our synagogues are torn between the competing forces of the "altar" and the "hall." Which shall triumph—the social hall or the sanctuary?—the parties or the prayers?—the platform or the pulpit?—the *dinim* or the dinners?—the "Bar" or the "Mitzvah?" By our own highest resolve we must determine that we can have both, with the *mizbeiach* always primary. We must reassert the *religious* nature of our lives and our public institutions, so that our non-Jewish neighbors, the *goyim,* will never have the occasion, as unfortunately they sometimes do, to ask, "Where is their God?," whether Jews are really a religious people. Our task is clear, and we must execute it successfully and fearlessly.

Fourth on my list is the *intellectual* challenge. In a way, the institutional problem is just a reflection of the intellectual crisis in which we now find ourselves. Because of the limitations of time, I cannot treat this matter with more than minimal adequacy and therefore apologise for it.

The thrust of the philosophic attack on Judaism today is not the same as that of the 19th century. I am amused at both the pocket-*apikorsim* and the over-anxious defenders of the faith who waste their mental energies and forensic talents debating such issues as Darwinism or Wellhausen. These are issues which are only peripheral to the concerns of contemporary man. And perhaps that is the real problem—they have simply been by-passed!

Our most serious threat comes from secularization and secularism. I say "threat" because we have not yet adequately dealt with it; but "challenge" would be more accurate, because it affords us opportunities as well—if we are astute enough and profound enough in joining the issue honestly.

Secularity is not just a philosophy. It is the mood, the very mental climate, of the contemporary city dweller in our technopolitan society—what Harvey Cox has called "the Secular City."

Three factors amongst many other relevant ones demand our attention in confronting secularity, and I shall sketch in what I submit ought to be our approach to them.

First, secular man is interested only in this world. He does not know and could not care less about that other world of which

Christianity has been preaching, and whose geography it has been mapping, and whose temperature it has been measuring for almost twenty centuries. Second, secular man is convinced of his own freedom and autonomy, and cannot accept a theocentric universe where God determines everything and man is shorn of all power. Third, he tends more and more to a commitment to ethics while casting away all traditional moral restraints which he does not consider as enhancing his personality, deepening his relationships, or fulfilling his potential.

Now, with regard to the rejection of other-worldliness, we Rabbis, as teachers of Judaism, must strive to clarify to contemporary men that we refuse to be caught on the horns of this dilemma. We confirm neither the exclusive affirmation of material existence, nor the classically Christian view that this world is of no significance save as a pale reflection of the other world. Indeed, we do not subscribe to the ultimate bifurcation between *Olam Hazeh* and *Olam Haba*, between body and soul, between Law and Love, between the letter and the spirit. Of course we know of these distinctions and we use them. But they are primarily analytic tools, not hypostatic realities separated by an unbridgeable metaphysical abyss. Both Christianity and modern Western man have inherited these dualisms from ancient Gnosticism, and therefore feel constrained to choose between them. But Judaism, in its mainstream, has always affirmed both sides of each dualism, accepting an ultimate monism, and in fact tends to emphasize the here-and-now. Indeed, in all of Mishnah there is only one reference to theosophy (in *Hagigah*, chap. 11)—and it is negative!

The question of the autonomy of man in the face of an omnipotent and omniscient God has been raised by a number of existentialist thinkers, such as Camus and Sartre. Here too we must teach our people not to confuse Judaism with Christianity. Christianity has taught the moral nihility of man who can be saved only by grace. Modern man, who has built a fantastic technology, cannot accept this denial of his innate value and power and freedom. He therefore proceeds to assert his own freedom as over against God's hegemony.

Here again Judaism is in a favored position. It is our task to elaborate the Jewish view which sees God as denying Himself freedom and omnipotence in order to endow man with power and choice—for better or worse. I am sure that you are as aware as I am of the relevant sources in Bible, Talmud, and Midrash. Interestingly, we read in the Tanchuma to *Tazria* of a debate on this very topic between Tyrannus Rufus and R. Akiva. R. Akiva pointed out that God did not finish creation, but left it to man. Holding up stalks of grain in one hand and a loaf of bread in the other, the Jewish Sage pointed out to the Roman general the superiority of the latter to the former thus did R. Akiva explain circumcision to the Roman pagan: God even left man himself unfinished and demanded that he create himself, that he perfect himself. So that man's right and even duty to assert his own creativity and inventiveness, his own freedom, is an integral part of Judaism and can certainly accord with this aspect of the thinking of secular man.

The third element is more troublesome. Contemporary man, in his anthropocentrism and his denial of transcendental morality, has but one rule: the respect for the integrity of his inter-personal relationships. Moral prohibitions as absolutes do not interest him. His only question is: Am I fulfilling myself without hurting anyone else? If the answer is "yes," he permits and encourages it; if "no," he considers it wrong.

That this attitude is pervasive should be obvious from the fact that it has infiltrated even the churches. Study *Sex and Morality* by the British Council of Churches in 1966 and you will discover the extent of the moral disaster. Read between the lines and you will notice how it gives its *hetter* to *Lady Chatterly's Lover,* a particular form of adultery. Only recently a convocation of Episcopalian priests in New York declared as "morally neutral" the act of homosexuality where there was true love between the two parties and no outsider is hurt. These are symptoms of the new "immoral ethics" that threaten the whole structure of Jewish morality, heretofore accepted unquestionably, at least in theory, by the Western world.

And here there can be no accommodation. As Rabbis we may applaud the stress on meaningful personal relationships; but we must stand fast and firm and remain unapologetic in our undisguised espousal of theistic morality. Before Christianity civilized the pagan world by teaching it Jewish morality, we were all alone in fearlessly proclaiming the Law of God to an unredeemed world. Even if now the rest of official Christianity will follow the avant-garde of the Church and revert to paganism, which I do not expect, we shall continue our lonely watch with dignity, with conviction, and without ever wavering.

Finally, a nettlesome challenge to the modern Rabbinate is what we may call the *professional* challenge. Unfortunately, in the eyes of our contemporaries and even, alas, our own eyes, we are no longer *Rabbanim* in the grand tradition, but professional generalists in charge of communal trivia, pious superficialities, and ritualistic irrelevancies. We have, under the impress of an all but inexorable sociological development, yielded one realm after another of special and significant rabbinic competence. We have surrendered our halakhic positions to the *Yeshivot* and *Rashei Yeshivah; machshavah* to the professors of religion and theology; and communal leadership to the professional fundraisers and executives. Even the function of the Rav in *Chessed* has been reduced from personal involvement to perfunctory service: we screen people in order to refer them to charitable organizations, psychologists, or marriage counsellors. What we are left with is enough to discourage any intelligent man—a required weekly sermon; ritualistic "prayers" dutifully pronounced at official occasions and listened to by no one, probably not even by the Deity; minor counselling; Hebrew school supervision; and the development of just enough dignity to stand on when our own spiritual "authority" is challenged. We even pay regular hospital visits and *shivah* calls as if these were professional obligations rather than human encounters obligatory upon all Jews. Once we have succumbed to this trivialization, to this vulgarization, there is little left to encourage us or to inspire bright and dedicated young people to the Rabbinate. No committed and ambitious young man should ever aspire to become a functionary in an arid community; certainly not to become a parish butterfly.

There are two responses to this situation that I regard as most urgent, and that I respectfully submit for your attention. One is programmatic, the other personal.

The first response to this professional challenge consists of an educational reform which I believe is worthy of serious deliberation.

Our trouble is that we are generalists in an age of specialists, and so we are gradually becoming superfluities.

Some wit once said: The generalist learns less and less about more and more, until he knows nothing about everything;

whereas the specialist learns more and more about less and less until he knows everything about nothing.

We Rabbis must avoid both these pitfalls. We can, on the one hand, hardly expect any longer to produce the kind of personality such as a Rambam, what the secular world calls a Renaissance Man. Our accumulated knowledge is too great, and such genius is too rare. Nor can we opt either for generalism, which has helped bring us to this sad state, or specialization, which would destroy the Rabbinate just as effectively.

My prescription is something I have always felt intuitively was implicit in the Rabbinate throughout its history, but which was consciously brought to my attention by the recent innovation in the English Rabbinate, introduced by the Chief Rabbi, namely, the Cabinet, whereby different individuals are assigned different and specialized roles. But what I have in mind is not administrative but personal, not a bureaucratic improvement but an educational reform.

We must learn, in essence, to combine generalism with selective specialization. As generalists, Rabbis must be trained to be competent in *all* fields in which Rabbis are and ought to be active—preaching, counselling, administration, youth, theology, writing, education, and it goes without saying—*lomdut.* Every Rav should have passing adequacy in each of these areas, and far more than the minimum in the last category. Even for Rabbis is it true that *Talmud Torah ke'nagged kulam,* study of Torah outweighs all other commandments (Rav Kook once said, in a light moment, that Rabbis or spiritual leaders are known as *einei ha-edah* and we therefore pray *ve'ha'er einenu be'toratekha,* that even Rabbis should study Torah . . .) Of course, this learned audience does not need to be reminded that *am-haaratzut* is the very antonym of *Rabbanut.*

However, in addition, our schools—and we ourselves—must encourage each Rabbi to specialize in *one* area without ever relinquishing passing ability in the other areas. For to do *only* one thing well means to become a "professional," not a Rabbi: a professional teacher or speaker or writer or psychologist. And this is tantamount to giving up our souls and surrendering the influence that *only* a Rabbi can have on the community by virtue of his manifold tasks and the large number of people with whom he comes in contact.

Thus, for instance, some of us must specialize in *Pesak*—which once was almost the exclusive function of Rabbinate. We must know that there are colleagues (and not only professional *Dayanim*) to whom we can turn for *she'elot nashim* others for *gittin,* others yet for *Choshen Mishpat.* Some must become pre-eminent in teaching Talmud and *Mefarshim*—in effect, to become *Rashei Yeshivah,* while at the same time retaining ties in the Rabbinate so as not to fall victim to the derisiveness that characterizes the approach of so many *Rashei Yeshivah* to Rabbanim, an attitude which effectively discourages many of their best disciples from entering the Rabbinate. Some must learn modern historical and biblical and theological scholarship, and develop approaches for religious intellectuals to contemporary problems—probably our greatest and most pressing need at present. Others must specialize in youth work, others in educational administration, and so on.

I do not mean merely that we have to be better in some things than in others. That happens to everyone all the time; rather, we have to be *expert* in some areas while not abandoning the others: sufficiently expert to be effective and acknowledged, and above all, to serve as a resource of knowledge and experience and assistance for our colleagues.

The second response to our professional challenge is that of a profound personal decision. It calls upon us to reassert our own innate strength and enthusiasm and spirit by a sheer act of will. Our personal dedication must be such as to shatter the professional fetters which threaten to diminish us and emasculate our leadership and influence. We must simply refuse to crawl into the little notch that the Jewish community has carved out for us. We must adamantly reject the role that it has prepared for us and the image it wishes us to project. We dare not become dignified mannequins presiding over a game of religious charades.

In Kabbalistic terms, we must strive for *chessed she'bi'gevurah.* That should be our special pride. Let us face our tasks with *gevurah,* with intellectual vigor and spiritual strength and idealistic commitment. But let us never be guilty of intolerance or belligerence. *Chessed she'bi'gevurah* means to be aggressive, but not offensive; tough, but not rough; to act with vigor, not rigor. It demands of us courage and heroism with personal graciousness and compassion and generosity.

Such an attitude may sometimes cost us popularity; but we did not accept upon ourselves the burdens of spiritual leadership in these difficult times in order to win popularity contests.

Apropos of this last point, I offer you an interpretation I heard from Rabbi Kreiswirth of Antwerp, Belgium.

After Naomi rejected the entreaties of her daughters-in-law to follow her, she succeeded in discouraging Orpah, but not Ruth. Subsequently, according to the tradition, Ruth became the ancestress of David, and Orpah the ancestress of David's great antagonist, Goliath.

Now, this is apparently an injustice. Did not Orpah too express a desire to follow Naomi and was it not Naomi who dissuaded her from pressing her noble ambitions? Is it not unfair that she should have been defamed by history as the grandmother of that Philistine brute, Goliath?

The key lies in the two verbs which describe the point of departure between these two young widows, *Va-tishak Orpah le'chamotah ve'rut davkah bah.* Orpah **kissed** her mother-in-law while Ruth **clung** to her. Both had good intentions, both entertained lofty sentiments, both meant well. But Orpah was satisfied with an externalized gesture, while Ruth cleaved with a superhuman devotion that would not let her go. And from this apparently innocent and slight difference did the fate of these two young women diverge so radically: the empty kiss of Orpah led to the vile blasphemies of the Philistine Goliath, while the selfless, devoted clinging of Ruth led to David, sweet singer of Israel.

That the difference in the destiny of the two sisters-in-law lies here, is attested by the Talmud which, describing the encounter between Israel and the Philistines, declares: *Yavo'u benei neshukah ve'yiplu bi'yad benei devukah* "Let the children of the one who kissed, fall at the hand of the children of the one who clung" (*Sotah* 42b).

One of the most glaring weaknesses of Rabbis has been our sweet disposition. Too often we have forgotten the revolutionary nature of Torah and the transforming quality of its precepts, and so we have been unwilling to rock the boat in our communities. We have permitted passivity to displace passion, and saccharine sentiments of "respect" for Judaism to substitute for the searing of the heart and the soaring of the soul. We have often failed to demand of our people, to challenge them by examples of conviction and profundity. We asked them to kiss the Torah, and both they and we failed to cling to it by studying it. We introduced politeness and manners and respect and aesthetics into our services—the *va-tishak.* But we forget that while these are certainly desirable, services demand much more than this; they require passion and depth and commitment and a willingness to risk your life. Indeed, we forgot that services themselves are not the totality of Judaism. No wonder we are so often the victims of superficiality and a creeping mediocrity that has become an accepted occupational hazard of the Rabbinate.

So if we are to break out of this professional trivialisation which has so diminished our roles and threatened to undo us, we must resolve to do away with our comfortable, pacific image of kindly ministers of religion who do not wish to disturb the peace. We must do away with that which is symbolised by the empty kiss. Instead we must surge forth with regained strength and renewed dedication and redoubled pride to perform our tasks with true *devekut,* to cling and cleave to our ideals with superhuman strength, and to arouse in our flocks the awareness that they are themselves *benei devukah.* We must not desist, we must not permit ourselves peace until our clinging has evoked a cry to us from our communities: "Thy God is our God, thy people is our people, thy Torah is our Torah, thy destiny is our destiny."

Let this resolve and this determination evoke in us the courage—moral, spiritual, and personal—and the heroism which brought us into the Rabbinate in the first place, so that we may restore it to its historic role; and that it, in turn, may restore us to the awareness of the dignity of our calling.

Our challenges are mighty. The obstacles are high. The path is difficult. But with strength and vigor we shall prevail.

We shall overcome.

~ 38 ~

NOTES OF AN UNREPENTANT *DARSHAN*

The art and science of homiletics have fallen into disfavor and even disuse in the course of a generation or two. Sociologists of contemporary Orthodox Judaism have yet to take note of this phenomenon, although it will surely some day merit at least a footnote in some historian's tome on the American Orthodox rabbinate in the last quarter of the twentieth century.

When I began my Semikhah studies at Rabbi Isaac Elchanan Theological Seminary (RIETS) of Yeshiva University, and when I entered the rabbinate two years later, *derush* was taken seriously by those of us who considered the rabbinate as a life-long career. True, the amount of time devoted to it in the curriculum was minimal relative to Talmud and *Poskim*. But at the end of the fifth and beginning of the sixth decades of this century, there was still a consciousness of *derush* as a respectable discipline with its own skills and traditions and methodology as well as an invaluable asset for the practicing rabbi. The significance of preaching was almost as overemphasized 35 years ago as it is underestimated today.

I do not pretend to be an historian of the rabbinate, and I have not consulted whatever data are available. My comments are subjective and impressionistic, and I offer my observations and anecdotal fragments for whatever use they may be, if any, to scholars who may ponder the fate of this genre of rabbinic literature and professional activity. I do so because I love *derush* and rue its eclipse in recent times.

When I say that *derush* was taken seriously in the '40's and '50's, I do not mean to imply that there was unanimity of opinion as to the value of any particular form of *derush*. The "generation gap" was particularly acute in that period. Older, European trained rabbis looked with undisguised contempt upon what they considered the blather that the younger, American born or educated rabbis were preaching to their congregations. The latter were amused at the irrelevant, arcane, and often involuted *de-*

This essay was published in the Rabbinical Council of America Sermon Anthology *in 1986 rashot* of their older colleagues. But each group was generally respectful of the genre as such.

The situation today is different—and worrisome. Senior rabbinical students and a growing number of young rabbis generally do not regard *derush* as a serious enterprise worthy of the attentions of a *lamdan*, and their aptitudes are usually commensurate with their attitudes. "*Derush*" has, for some, become a pejorative synonym for a form of rhetoric that is pretentious, superficial, and lacking in intellectual value or respectability. Moreover, those laymen who are more educated in Talmud and traditional Jewish lore, and whose world-view is more pronouncedly halakhocentric, expressly prefer rabbis who are *talmidei chakhamim* and who will *not* preach on Shabbat or Yom Tov. A *sheiur*, yes; a *derashah*, no. An inverse snobbism seems to be developing: incompetence in *derush* is taken as a distinguishing characteristic of the "real" scholar.

I recall talking to a newly minted *musmakh* of RIETS three or four years ago. I was interviewing him for entry into one of our Kollelim, and after a period of "talking in learning" (a less threatening form of *bechinah*), I asked him about his career plans. He professed interest in a congregation—but was careful to inform me that he intended to give *sheiurim* in place of sermons. This piece of good news was accompanied by a triumphant smile of self-satisfaction. I reminded him that Tannaim such as R. Meir and R. Akiva and R. Judah ha-Nasi gave *derashot;* that his "rebbe" and mine, the Rav (Rabbi Joseph B. Soloveitchik), is [was] one of the most gifted and distinguished homileticians of our generation; and that his future congregants may seek instruction not only in the practical aspects of *melichah* or the construction of an *eruv,* but also in problems of morals and questions of destiny and death and how to react to current issues—matters that do not always lend themselves to solutions readily available in *Mishnah Berurah* or *Iggerot Mosheh.* He was not impressed. But apparently the word got out that I was easily swayed by a *gut vort,* and thereafter senior students who came to my office for brief sessions of scholarly discourse before being certified as *rabbanim* by the Yeshiva appeared well armed with homiletic nuggets of all sorts. I had to force them back to discussions of Halakhah. After all, my reputation was on the line. . . .

In truth, this attitude is not as radically new or unique as I have implied. Practitioners of "hard" disciplines generally tend to dismiss those in the "softer" areas. Natural scientists feel superior to social scientists, psychologists ridicule social workers, and historians refer to shoddy scholarship in their field as "journalism." In the same manner, homiletics is less demanding intellectually and therefore less prestigious than Halakhah. Indeed, the analytic prowess necessary for successful execution of halakhic discourse is far greater and deeper than, as well as different from, the cognitive abilities required for good *derush*.

But this, of course, begs the question. Granted that Halakhah is more impressive in its rational powers, and more important for Jewish continuity, and occupies a higher role in the hierarchy of Jewish values than *derush* or Agadah—does this imply that the latter is of *no* significance? Granted that *devar Hashem zu halakhah*—is not all of (non-halakhic) Genesis too "the word of the Lord?" Bread may be "the staff of life"—but how many of us are satisfied with bread alone and willing to forgo the other staples of our normal diet? If Halakhah is the science of Jewish religious life, *derush* is its art, and esthetics needs no apology in its claim to a rightful place in the sanctuary of Torah.

Whence the low esteem of homiletics and preaching in general?

A number of different elements seem to have coalesced in creating this shifting pattern. For one thing, it is a reflection of the newfound strength of the Roshei Yeshivah as opposed to congregational or communal rabbis. This phenomenon is, in turn, but one aspect of an interesting sociological change in our community which in many ways parallels the communal structures introduced by Hasidism, except that today the role of the Hasidic Rebbe is being filled by the Mitnagdic Rosh Yeshivah. Where once the religious authority of the community was vested in the Rav of the Kehilah, Hasidism substituted for this geographic form of authority an ideological cohesiveness: you were subject not to your local Rav, but to the Rebbe, no matter how far away his locus. Today too, many a young professional or businessman who spent his formative years at a yeshivah will consult not the Rav of his Shul (if he has one—more often he will "daven" in a "Shtibel" whose pride is in its *not* needing a rabbi) but his Rosh Yeshivah from his yeshivah days. But the strength of a Rosh Yeshivah (despite any talents he may possess in *derush*) lies in his halakhic scholarship, the medium of his discourse and the badge of his authority; whereas the Rav, who may be equally learned or perhaps an even greater *lamdan* and may spend most of his time and intellectual energy in his capacity as halakhic decisor and teacher, must reach his *entire* community, not only his pupils, and his medium of religious communication is more the *derasha* than the *sheiur.* The downgrading of *derush* is therefore a reflection of the unconscious grasp for the symbols of power and authority.

A second contributor to the phenomenon we are investigating is the need to establish a sharper ideological identity. The growing polarization in the Jewish community between Orthodox and non-Orthodox results in increasing emphasis upon what sets us apart from each other rather than upon unifying factors. Hence, the search for easily identifiable differentiae such as darker clothing (especially the black fedora) and the peculiar yeshivah patois that has become the "insider's language" in our *frum* or *frummer* community. The same intuitive reasoning leads to the conclusion that in our professional rabbinic activity we must stress our differentness, and if the non-Orthodox, for whom Halakhah is marginal, express their clerical roles by means of the sermon, we must choose the lecture or *sheiur.* (The same dynamic may account, at least partially, for the rather skimpy record of Orthodox rabbis on social justice issues—even when the cause is Russian Jewry and the like.)

A third element is one that is common to all segments of American society: the loss of verbal potency. Teachers throughout the country—and perhaps much of the world—complain about the disrepute into which language has fallen in the eyes of young people. Not only do students lack facility in language, and ignore its powers, subtleties, and nuances, but they consciously deprecate it. Now, preaching is a form of communication; rhetoric demands verbal skills. And the art of homiletics therefore suffers along with all other forms of verbal communication. Even if one is endowed with the requisite talents of imagination in interpreting a text, he too often lacks the skills needed to express himself cogently.

Fourth, I suspect that many of the younger men who express a measure of disdain for *derush* simply have not heard good *derush* and therefore generalize from their very limited experience. Those who grew up in more formal *shuls* and were exposed to competent and inspiring preaching know how valuable, edifying, and inspiring a first class *derashah* can be. A good sermon, like a *mitzvah,* begets other good sermons.

There are, I believe, also more profoundly theological reasons that go back almost two centuries. All contemporary yeshivot are, in one way or another, derivative of the Yeshivah of Volozhin, founded by R. Hayyim Volozhiner. It is R. Hayyim's thought, most clearly formulated in his *Nefesh ha-Hayyim,* that shaped the character of the whole Mitnagdic yeshivah movement. R. Hayyim raised the study as well as practice of Torah to unprecedented heights, and in Torah itself it was Halakhah that was considered preeminent. R. Hayyim refers to a statement by the Sages that King David prayed that the reading of his Psalms be accounted as worthy as the study of *Nega'im* and *Ohalot*. Since we nowhere find that his prayer was answered, we conclude that the reading of Psalms (or other non-halakhic parts of Tanakh) is less praiseworthy than halakhic study. The burden of this attitude, as well as the rest of his *Nefesh ha-Hayyim* (which is largely a statement of the Mitnagdic ideology in response to the challenge of Hasidism), is thus the centrality of Halakhah with the concomitant downgrading of all other branches of Torah study. This halakhocentrism appears in our own days in both the high status accorded to Halakhah and the negative evaluation of *derush* as well as Agadah, Tanakh, etc.

Closer to our own times, the publication by the Rav of his *Ish-ha-Halakhah* some forty years ago had a profound influence over two generations of Orthodox rabbis raised under his tutelage. This powerful essay, a species of intellectual psalmody in honor of the archetypical "Man of Halakhah," gave philosophical grounding and analytical respectability to the classical Mitnagdic esteem for the study of Halakhah over all else. The Rav's magisterial authority and elegant conceptual prowess has thus given credence (unintended, to be sure) to this deprecation of all non-halakhic expressions of Torah Judaism.

However, the question that must be dealt with in the education of our Semikhah students is: Are these explanations also excuses? Are these conclusions valid, given the premises, or are they wanting? Granted the preeminence of Halakhah (and not only for argument's sake), is the teaching and practice of *derush* illegitimate, a waste of time?

I feel most strongly that *derush* is an integral part of the authentic Jewish experience, that it remains and will indeed become even more significant as a medium of religious communication with our Jews in the years to come, and that rabbis ignore it at their own peril.

The rationales, both explicit and implicit, conscious or unconscious, for the disesteem of *derush* in the eyes of some of our younger Orthodox rabbis are inadequate and fallacious. The Rosh Yeshivah may indeed take more naturally to rigorous halakhic analysis than to the exhortations and imaginativeness of *derush,* but congregational rabbis are heirs to an old and worthy tradition and they should aspire to be what they intended to be, not what is more popular or prestigious or powerful, or what they would want to be in another *gilgul.*

Halakhic fealty and creativity may be more characteristic of Orthodox rabbis and set them off from others, but that is no reason for abandoning homiletics, a form of religious communication and expression that is thoroughly Jewish. The authenticity of the Orthodox rabbi should consist of the content of his message, not in rejecting whole genres of rhetoric or literature because ideological antagonists make use of them. Historians tell us that the reverse process took place during the period of the Geonim and Rishonim: When the Karaites developed the field of Biblical exegesis and grammar, Rabbanites such as R. Saadia and Ibn Ezra accepted the challenge and did not shy away from the field; they entered it with gusto and mastered it.

The centrality of Halakhah does not imply a deprecation of other modes of legitimate religious expression. R. Hayyim Volozhiner did occasionally preach *derashot,* although not of course the weekly regimen contemporary rabbis struggle with. And the Rav, for all his greatness as a giant of Halakhah, is the most creative *darshan* and most effective speaker I have ever heard. Setting up Halakhah and *derush* as opposites is erroneous—and silly.

Moreover, halakhocentrism is a theory that is always articulated in a *non*-halakhic medium! The *Nefesh ha-Hayyim* is a theological tract (I know of no better way to describe it), not a halakhic essay or responsum. And the Rav has elaborated his conception of Halakhah in philosophical idiom and in a variety of *derashot* throughout the years. (One should add that *derashot* may make use of halakhic material as well as agadic sources, depending upon the erudition and resourcefulness of the *darshan*.)

It is true, of course, that Judaism is unthinkable without Halakhah; but it is equally inconceivable without Agadah and *machshavah* and *derush*. After all, what is life without poetry? *Derush* has been ubiquitous throughout the history of Rabbinic Judaism and is largely coextensive with it. There is no reason for authentic *derush* not to serve a creative function for our times as well. It is fortunate that more people want to "learn" today and that they recognize the spiritual hegemony of the Halakhah—although there remain thousands of members of Orthodox synagogues whose knowledge is still quite limited and compares inadequately either with their aspirations or pretenses. But people not only want to *know*. They—*benei Torah* as well as "ordinary" *baalei batim*—also seek and need to be *inspired* and *motivated*. "If you want to know Him through Whose word the world was created, study Agada, for thus will you get to know the Holy One and cleave to His ways," said the Sages (Sifre, *Ekev* 49). It is the *derashah* which can most effectively engage both intellect and emotions and tap into the vast unconscious reservoir of Jewishness. An irrepressible hunger for the spirit abounds in the land, and it will seek out not only metaphysical ends and halakhic discipline but also the esthetics of the agadic tradition. The *neshamah* as well as the mind of a Jew thirsts for the *devar ha-Shem*, and it is sinful to neglect it. It is one sure case where "the medium is the message."

The question, to my mind, is not whether *derush* will survive, but what form it will take and how it can best be oriented to serve a vital function in the teaching of Torah.

Several paragraphs back I mentioned the criticisms leveled at each other by the older and younger generations of Orthodox rabbis in the early and middle years of the century. Both, I believe, were correct in their assessments. The older, European trained rabbis were usually irrelevant to their congregants, mostly because of their cultural orientation and the form of their homiletics—and not only because of their difficulties with the English language. And the American Orthodox rabbis, in their desire to be as relevant as possible, met their audiences not half way, but all the way, and thus diluted the message of Torah in a thin soup of superficial "relevance." I suspect that neither group truly respected its audience. The Europeans therefore retreated into a mode of traditional *derush* with which they were personally comfortable even though it was alien to their congregations, and the Americans gave their listeners what they thought they wanted and could absorb—which was poor pabulum indeed, and which neither elicited nor deserved respect.

The Americans, moreover, failed in another way. The more thoughtful and worldly of their people were troubled by genuine philosophical and theological problems occasioned by the clash of cultures in open, pluralistic America: the Holocaust; the rise of the State of Israel; a society becoming progressively more hedonistic; the dogmatic aggressiveness of scientism, relativism, certain schools of psychology, etc. They sought guidance for these problems—often inchoate and only vaguely intuited—and received few answers that addressed their concerns seriously and directly. Instead, they received *"derashot"*—a *bon mot,* a Hasidic story, an awkwardly interpreted Midrash or *maamar*—which not only were totally inadequate but, in their evasiveness, betrayed a lack of sympathy for the religious crises Jews were experiencing. This did not give *derush* a good name.

It was the *darshanim,* not *derush* that failed.

Yet there were a number of gallant exceptions, and they have much to teach us about what is right about homiletics and how it must be reconstructed for our age. Some have published their sermons, whether in separate volumes or in the *RCA Manual,* and I have heard others' *derashot* recounted by them or in their names. I had the privilege of hearing still others directly, upon delivery.

An autobiographical note is in order. When I first began my rabbinic career, I discerned three sources of influence on my homiletic development. One was my uncle, Rabbi Joseph M. Baumol, then of Crown Heights Yeshiva and now retired, representative of a whole class of men in the Bronx and Brooklyn, some few of whom are still "darshening" today. The second was the late Rabbi Joseph H. Lookstein, o.b.m., my teacher of homiletics at RIETS and whose assistant I later became. And the third was our master and teacher, Rabbi Joseph B. Soloveitchik, "The Rav," *zekher tzaddik li'verakha*. These three Josephs taught me to interpret not dreams but texts and ideas. Each had his own characteristic approach—"no two prophets prophesy in the same style"—and both their differences and similarities are instructive.

Each of them succeeded because he spoke to *his own* listeners, not to some imagined or stereotyped or idealized audience.

My uncle, who first taught me how to take advantage of the marvelous adaptability and versatility of a text, spoke to a largely immigrant and first-generation congregation whose members were intelligent if culturally limited. The basic sources of Judaism were familiar to them, even if not always with great detail or accuracy. His sermons could be peppered and nuanced with classical Jewish references, without having to translate or identify every source. The form of the sermon—basically the one most of us were taught and used—was quite stylized although not rigidly so. There was a text, an interpretation (usually in the form of question and answer), illustrations, applications, a "story" thrown in here and there, and an occasional Hasidic or Musar *vort*.

Rabbi Lookstein, who was a master rhetorician, practiced a kind of schizoid homiletics. Reading or hearing his weekly Shabbat sermons and his High Holiday talks, one would not suspect that they came from the same source. His Shabbat and Yom Tov *derashot* were on the same pattern as those I learned from my uncle. The differences were mostly those of personal taste and style: his skillful use of epigrams and his splendid sensitivity to the English language. His dramatic pauses and his perorations were often spectacular; they seemed to come so naturally to him—sometimes too much so. But at bottom these were the same fare his Brooklyn and Bronx colleagues were giving to their congregants, with the necessary rhetorical shift for speaking to an Upper East Side audience. This was not the case when it came to the High Holidays. (The late Rabbi Harry Wohlberg, who taught me Midrash at RIETS, used to say that, for Rabbis, *Yamim Noraim* should be translated not as "The Days of Awe," but as "The Awful Days." He had a point, other than the humor involved: the three-times-a-year people changed the character of the congregation, and as a result rabbis tended to overprepare their sermons and succeeded in sounding strained and stultified.) Then, he would depart from this norm, and almost always give a "project sermon," i.e., one centered on a theme rather than a text. On Rosh Hashanah and Yom Kippur he preached (not "*darshened*") to his elegant and wealthy Park Avenue worshipers (not really "daveners") who were relatively estranged from full Jewish observance, and both his style and substance were radically different. Stylistically, one could tell that he had been influenced by Harry Emerson Fosdick. Even when he creatively introduced a *gut vort*, it was—well, uncircumcised. The sense of Jewish immediacy was simply absent; it was like the "yeshivah bochur" who returned to his *shtetl* after a couple of years in America—you recognized his eyes and ears and voice, perhaps even his conduct, but somehow the language and dress and mannerisms made him no longer the same person. But it was not only the style—the Looksteinian turn of phrase, the wit and sarcasm and irony, the "project" construction—that was different; the substance, or at least the content, changed too. The outlook was more universal—often at the expense of the particularistic bias of Judaism. The use of classical texts was augmented if not partially displaced by the tokens of Western sophistication: Shakespeare and Wordsworth and Freud and Buber and other icons of the pantheon of rapidly acculturating Jews. Yet, considering the nature of his High Holiday congregation, his commitment to keep them within the Orthodox fold, and his highly sensitive atunement to the subtleties of effective communication, he was no doubt correct in his change of stylistic pace. And the results were gems of construction, style, and creative interpretation—and they helped keep more than one generation of upper-class Jews close to Judaism.

The Rav as *darshan*, as in all else, is [was] in a class by himself. His use of language (including English), his facility in formulating profound ideas clearly and cogently, his dramatic perorations, his creation of a sense of excitement and anticipation, the elegant architechtonics of his addresses, his almost theatrical flourishes at exactly the right time—all these are aspects of his virtuosity of technique. But they are as nothing compared with his insistence upon the *derashah* as a medium for the teaching of ideas. He has essentially resurrected, in his own personal style, the medieval tradition of philosophical *derush*, geared to contemporary man.

My desire to use him as a role model caused me no end of grief. Every time I heard him, I suffered genuine frustration—not only because his genius created a chasm which made imitation all but impossible, but also because he was able to use any and all sources without having to explain them in a most elementary manner, and because he was able to ignore that most tyrannical of all disciplines—the clock. The Rav did what none of us could afford to do—he *luxuriated* in his *derashot*, freely choosing his texts not only from Midrash and Agadah and classical exegetes, but also from Halakhah and Kabbalah and Jewish thought and family traditions, and all these supplemented by the whole range of Western philosophy and mathematics and history of science, cited for their substance and not as mere ornamentation. And all this—with aristocratic disdain for the hour hand! Could the inspiration and religious experience of a Soloveitchik *derashah* be duplicated by me, even in miniature, given the absence of his virtuosity, the restraints on the kind of source material my audience would find congenial and even comprehensible, and the constraints of a twenty-minute discourse? The answer was obviously No. But the challenge to learn from him how to inform and inspire at the same time, teaching and preaching simultaneously; how to lend passion to the cognitive and intellectual dignity to the emotive; and how to evince a healthy respect both for one's audience and his source material—that challenge was too great to abandon. Hence, the frustration.

But this frustration was terribly important for me. I could not hope to duplicate what was *sui generis*. I was not speaking to an audience of elite *lomdim*. I had to conform to the strictures of a limited "service." But I could, nay had to, speak about *real* issues, *real* ideas, *real* concepts. I tried to learn from him to trust my listeners' intellectual capacities if not their erudition, to impart to them a sense of excitement about ideas in general and Jewish teachings in particular, and to share with them the awareness of the pertinence of even the most abstract of concepts. Somehow, I too must learn the secret of this homiletic and rhetorical wizardry by means of which the message I chose seemed both authentically Jewish, indeed necessary, and yet swam gracefully and freely with the greatest ideas and discoveries in the currents of Western man's mentality and culture. If I could not be the Rav, I had to be a responsible *talmid* of the Rav. The frustration would always be a creative one, at least subjectively, even if the results objectively fell far short of the ideal.

All these point to indications for a new effort at *derush*. The current lugubrious indifference to homiletics will not endure. It cannot, because there has to be a way, other than direct teaching of Halakhah, for inspiration to occur and for metahalakhic ideas to be imparted.

What kind of *derush* will emerge? With a few notable exceptions, I believe that for the near future technique and form will be mediocre. Two generations of sloppy language teaching throughout the United States will not be rectified in two hours of "Homiletics" per week as part of "Supplementary Rabbinics." At RIETS we do what we can in the few hours at our disposal; there is no way or reason to expand the hours much beyond what they are now. "Lomdus" is and always will be given priority. We shall explore new ways of instruction. We now emphasize, more than before, rabbinic *shimmush* or internship. With all this, the differences will not be marked. Personal talent and disposition will, as always, play a greater role than formal instruction.

What will change, I believe, is the content of the sermons the new generation of rabbis will be delivering. Their inherited approach and their own ideas will be modified by their experiences with a new type of congregant—one who will still demand of his rabbi inspiration and guidance in current communal and international affairs, but who will be more committed to Torah and especially to Halakhah, and who will take the whole religious enterprise with a great deal of seriousness. Rabbis will be forced to deal with real and cogent ideas and to support them from the array of sources available to them as a result of their years of study at Yeshiva. They will have to supplement, on their own, the study of theological, Hasidic, and Musar material sacrificed, during their student years, in favor of ever more intensive study of Gemara and Rishonim. If they are sensitive, experience will force them to acknowledge in practice what we teach them expressly: that each kind of talk requires a different methodology, that a sermon and a *hashkafah* lecture and a *parashat ha-shavua* talk and a halakhic *sheiur* all have their own immanent rules and make their own individual demands on the rabbi. As congregations become more conforming with Halakhah, as the nature of their memberships changes, and as new rabbis emerge to deal with them, the *derashot* will, I suspect, be more substantive and more meaningful, though less effectively constructed or delivered and less resourceful in taking full advantage of the classical modes of *derush*. The *gut vort* will remain in eclipse until such time as halakhically committed rabbis and laymen will feel enough self-confidence to foray into those areas of Torah discourse that are more fanciful, imaginative, symbolic, esthetic, and subjective, and do so in a disciplined manner.

The ascendancy of the cognitive in the fine equilibrium between substance and technique is nothing to rue. If indeed one has to choose, clearly the substantive must take precedence. What is regrettable is the feeling that one is forced to make a choice, that the two are incompatible.

But if *derush* is to have a future, with benefit for both rabbis and congregations, there must be some changes in the way rabbis approach their craft.

For one thing, the rabbinate that is now emerging will have to exercise more homiletic discipline. Homiletic talent often brings with it the danger of abuse. *Derush* is appropriate to a *derashah;* it is awkward and out of place in a philosophical article or an analytical discourse on *Machshavah.* A serious essay may occasionally benefit from a homiletical flourish, especially in the hands of a master craftsman, but the overuse of *derush* in a genre for which it is unsuited and alien succeeds only in holding up to opprobrium the whole homiletic enterprise as superficial and dilettantish.

A second area of self-restraint that *darshanim* must exercise if they are to be taken seriously is the tendency to stray too far from the original intent of a passage. *Derash* is not the same as *peshat,* but it is most certainly limited by it to a large extent. The untrammelled use of plays on words and exploitation of homonyms and language similarities to make a point at the expense of completely ignoring the *peshat* is a form of *megaleh panim bi'derush.* Too often, a pedestrian pun displaces a significant text or a cogent idea as the focus of a sermon, and the result is a banal sermon that does not deserve the attention of a congregation. Even in the realm of imagination, symbol, and inspiration, one must play the game by rules, lest the game be discredited and the players be dismissed as impostors.

I have always felt that the seductive powers of a novel homiletic insight are often so overpowering, that I exclude almost all *derush* from writing and speaking on Halakha, *Machshavah,* history, or whatever. The *darshan* has to play it safe if his work off the pulpit is to be considered as sober and thoughtful. Hence—my apology for the absence of *derush* in this essay on *derush*. . . .

Finally, both rabbis and congregations will have to understand that changes must be made in the scheduling of sermons. It is simply impossible to be creative on a weekly schedule. Neither babies nor rabbis respond well to nourishment by the clock.

For the rabbi to say something significant, he must prepare—and that means learning and reading and thinking as well as organizing and writing. And the burden of being fresh and original every week is beyond the powers of most mortals.

For most of my 25 years in the rabbinate. I was fortunate in being able to alternate with Rabbi Leo Jung in the pulpit of The Jewish Center. During those times when I occupied the pulpit alone, I kept to the weekly schedule. But the results were evident to me, and probably to my people—and I resented it.

Hence, some new system will have to emerge whereby teaching and preaching will alternate, without a consensus necessarily developing as to its exact forms. Different experiments are already being conducted here and there, allowing rabbis and congregations to adjust to each other's needs.

In the long run, all will have to remember that the choice of *derashah* or *sheiur* is a question of medium. The end of both is and should be identical—*le'hagdil Torah u-le'haadirah.*

~ 39 ~

THE SELF-IMAGE OF THE RABBI

A good part of the functioning of a rabbi, in the many aspects of his career as a teacher of Torah and leader of his community, depends upon his self-confidence—a psychological and also spiritual issue which involves his self-image as a rabbi and student of Torah, and his conception of his role, his identity, and his destiny.

Maimonides on Pride

At first blush, the problem is a rather simple one. Self-image is a question of *gaavah* (pride) or *anivut* (humility), and Maimonides in his *Hilkhot Deiot* is quite clear on this. In all other attributes of character, as a matter of Halakhah, Maimonides demands that we follow the middle way between the extremes. We are to shun the extremes and follow the path of moderation, the mean between the two polar opposites. This middle way, what is popularly known as the "Golden Mean," Maimonides identifies as "The Way of the Lord." But there are two exceptions that Maimonides makes in formulating this *halakhah* of character, and one of these is self-assessment. Here Maimonides identifies the two extremes as *gaavah* (pride) and *shiflut* (lowliness), and the middle way as that of *anivut* (humbleness). Unlike other characteristics, or *deiot*, a person here must choose the extreme of *shiflut*—of self-abnegation or lowliness. Thus, we read concerning Moses that, "and the man Moses was very humble" (Numbers 12:3). Maimonides interprets the intensive as indicating the extreme; thus, "*very* humble" *(anav me'od)* equals "of lowly spirit" *(shefal ruach).*

Similarly, in the fourth chapter of *Avot* we read that R. Levitas of Yavneh says, "Be exceedingly careful *(me'od, me'od)* to be lowly of spirit." Hence, with regard to a person's self-definition, the "golden mean" or middle way does not apply and, instead, one must opt for *shiflut* or lowliness—the extreme or intensive form of *anivut*, humbleness.

Address at the Chag Ha-semikhah (Ordination ceremony) of the Rabbi Isaac Elchanan Theological Seminary, March 29, 1981.

However, the matter is too complex and too consequential to leave it at that. An analysis of Maimonides' view leaves us with a number of troubling questions.

For one, does not *shiflut,* as Maimonides explains it, seem to conflict with *emet,* truth or honesty? If, e.g., Maimonides thought of himself as an ignoramus, that might be an instance of *shiflut;* but is it true?

And is it psychologically desirable? How many of us consciously conform to the norm of such *shiflut,* and how many of us are prepared to raise our own children and educate our own students towards the ideal of feeling worthless? One need not subscribe to the contemporary ideology of narcissism to be worried by its extreme antonym as a norm of self-perception and conduct.

Moreover, there are alternative sources to Maimonides' invocation of R. Levitas. Whereas R. Levitas of Yavneh demands *shiflut* as *me'od me'od,* we read in the same chapter of *Avot* that R. Meir says: "Be lowly of spirit before every man." Notice: there is no demand for *me'od me'od,* of going to the extreme, and R. Meir addresses himself not to substantive self-image but "before every man," in other words, only to one's conduct in relation to and in the presence of others.

An Alternative to Maimonides

I believe, therefore, that a legitimate alternative to the opinion of Maimonides exists within the writings of the Sages, even though this view may not have been formally articulated. This approach, which would follow R. Meir instead of R. Levitas, would hold that *gaavah* is a homonym for two related yet different characteristics. The first of these is self-importance, vanity, egotism; its opposite is *shiflut*—humility, low self-esteem. The second form of *gaavah* is arrogance, haughtiness, and aggressive self-assertion—more of an attitude to others than a vision of one's own place in the scheme of things. Its antonym at the other end of the spectrum is *anivut*—meekness, a willingness to abide insults without reacting in kind. *Shiflut,* humility, is a matter of self-deprecation; it is a psychological condition. *Anivut,* meekness, implies self-effacement; it is a behavioral reaction. They are polar qualities on two different spectrum bands of character.

Thus, when R. Meir demands that we be "lowly of spirit before every man," he is elaborating a social, not an existential or psychological attribute, and his "lowliness of spirit" is a synonym for a moderate form of self-image, or: *anivut*. It is a moot question whether, using Maimonides' general system of *Deiot*, R. Meir considers *anivut* an extreme which, in this case, is desirable; or whether he holds it to be a mean between *gaavah* (as aggressive self-assertion) and some unarticulated extreme form of meekness.

Despite their assaults upon him, Moses (in the passage mentioned above) keeps his peace, he does not respond. Instead, it is the Almighty who takes up the cudgels on behalf of Moses. The silence of Moses is the result of his *anivut*, his meekness.

According to this definition, there is no conflict between the proper form of self-definition and honesty, *emet*.

Interestingly, this will explain as well an otherwise startling passage in the Talmud at the end of *Sotah*. In the last mishnah of that tractate, we read that when Rabbi (R. Judah the Prince) died, *anavah* (the same as *anivut*) and the fear of sin vanished from the world. In the gemara on that mishnah we read that R. Joseph said to the Tanna, "Do not say *anavah* (in other words, the fear of sin may have vanished upon the death of Rabbi, but not *anivut*), for I am here." Now, this is an astounding statement. Surely, the very self-awareness of humility undoes it and disproves it!

However, if we interpret *anivut* not as humility but as meekness (an interpretation suggested to me by my late, dear friend Dr. William Zev Frank), the passage makes eminently good sense. One can be aware of one's meekness without destroying it, even as one can be aware of one's musical talent or height or fair complexion without subverting any of these qualities. A man can recognize that he is meek, that he never answers an insult in kind, and the statement is not at all self-contradictory or paradoxical. (This redefinition of *anivut* is mentioned as well by the Netziv, who cites the passage in *Sotah* as proof. See his *Haamek Davar* and *Harchev Davar* to Nu. 12:3.)

Hence, with regard to both *shiflut* and *anivut*, we may insist upon the middle way instead of the extreme, as we do with other attributes of character.

It is this doctrine of moderation with regard to self-definition which, I submit, is crucial for the rabbi of today. And even if one were to disagree with my thesis concerning this alternative to the decision of Maimonides, surely a community, like a nation, must operate according to different rules from those of an individual (a topic too involved to discuss here, but *kavod* and *kinah* come to mind immediately as examples)—and a rabbi in his role of communal leadership should be viewed as representing the community as well as an individual.

It is imperative that our *musmakhim,* who bear the burden of Torah leadership and of continuing the heritage they have learned in these sacred precincts, guard against both extremes in their rabbinic role—that of *gaavah,* as exaggerated and overweening self-confidence and self-importance; and *shiflut* in the form of a weak self-image, the lack of self-esteem and self-worth.

Occupational Dangers

Young rabbis must be forewarned of one of the occupational dangers of the rabbinate: laymen sometimes look up to a rabbi (and, occasionally, to a teacher) deferentially and thus distort his perspective on himself. It is too easy to emerge from your studies here, in this atmosphere of intense intellectual competition and spiritual ambition, and the attendant deflation of ego, and suddenly find yourself on a pedestal where you believe some of the adulation you will receive. My advice to you is: be wise, don't believe it. It is dangerous to your spiritual health.

Moreover, a rabbi must be careful never to practice *gaavah* towards his own laymen, his "baalebatim." The layman is not the natural enemy of the rabbi. He is his *talmid,* his disciple, in ways both formal and informal, and like students of all ages he is sometimes resistant to instruction. But this only constitutes a greater challenge to the rabbi to marshal both his inner resources and his acquired techniques to teach, educate, inspire, and instruct. But never, never look down upon the men and women of your community. That Jews come to *shul* or study Torah or work for the Jewish community or contribute to Israel—in this atmosphere of widespread assimilation and assertive ignorance—is already a "plus" and a sign of the Jewish dignity of your people. You will find many of them considerably talented, learned, experienced, devoted, charitable, and self-sacrificing—even if very few will not have all of these qualities, and some will have none.

They deserve not your obedience, but certainly your respect and your love.

You must live up to their highest ideals of what a rabbi should be—a man of integrity and spirituality. Scholarship and piety are necessary but they are not sufficient. A spiritual person is one whose ideals and practice transcend his self-interest, whose deportment and, indeed, very presence symbolize the values of Torah. Your people want and need and deserve a symbol not of other-worldliness, but of the sanctification of this world: a man who, together with his sophistication and secular learning, is living proof that Torah creates a spiritual personality in this very world of technology and high finance, of hedonism and narcissism.

By all means, a rabbi should have a good living salary, no less than others, but his material ambitions should never be his priority. A rabbi should always have his hand stretched out to his laymen to solicit their help and substance for *tzedakah*—but never, never may he have that hand out for a personal gift or fee.

But mostly, do not succumb to the *gaavah* that you are an accomplished scholar of Torah, that you already are a *Talmid Chakham,* that you have gotten enough Torah erudition from your masters to last you a lifetime. Semikhah is not only, as it is classically known, *heter hora'ah,* but also a *horaah lilmod.* . . . Smugness at this stage of your development is the sure road to lasting and pervasive ignorance.

Remember always the astounding tale that the Sages tell us (*Shab.* 147b) about one of the greatest of all the Tannaim, R. Elazar b. Arakh, who one time went to visit two places that were renowned in antiquity for their fine wine and sparkling waters. According to the Sages, R. Elazar overstayed his visit; the spa apparently attracted him more than it should have. As a result, he slowly but surely began to forget his learning. So much so, that when he returned to the great Academy of Yavneh, the greatest academy of learning in the history of our people, and he was invited to read in the Torah the portion that begins with *ha-chodesh ha-zeh lakhem.* ("This month shall be for you . . ." Ex. 12:2), he mistook the text for three similar words that had a totally different meaning: *ha-cheresh hayah libam* ("Their heart was mute"). His learning did not return to him until the Rabbis prayed for him. The lesson from all this, our Talmudic text continues, is the statement in the Mishnah by R. Nehorai that one must always go to a place of Torah learning even if it means going into exile: "And do not rely upon your own intellect."

If this is true of the great R. Elazar b. Arakh, whom his teacher R. Yochanan b. Zakkai (according to Abba Shaul) considered the greatest of all disciples, how much more so is it true of us lesser mortals. There will be a thousand reasons for us to be distracted from regular study of Torah—from the professional demands upon us to community concerns, from family obligations to the leisure pursuits of our own laymen. Excessive self-confidence in our own learning can, as R. Elazar b. Arakh learned, deaden our sensitivity—make our "hearts mute"—and pave the way to forgetfulness and corrosive ignorance.

It is only a consistent and creative uncertainty about ourselves that can motivate us to keep up our learning and to develop into mature *talmidei chakhamim.*

But I feel that I must caution you even more against the other extreme, that of excessive *shiflut,* which afflicts the Orthodox Jewish community generally and us, often, in particular.

Our Collective Self-Image

I address myself to our weak collective self-image in several respects—professionally as rabbis; communally as Orthodox Jews; and institutionally as alumni of Rabbi Isaac Elchanan Theological Seminary and Yeshiva University.

As rabbis, our humility has its source in our perception that the rabbinate has come upon bad times. For a variety of reasons, not irrelevant but too extensive for us to address here, the rabbinate as a career has become devalued in Jewish life.

In the secular Jewish world, some of its functions are being taken over by professors of Judaic studies, and others by executives of the various federations and other Jewish agencies. In the Orthodox world, *rashei yeshivah* and Hasidic *admorim* have captured much of the authority and esteem previously held by rabbis. Prestige and influence—sometimes even *shiddukhim!*—often can be seen slipping away from rabbis to these other groups. As a result, Orthodox rabbis emerge with a sense of inferiority, an awareness that they are no longer in the center of things, that they are marginal.

But as young *rabbanim,* as students of Torah educated in our holy Yeshiva, you must accept this as a happy challenge "to restore the crown (of the rabbinate) to its ancient splendor," perhaps in new and unforeseen ways.

Do not allow humility to interfere with your life's mission.

Remember the immortal rebuke delivered to King Saul by the prophet Samuel: "Even though thou be small in thine own eyes, thou art head of the tribes of Israel" (I Samuel 15:17).

Never mind your self-doubts and the new competition to the rabbinate. If you have a clear consciousness of serving as "the head of the tribes of Israel," of your responsibility to create and to lead a *kehilah kedoshah,* a truly "holy community," you will enhance the dignity of the Torah and the rabbinate and raise it to a new plateau.

You will learn to speak out clearly, fearlessly, attractively, cogently, and unequivocally on issues affecting the Torah of Israel, the people of Israel, and the State of Israel.

You are rabbis. Bear your mission with pride and dignity "even though you be small in your own eyes."

Extremism in Our Time

There is yet a second area in which this pervasive lowliness has insinuated itself and caused great difficulty. In the Orthodox community generally, I see *shiflut* as the root of certain pathological manifestations of extremism that have become a source of humiliation and chagrin to all of us. Any psychologist will discern a sick sense of inferiority and grave self-doubt as one of the main causes of this violent, militant, and contemptible extremism that has created a massive *chillul Ha-shem* for all Jews, and especially Orthodox Jews. Riots, violent demonstrations, rock-throwing—this is not our way. "The words of the wise spoken softly are more acceptable . . ." (Eccl. 9:17).

I have no doubt about it; this contemptible extremism which has so sullied the good name of Torah—whether this militantism manifests itself in physical violence or verbal abuse or in self-righteous contempt for others—is a faithful indicator of a faithless man, and one who is *mi'ketanei emunah,* plagued by inner doubt and religious insecurity.

I bring this to your attention not because I suspect that there are extremists among you, but because we must all of us beware of a dreadful error that some of us make if we think, in the privacy of our consciousness, that somehow it is the extremists who are "authentic" and that moderation is merely pragmatic rather than principle and thus an unworthy compromise.

Not so! Those who throw rocks do not represent the "Rock of Israel!" Those who suffer a wrenching inner self-contempt and express it in arrogant self-righteousness—they do not represent Torah and Judaism. Remember: it is the way of moderation which Maimonides refers to as the "way of the Lord."

The teaching of moderation is not a policy of prudence but a philosophy of character and society. Extremism may be far more successful in whipping up passions and fostering the illusion of principle. But it is fundamentally inimical to Torah and to reason and it is hospitable to bigotry. Its "idealism" is meretricious, and its claim to Jewish authenticity rings hollow and false.

Both American society and the Jewish community must be alert to the perils of political and religious extremism, whether of the Right or of the Left. The allure of the quick fix is all too prevalent in times of crisis or transition, and we must not fall victim to it.

Radical Moderation

One of the main contributions that a renewed and dynamic Jewish spiritual leadership can make to our community and our times is a dedication to moderation without blandness, to a kind of radical or extreme moderation which is based upon high principle, great ideals, deep faith, respect for people—together with a healthy skepticism of easy solutions and a contempt for small-mindedness and meanness of spirit.

This leads me, finally, to a few words about our institutional self-image as rabbinic alumni of RIETS and advocates of our institution and what it stands for.

I am often dismayed at our inferiority feelings, our defensiveness, our lack of self-esteem.

Let me remind you. As a group, your cultural-educational credentials are no less impressive than Conservative or Reform or secularist or lay leaders of any stripe in the Jewish community.

And your *lomdut* and the *derekh* you learned here at the feet of some of the greatest *Rashei Yeshiva* anywhere in the world are not one whit inferior to those of other Yeshivot, despite the perennial criticism, cynicism, and *bittul* that are as old as our Yeshiva is—which means about four times as old as any of you!

We have for too long tended to internalize the carping criticism of certain scoffers, and have developed a rankling lowliness, one that is unworthy and even corrupt.

If our view of Torah in the world is subjected to respectful critical analysis by the other *benei Torah,* let us listen and assess and evaluate it openly and honestly, and respond truthfully and forcefully and respectfully. But if the criticism is petty and mean-spirited—simply ignore it. Do not dignify it with either your remonstrance or your concern. Treat it with the studied contempt it so richly deserves.

Remember that the *Torah Umadda* we aspire to is an ideal and not a compromise, a *le'khat'chila,* and not a *bi'di-avad,* that it is ideologically grounded in our Torah *Anschauung.*

The RIETS Record

Bear in mind what Rabbi Isaac Elchanan Theological Seminary has done for Torah and for the Jewish Community:

- We have reproduced ourselves in kind: so many of our own *Rashei Yeshivah* are themselves alumni of our Yeshiva;
- We have 367 rabbis now serving in congregations throughout the United States, and another 337 now active in various forms of education and community service;
- 157 of our alumni have made Aliyah, and are significantly involved in education and the rabbinate in the State of Israel;
- 21 of our rabbis are now serving in Canada, 4 in Australia, and others in other countries;
- This Yeshiva is involved in an effort to open up new communities where the influence of Torah will make itself felt. Its work in the Division of Communal Services, and especially its Youth work and Seminars, continues to inspire hundreds and thousands with our out-reach.

How many other yeshivot can show such a record of achievement towards the sacred goal of the advancement of Torah, *le'hagdil Torah ule'haadirah?*

It is true that most of our rabbis and students do not necessarily affect the garb or other accoutrements that many students of other yeshivot (and some of our own) do. So what? I refuse to identify halakhic authenticity with sartorial style or hats of a particular hue.

As you go out to do battle with the forces of ignorance and assimilation and hedonism in the "war of Torah," be proud and strong, never fearful and diffident and self-denigrating, never a *shefal ruach* (according to both interpretations of *tannaim* in the *mishnah* in *Sotah*). Excessive self-doubt, lack of confidence, and extreme humility are both dangerous and false!

In a remarkable story, the Sages *(T. de'b E.Z.)* relate that a young man accosted the prophet Elijah and insulted him. The response of the prophet was immediate and penetrating: "How will you answer for this to your Creator on Judgment Day?"

Elijah's telling retort had its effect. The young man answered, "Intelligence and knowledge were not granted to me."

Elijah was not satisfied with this answer, and pursued the matter: "My son, what do you do for a living?" The young man responded that he was a fisherman by profession.

"Ah," cried Elijah, "for the art of fishing you do have intelligence and knowledge, you know how to spin the flax and weave the nets and identify the migrations of the fish, when to throw in your nets and when to pull them up, how to prepare your product and how to market it. But Torah—concerning which it is written, 'this matter is very close to you, it is in your mouth and in your heart that you may do it.' (Deut. 30:14)—for this you do not have enough 'intelligence and knowledge?'"

Extreme self-deprecation leads to evil conduct; even worse, such diffidence is spurious and false! Those who fall prey to it will someday have to answer for it when judgment will be made.

The Sense of Being Chosen

You are a group of intelligent and bright young men who could have become doctors and lawyers, businessmen and scientists, psychologists and computer experts, as easily as your colleagues who graduated with you from Yeshiva College. You do have the blessing of abundant "intelligence and knowledge." But you chose to use it for Torah, which is "in your mouth and in your heart in order to do it."

Remember that—and, without becoming supercilious, bear yourselves with pride in your life's mission, in your rabbinic calling, in your Yeshiva, and in the Torah you teach. In the words of R. Nehorai (whom some Sages identify as the self-same R. Elazer b. Arakh!), "Do not rely upon your own intelligence." Do not *rely* on it—but also do not *deny* it!

Your task is a psychologically difficult one, but one that is a sacred and inescapable obligation: to choose the right theme at the right time, to shun both arrogance and humility in their extremes, to know when to be more humble and when to be more proud. Such moral moderation requires an abundant intelligence and a high degree of wisdom. But without a sense of balance, without that dynamic equilibrium, you will have failed in your mission—and "how will you answer for this to your Creator on Judgment Day?"

All that we have said is summed up in a comment of Rashi on the verse, "And Moses said to Aaron, 'Draw close to the altar'" (Lev. 9:7). Rashi comments: "Aaron was diffident and afraid to approach the altar. Moses said to him, 'Why are you diffident, seeing that this is what you were chosen for?'"

The author of *Sefat Emet* comments that from this we learn that one who prepares for a life of sacred service must wrestle with two opposing forces within him—the ambivalence of *bosh ve'-yarei la-geshet* on one side, and an awareness of *ki le'kakh nivreta* on the other; it is a struggle of the dialectic of personal humility and a sense of destiny.

Never lose that healthy consciousness of shyness, diffidence, and apprehension about taking on too much responsibility: it is an excellent antidote for *gaavah.*

And never be without a sensitive and historical awareness that, "For this you were chosen," that you are entering a "calling," a great and noble and historic mission—that of the rabbinate and the teaching of Torah.

And so, with this awareness—"draw close to the altar, and atone for yourself and for the people."

~ 40 ~

THE MAKINGS OF A *BEN TORAH*

To be a rabbi, one must first of all be a *ben Torah.*

What or who is a *ben Torah?* The translation, "a scholar of the Torah," does not do the term justice; it is far too restrictive. A better definition would be "a Torah person"—bearing in mind that one cannot truly be a "Torah person" without first being an accomplished Torah scholar.

What, then, are the extra ingredients, beyond talmudic learning, that go to make up a Torah person, a Torah personality?

Someone once said that education is what a person has left after he has forgotten all that he has learned. Applying this to a *ben Torah,* we might then ask what distinguishes a *ben Torah* from others after you have subtracted all that he has learned of Talmud *Bavli* and *Yerushalmi,* of Rashi and *Tosafot,* of *Rishonim* and *Acharonim,* of Rambam and Ramban, of *Tur* and *Shulchan Arukh,* of *Shakh* and *Taz,* of R. Hayyim and R. Akiva Eger. Remove all that and ask: What makes (or should make) us different and special? What, in other words, are the attitudinal foundations that inform the mentality of a *ben Torah?*

THE MOST OBVIOUS and the primary answer is that a Torah person loves and esteems the Torah and Torah learning.

So, if a *ben Torah* forgets all that he has learned, his first task is—to learn it all over again. "For they [the words of Torah] are our life and the length of our days" *(Siddur).* Inscribed in the cornerstone of our yeshiva is the principle that R. Hayyim of Volozhin cemented 180 years ago into the foundation of his yeshiva, Yeshivat Etz Hayyim, the mother of all yeshivot since. This mishnaic dictum, *ve'talmud Torah ke'negged kulam*—the study of Torah outweighs all other commandments—is to be taken not quantitatively, but functionally. The study of Torah is not only

---

Adapted from an address at the Chag Ha-semikhah (Ordination ceremony) of the Rabbi Isaac Elchanan Theological Seminary, March 6, 1983, and printed in Moment Magazine, *September 1983.*

greater than the sum of all the other commandments; it is their very source. Torah is the "tree of life"; all the other commandments are the branches of that tree. Accordingly, the study of Torah is the source of all Jewish life.

That is why your overarching commitment is to learn, and then learn more. The day you stop studying, the day you stop climbing the road to Torah excellence, is the day you are no longer a *ben Torah.* On that day, all that is written on your rabbinic diploma is rendered meaningless.

I have long wondered about an imbalance between our early morning and our late evening prayers. Upon arising in the morning and upon going to sleep at night we recite two blessings that are quite parallel to each other. In the morning we bless God "who removes sleep from my eyes and slumber from my eyelids." Similarly, after reciting the *Shema* before retiring, we bless God "who closes my eyes in sleep and my eyelids in slumber." However, accompanying these blessings are two additional petitions that are not really analagous. The night prayer seems reasonable enough: "May it be Thy will . . . to grant that I lie down in peace and that I rise up in peace. Let not my thoughts upset me—nor evil dreams, nor sinful fancies," etc. By the same token we should expect that the morning prayer should ask that God grant that we rise up in peace, that we prosper, that we be spared all misfortune. Instead, we pray, "May it be Thy will . . . to habituate us to thy Torah, and to cause us to adhere to Thy precepts," etc.

Why the asymmetry?

Because a true *ben Torah* must know and understand that without Torah, he cannot know that he is awake. How do we know that our lives are not but dreams—and not necessarily pleasant ones, at that? Without our daily contact with the eternal, without this glorious communication with the transcendental to elevate and transform the routines of daily life, what difference does it make whether we are sleeping or not sleeping?

A *rav* who does not practice "habituate us to thy Torah" is not only in a state of somnolence; he is inauthentic. His mind and his heart are sealed even if his eyes are open. Moreover, he is cut off from his moorings, alone in the world. A *ben Torah* without Torah is an orphan.

So the love of Torah is an absolute prerequisite in the mentality of a *ben Torah.* We expect you, therefore, to enhance your own love of Torah. Let it motivate you to greater learning, let it inspire you to goad your fellow Jews until they, too, achieve the status of being Torah persons, and always know that a rabbi is not a rabbi if he is not a *ben Torah.*

After your years here, so much must by now be obvious to you. Are there, then, other ingredients, beyond study, that are required of the *ben Torah*?

THERE IS *ahavat Yisrael,* the love of Israel; this is the love that complements your love of Torah.

Remember always that Torah was not meant exclusively to provide for your *own* spiritual needs, your *own* religious integrity, your *own* intellectual creativity. The Talmud refers to the study of Torah for its own sake as "an elixir of life." But it is the kind of medicine of which you must be not only the consumer but also the pharmacist. It is a medicine that if kept on the shelf and never dispensed is no longer a medicine but merely a chemical, one that in time can become dangerous.

The problem with too many of us in the yeshivot is that we have somehow managed to assimilate—excessively—the spirit of the times. Society today is highly narcissistic. Everywhere it seems, we are admonished to undertake the quest for self-fulfillment, for self-expression, for self-realization. Unfortunately, we have too often adopted that self-centeredness in its spiritual form, and we have thereby become religious narcissists. We are too concerned with our own Torah growth, and the result of this spiritual introversion is an indifference, at times even an antipathy, to Jews who are unlike us, who are, by our standards, deficient in learning or in commitment or in observance. As a consequence, even those who admirably devote their lives to the teaching of Torah, as rabbis or as educators, confine themselves to preaching to the converted, and come to see themselves as halakhic technicians. Their sense of responsibility for others' lives—physical as well as intellectual, worldly as well as spiritual, psychological as well as scholarly—is inadequate.

From this there derives a deep malaise in our community, a malaise that must be exposed if it is to be uprooted. For Torah was meant for *all* Jews, not just for a small circle of the religiously privileged, the halakhic cognoscenti. It was meant for laymen as well as rabbis, for those who yearn for the poetry of Torah as well as for those who revel in its intellectual rigor, for those who are not yet observant as well as for those who already are.

And that means that rabbis, whether in the pulpit or the classroom, must use all the forms of communication in order to bring Torah close to Israel—not just those forms that confer prestige in the halls of the yeshiva.

Perhaps that is why, right after we ask God that it be His will that He habituate us to Torah, we add, "Lead us not into sin, transgression, iniquity, temptation or disgrace." The temptation of smugness? The disgrace of ignoring or denigrating those who are not yet within the circle of Torah and *mitzvot?*

I DO NOT want to be unkind or unfair. I recognize the psychological reality: After such deep immersion in the study of Torah here at Yeshiva, with criteria and standards so very different from and so far beyond those that prevail in the "outside" world, it is understandable if we sometimes feel discomfort with those who have not attained such a level, who have never aspired to it, who—perhaps—look down upon it because they have never experienced its intellectual stimulation, its moral beauty, its ethereal sanctity, its transcendental significance.

Let me confess to you: I, too, am uncomfortable with many Jews and with many types of Jews. Any rabbi, any principal, any Jewish leader, any president of Yeshiva University has to deal with a variety of people of whose views he may not approve, whose life-styles he may not share, whose company he may not enjoy—or whom he simply does not like.

I can give you a whole list of my own pet peeves, of Jews with whom I do not feel particularly relaxed: Jews who are either enarmored of or intolerant of non-Jews; Jews who are embarrassed by their Jewishness or who are aggressively holier-than-thou; zealots who burn the Israeli flag and Israelis who believe that now that we have a Jewish state we do not need Torah; Jews who are indistinguishable from WASPs and Israelis who regret that they are not WASPs; Op-Ed page writers who loudly proclaim their Jewishness and then go on to excoriate Israel with venom. And the list goes on and on.

But—and this is my point—so what if I am not comfortable with them? The love of Israel means that even if I do not approve of them or endorse their views or relish their company or even *like* them—I must *love* them. I must dedicate my life to saving and enhancing and enriching their lives, to healing them spiritually and physically, to comforting them, to bringing them to Torah and Torah to them—and them to each other.

That is what the love of Israel is all about. It is not an easy *mitzvah*. And it is especially incumbent upon Jewish leaders and *benei Torah*.

THIS DUTY OF the *ben Torah* towards his fellow Jews was already adumbrated by Moses. I believe, I suppose rather shockingly, that Moses did not especially like his Jews. He did not find them congenial, he was not comfortable with them, he did not enjoy their presence. He had little respect for them, he had no desire to impress them, he did not seek their approbation, there was virtually no mutuality between him and the people.

Truth to tell, Moses was not the sort of man who could be easily pleased. It is usually difficult to develop an easy relationship with a perfectionist, let alone the greatest prophet who ever lived. And it is also true that there wasn't much to like about these Israelites. They were an impetuous and whining and capricious lot. Moses broke open for them the horizons of Heaven, and they concentrated on their trivial needs and petty wants. He offered them a career of holiness, and they snivelled about leeks and onions and garlic. He offered freedom, and they complained that they were thirsty. He pointed to the heights of the spirit, and they yearned for the fleshpots of Egypt and coveted another *fleishig* meal. They were ungrateful, stubborn, slow to learn and narrow.

But Moses was passionate in his love for Israel. Remember that Moses was the only human being in history to whom God made the offer that, for his sake, He would abandon the Children of Israel and raise up a new people from his, Moses's, loins, and that this new people would be the Chosen People, descendants of

Abraham, Isaac, Jacob and—Moses. But Moses refused. He gave up this stunning opportunity. Not only that; his refusal bespoke his feeling of injury on his people's behalf. For after he asked God to forgive his people, he went on to say, "And if not, erase me from Thy Book" (Exodus 32:32). He loved the Jews so much that he was willing to forfeit, for them, his life, his fate, his destiny and eternity.

Moses loved them enough to risk and sacrifice all for them—but he did not like them very much. As a result, he was impatient with them, intolerant, angry and upset.

So Moses teaches all Jews, and especially Jewish leaders imbued with Torah, that love transcends liking. (My friend Michael Tabor of Manchester, England, said, "You like because; you love despite.") You will recall that Ramban interprets the commandment "Thou shalt love thy neighbor as thyself" as dealing with function, not emotion; act lovingly towards your fellow man even if you do not particularly like him. Similarly, *ahavat Yisrael* is volitional, not affective. To possess true love of Israel means to overcome your dislikes and your distastes, your peeves and your plaints, and to serve your people heroically.

Moses was the ultimate archetype of the *rav,* the *rosh yeshiva,* the *talmid chakham*—the *ben Torah.* His difficulties, his challenges, his ambivalences and his resolutions are all a model for Torah leadership in the personal and social problems that confront us.

It is this love of Israel that will inspire you to devote your lives, whether vocationally or avocationally, to the sacred service of Torah and Israel; to risk problems and peacelessness of mind; to travel far and wide to seek out our people. The mission upon which you now embark is, truly, a mission of love.

THESE TWIN LOVES, the love of Torah and the love of Israel, are what a true *rav,* a true *ben Torah,* has left even after he has forgotten all that he has learned. These are the basic attitudes that inform and orient and motivate him.

Your teachers have found you worthy of bearing the mantle of the rabbinate. This means that they have trust and confidence in your learning—and also in your love of learning and in your love of your fellow Jews, all of them.

I have no doubt that that trust and that confidence will be vindicated as you go forth, each in his own way, to spread the learning of Torah and to serve your people Israel and, in the process, bring much comfort and pride to your families, your teachers, your yeshiva.

On your behalf, I—and, I am sure, all our people—pray for you, in the words of the latter half of that morning prayer I discussed earlier, the prayer that begins with a petition for habituating us to His Torah and letting us cleave to His commandments:

> "GRANT US TODAY and every day, grace, favor and mercy, both in Thy sight and in the sight of all men, and bestow loving-kindness on us. Blessed art Thou, O Lord, who bestowest loving-kindness on Thy people Israel."

~ 41 ~

THERE IS A PROPHET IN ISRAEL

This address is dedicated, as is my *sheiur* tomorrow, to the memory of my revered teacher Dr. Samuel Belkin *zatzal*, whose tenth yahrzeit we commemorate during Chol ha-Moed Pesach.

Because Dr. Belkin was not only my teacher for one year—the last that he taught—but also my predecessor as President, I had the opportunity to appreciate the full scope of his prodigious talents and insights—his greatness not only as a *talmid chakham* and as an educator, but also as a leader. And it is this quality of leadership that I choose to discuss on this, his tenth yahrzeit and the one hundredth birthday of our Yeshiva.

Dr. Belkin taught us by example that to be a *talmid chakham* you need "lomdus"; to be a *yerei shamayim* you need *emunah*; to be a teacher you need love of your pupils as well as your subject matter. But to be a *Rav*, a rabbi in the classic Jewish sense, you need all these and much more: you need the gift of leadership.

Dr. Belkin himself was an orphan from Lithuania who became a renowned *talmid chakkam* at a young age, wandered to the United States, got himself a doctorate at Brown University, and then came to Yeshiva as both a Rosh Yeshiva and professor of Greek. His contribution to the Jewish world, however, was not confined to what he knew and what he taught, but was distinguished by the way he combined these with his vision, his goals, his determination, his readiness to use either gentle persuasion or confrontation—in a word, his leadership. It was the ability to integrate his Torah and his *Madda* with his leadership qualities that ensured his place in Jewish history.

Dr. Belkin was blessed with great gifts, both intellectual and personal, and few of us indeed can aspire to equal his achievements. But we can learn from him, each in his own way and in accordance with his own personality, to exercise leadership in our careers as rabbis; to bear in mind that the rabbinate is neither

---

Delivered at the Chag Ha-semikhah (Ordination ceremony) of the Rabbi Isaac Elchanan Theological Seminary, April 6, 1986

a service profession nor a lifelong *kollel* at the expense of a congregation, but a challenge to take the initiative to dream dreams for the greater glory of God and Torah and Israel—and implement them; to teach, but also to direct and orient and mold and build and create.

Do not take this charge lightly. Leadership is not for the faint of heart, but neither is it for the light-hearted and the frivolous. If an ordinary person makes a mistake, he merely makes a mistake; if a leader errs, he *mis*leads. Indeed, according to the Pesikta Rabbati (ch. 22), misleading, or the failure of a leader to exercise leadership, is a violation of one of the Ten Commandments! Thus, the Pesikta interprets the verse not to take the Name of the Lord in vain, to mean: not to accept an office when you are not worthy of it. The Netziv explains: the name *Elohim* can be either sacred or profane, depending upon whether it refers to God or to a human source of power, such as a judge or a prince. One who is designated a leader therefore shares with God, as it were, the title *Elohim* and if he proves unworthy of it by neglecting his responsibilities, he weakens and desecrates that Name—thus violating *lo tissa* and taking the Name in vain.

But there is not only danger in undertaking leadership, there is also glory. If abuse or disuse of responsibilities as a leader puts one in violation of *lo tissa,* then the proper execution and positive assertion of one's leadership is nothing less than a *Kiddush Hashem,* the sanctification of the divine Name.

Let me explain this by referring to a fascinating story recorded in Tanakh (II Kings, ch. 5):

Some 2,800 years ago, there was a king in ancient Israel—Jehoram, and a prophet—Elisha, the disciple of Elijah. The Kingdom of Israel was then effectively a satellite of Aram or Syria, and the Israelite king was a vassal of the king of Syria.

Naaman, the general of Syria, was a leper. A captive Israelite girl told Naaman that he could find relief by consulting Elisha the prophet. The king of Syria thereupon sent his general to Jehoram, the king of Israel, asking that the latter provide the cure from his leprosy. Jehoram panicked, for he had no idea how to cure lepers, and suspected that the Syrian king was using this as a pretext for attacking him.

When Elisha heard about that, he sent word to Jehoram that he, the prophet, will effect the cure: "Let him know that there is a prophet in Israel." Elisha then sent a messenger to Naaman telling him how to proceed in order to be cured. Naaman's advisors prevailed upon him to follow the prophet's advice, which he did, whereupon he was healed.

The story then reaches it climax in the words of Naaman: "Now I know that there is no God in all the world save in Israel." It is the act of *Kiddush Hashem,* the glorification or sanctification of God's Name.

Three things stand out in this story, and they make of it a parable of eternal and cogent relevance.

First is the description of Naaman: *gibbor chayil ish metzora,* the man was a mighty hero, but a leper.

What a startling juxtaposition, what a striking contrast: mighty, but a leper . . .

The *gibbor chayil metzora* is a symbol and picture of modern society, expressive of a painful paradox of Western civilization: technologically powerful, but ethically leprous; scientifically progressive, but spiritually regressive; materially mighty, but morally a midget. From the distance, when you behold this *gibbor chayil,* this mighty warrior who symbolizes modern society, you think he is self-confident, assertive, optimistic, problem-solving. But draw closer to him and you see that he is—a *metzora,* a leper, corrupt, frightened, in despair and disrepair, uncertain and perplexed, rotting and withering away inside.

Second, within the camp of Israel itself, there is a troublesome tension between king and prophet. The captive girl recommends the prophet, but the king of Syria sends Naaman not to the prophet, but to the king of Israel. The latter, in his despair, rends his clothes out of sheer frustration and worry—and he does not even think of sending the leper to the prophet! Ultimately, however, it is only the prophet who can, by imploring God, heal the leper: so that all may "know that there is a prophet in Israel."

In Israel there is always the tension between prophet and king, between the sacred and the profane, between that aspect of the life of Israel that is represented by the king—wordly knowledge, power, material wealth, cleverness—and that represented by the prophet: *kedushah,* holiness, the supreme word of the Lord, Torah, the spirit, and Jewish way of life. We have often erred and misled others, by offering to the world the king instead of the prophet as the source of Jewish healing. We have told ourselves and others that the ancient vision of salvation from Israel will come through a Jewish government or through Jewish nationhood, through Jewish scientists or Jewish Nobel Prize winners, through Jewish wealth or through Jewish writers or Jewish intellectuals.

Not so! Those who are symbolized by the king of Israel can help; they are, indeed, indispensable. Without *Maada,* without a material framework, without a proper natural and national context, without secular knowledge, without the profane, the prophet cannot flourish. But the main task of healing the Naamans of the world of their spiritual ills, of resolving their inner contradictions, of banishing the leprosy of the heart and soul, can come only through prophecy and Torah. "Let them know that there is a prophet in Israel."

The third thing we learn from this passage is that if and when the prophet is ready to take the initiative and let the kings, Jewish and non-Jewish, know that there is a prophet in Israel ready to heal the moral sickness that plagues the world, the result is—*Kiddush Hashem,* the sanctification of the divine Name.

What held true for Elisha the prophet holds true for each of you: Lead, for Heaven's sake; lead *le'shem shamayim;* and let the world know that there is a new and reinvigorated and energetic and authentic rabbinate, that there are still prophets in Israel! There is hardly a greater *Kiddush Hashem* than the awakening awareness that the *rabbanut* is alive and well and that Torah is thriving in Israel!

As we induct you officially into the *rabbanut,* we charge you with the holy burden of spiritual, Torah, intellectual, and communal leadership.

Leadership means creating, encouraging, and inspiring followers. *Ein melekh be'li am,* there can be no king without a country. And this task will demand of you new talents, largely untried during your student days—talents of motivation and organization and personal vigor and communal relationships. Rabbis must have "baalebatim" and congregations, and teachers must have pupils and schools. And if they're not there waiting for you, go out and beat the bushes, find them and mold them and elevate them, and "let them know there is a prophet in Israel."

Yeshiva is, in many ways, a social cocoon. Although we are much more open to variety than other yeshivot, nevertheless, we are more or less homogeneous. In the exercise of rabbinic leadership, you must learn to be open to *all* Jews from *all* backgrounds—Ashkenazim and Sephardim, old and young, men and women, Orthodox and non-Orthodox, affiliated and non-affiliated, those already on the way to *teshuvah* and those not yet at that level, confirmed secularists and those who simply go along with the crowd unthinkingly—you must be the *Rav* of all of them, whether or not they belong to your shul, whether or not they identify with our worldview. They—all of them—must know that you represent the prophet in Israel, the *masorah* of the *nabbanut;* that you bear the ring of authenticity; that your love and concern are broad and not parochial; that even the Naamans of life can come to you for help.

At a time when the vacuum in Jewish leadership in the community is being filled by well-meaning people who often lack any Torah orientation, it is time for our Rabbis to take their place in community leadership—whether of *vaad ha-kashrut* or *mikveh,* UJA or Federation, Soviet Jewry or PACs. You must breathe a *neshamah* into the established Jewish leadership by forthrightly articulating what we stand for, and doing so with *darkei no'am,* the "ways of pleasantness."

But, of course, you must never become just another "macher." You must ever remember that the source of your legitimacy as rabbis is—your status as *benei Torah* and *talmidei chakhamim* scholars of Torah. Unless you continue and deepen your study of Torah, unless you teach and are *marbitz Torah,* your credentials are suspect, your legitimacy is in question, your effectiveness is crippled.

This is a time of growing Jewish literacy among an emerging group of our Orthodox "baalebatim," and many of you will be undergoing a *bechinah* every time you give a *sheiur* or *derashah* or answer a *she'elah.* Only through your knowledge of Torah will people know that "there is a prophet in Israel."

To be a *talmid chakham* you need a head. To be a *yerei shamayim* you need a heart. To be a *gomel chasadim* you need hands and feet. To be a *darshan* you need a mouth. But to be a leader—you need a *chut ha-shedrah,* a spine, a backbone. And in age when, as we are told, the majority of the population suffers from back pain, that is no simple matter.

Leadership means not only marching at the head of a column

of loving and admiring followers, but also the ability to put up with criticism, justified and unjustified, often harsh and pitiless; with sarcasm and innuendo and vicious rumors; with yes-men who shield you from the truth and, more often, implacable adversaries who expose you to falsehood; with inertia and with hysteria; and with a lot more. Leadership means to put up with all this, and yet to hold fast to your principles despite all; to draw strength from your supporters—and even from your critics.

This has been the policy which our Yeshiva has followed for itself for one century—and *be'ezrat Hashem* will do so for at least another one. We did not become what we are by timidity and fear of criticism.

I have been connected with Yeshiva for 40 of its 100 years, ever since I came here as an 18-year-old student. I know something of its previous history. The way that Drs. Revel and Belkin chose for us was often beset with pain and controversy. It was never easy. We were told by Jews who were authorities in the world of secular education that "yeshiva" and "university" were antonyms, that they could never coexist in one institution. And the rivals of Yeshiva in certain non-Orthodox camps which today speak so admiringly of "pluralism," sneered at us, mocked us, wrote our obituaries. We were too Orthodox, too East European, too Old World.

At the same time, other yeshivot refused to recognize our existence; they too believed that "yeshiva" and "university" could never live together, conveniently ignoring the tradition of "the beauty of Japhet in the tents of Shem." For them, we were too modern, too American, too New World. To this day, at a wedding or at a funeral where our people mingle with those of certain other yeshivot, the others will be announced as the Rosh Yeshiva of this or that yeshiva, this or that Kollel, this or that Beis Medrash. But our Roshei Yeshiva, distinguished *geonim* and *gedolei Yisrael* of this, the mother of American yeshivot, are introduced with all kinds of devious euphemisms—the Rav of such and such a shtetl, the *talmid* of such and such *gaon*, the son-in-law of such and such *gadol*—but rarely as *Rosh yeshiva bi'yeshivat Rabbenu Yitzchak Elchanan.*

Yet the greatness of our Yeshiva is that we kept to our *derekh* with strength and with courage, that we conducted ourselves with individual and institutional dignity, that we refused to reciprocate petty insults and trade invectives, but continued to relate to others according to the principles of *kevod ha-beriyot* and *kevod ha-Torah.* This will continue to be our policy—one from which we will not be deterred, neither by flattery nor by threats.

What is true for Yeshiva as an institution is true for each of you as individuals. Only a few years ago, the rabbi of a significant congregation in this city was beset by problems and attacked viciously for a ruling he had made in good faith. He was pressured and buffeted by all sides.

Because he was not a *musnakh* of our yeshiva, he asked me to introduce him to our revered mentor, the Rav. I did so. It was *parashat Va-yetzei.* The Rav heard him, thought silently for a few minutes, and said to him the following: "Our Sidra ends with the words, 'and Jacob went upon his way, and he was met by the angels of God.' That is my advice to you: Go upon your own *derekh,* your own way, without looking right or left; and if you do so with sincerity and truth and honor, with the conviction that this is what Torah demands of you at this time and in this place, then you will be met by 'the angels of God.'"

That wisdom is worth sharing with you, our newest *musmakhim.* If you are to be leaders, if your goal is the honorable one of *kiddush shem shamayim,* then don't be overly concerned with what others say or press you to say; don't pander to the Left and don't cower before the Right. In Torah there is neither left nor right—if your "way" is that of a Jacob, then what follows is the meeting with the angels. There is only one way: straight ahead. Only with such firmness of method wedded to sacredness of purpose will the world know that "there is a prophet in Israel."

I hope I have not frightened you with this charge of leadership. Truth to tell, it is a hard, often painful way. But remember: nothing is easy. The Chazon Ish writes wistfully, in one of his letters, "everything comes with difficulty, and I have rarely encountered anything that is easy." If it was so for him, how much more so for us!

It is a mission that you dare not take lightly, but of which you must not despair. It will raise you up even as it wears you down. It will both exhilarate you and exhaust you. It will inspire you and scare you. You have chosen it—and it has chosen you. "Yours is not to complete the work, nor are you free to desist from it" (*Avot* 2:16).

You will not, in the exercise of your rabbinic leadership, avoid mistakes. But if you approach your tasks with a stout heart and deep commitment to the Almighty and to Torah; if you are frank enough to admit an error and correct it; if you are bold enough to stand up to others in the name of what you know to be right and proper and truthful—you will ultimately bask in the warmth of knowing that you brought to bear in your communities the presence of the contemporary counterpart of a "prophet in Israel"; that you made a genuine and lasting contribution to reducing the manifold leprosies of our ailing people and diseased times; that you did your share in effecting a *kiddush Hashem;* that you made it possible to be met by the angels of God in the form of children you sent to yeshivot, adults who deepened their life of Torah and Mitzvot, of a community endowed with a new and proper respect for Torah Judaism, of other young people whom you directed to our Yeshiva and who will some day take their places as *musmakhim* and as leaders.

Such rewards are enough to give you the courage to survive all the tests and rigors and pains of leadership. Not all of you have all the requisite personal attributes for great leadership, but each of you has some capacity for moving ahead and inspiring others to follow you, whether in the congregational rabbinate, in education, or in any area of *avodat ha-Kodesh.* Take that capacity, great or small, work on it, develop it, and express it *le'hagdil Torah u-le'haadirah.*

The mantle now is given to you as the dawn breaks on a new century for our beloved Yeshiva. You are not only our alumni, but our pride and joy, our emissaries to the Jewish community.

Wear the mantle, the mantle of the prophet who wanted all the world to know that "there is a prophet in Israel," with distinction, with resolve, with hope.

And may the Almighty grant you and your families the years, the health, the strength, some day to pass it on to a new generation, and another one after that, *ad biat ha-go'el.*

~ 42 ~

A RABBI INSIDE AND OUT

Every morning, at the introduction to our *Shacharit* prayers, we recite the following words: *Le'olam yehei adam yerei shamayim ba-seter uva-galuy,* "a person must always be in fear of Heaven, both in private and in public."

The source of this statement is the *Tanna de'vei Eliyahu,* where it appears in a slightly different form, omitting the word *uva-galuy,* thus reminding us to be God-fearing in private. This reading, which is also that of Rambam in his version of the Siddur, is obviously meant to encourage Jews living under oppression not to forsake their faith within the privacy of their own homes and hearts even if they are forced to do so in public.

However, the popular version, which we recite daily, is puzzling. Why was it necessary to include *uva-galuy?* And if it was done in order to emphasize that for Jews living under comparative freedom piety had to be pursued at all times and occasions, why not simply say *Le'olam yehei adam yerei shamayim,* that a man should always be God-fearing, without specifying that he should do so both *ba-seter uva-galuy?*

I suggest that a hidden nugget of wisdom lies here—a teaching that there really are two different kinds of piety, one for *ba-seter* and one for *uva-galuy,* and that the two realms of the hidden and revealed, or private and public, are distinct from, although continuous with, each other. The *ba-seter* or "Inside" fear of Heaven is a piety of and for oneself; it fills one's inner space. Such a person is concerned only with his own spiritual welfare and growth in Torah. He experiences a kind of noble egotism of the soul, one which may, however, lead to spiritual narcissism. His untiring efforts are focused only on his own *avodat Ha-shem* as he shuts the world off in order for this kind of devoutness to flourish. Such an Inside person is, in effect, reliving the condition of Moses who was commanded to ascend Sinai by himself: "no other human may accompany you." The Inside piety is fashioned out of soli-

---

Delivered at the Chag Ha-semikhah (Ordination ceremony) of the Rabbi Isaac Elchanan Theological Seminary, March 18, 1990.

tude and loneliness and the stillness of one's heart and conscience.

The *uva-galuy* or "Outside" piety is an outgoing experience. Here, the emphasis is not on oneself but on others, on the world. This kind of devout person is deeply concerned about the welfare of others, both spiritual and material. He is seized by a kind of spiritual altruism as he feels himself bound by a common creatureliness to all Jews, to all humans—indeed, to all forms of life. His religious experience reflects the Psalmist's triumphant cry, *kol ha-neshamah tehalel Yah halleluyah,* "let every soul praise the Lord"—as all of creation, in all its richly resplendent forms, joins the worshipper in offering praise to the Creator. This is the *uva-galuy* form of piety.

Therefore, *Le'olam yehei adam yerei shamayim ba-seter uva-galuy.* One must forever be devout, both Inside and Out.

And what is true for people generally is doubly true for rabbis. The rabbinate must be lived and practiced on two levels: Inside and Outside.

Inside

The special *yerei shamayim ba-seter* of a Rav, that piety which relates to his private sphere, comprises a number of areas.

Above all, there always stands the high demand for continuing *Talmud Torah.* True, the study of Torah is incumbent on all Jews, but it holds special significance for and makes unusual demands upon rabbis who are, after all, teachers of Torah.

As such, you who today are officially inducted into the rabbinate as we carry out the *shelichut* of yore, are doubly fortunate: as *rabbanim* and *mechankhim,* you both learn and teach—and this is an expression of the love of both Jews and Torah. Bear in mind the incisive comment of the Kotzker Rebbe who, on the well known statement of R. Akiva that "thou shalt love thy neighbor as thyself" is a *kelal gadol ba-Torah,* a great principle of Torah, added: the greatest way to express your love of your fellow Jew is to teach him Torah . . .

So never entertain any excuse to become lax. I am confident that you will continue to learn throughout your lives. I caution you only that you must never be satisfied with the level and depth that are required of you when you instruct children or teach adults who are relative novices. You must continue to analyze and probe as if you never left the *Bet Midrash,* no matter how little you are challenged by your pupils.

In addition, you must make up by yourselves for all that we did not have time to teach you in class: the rest of *Shas;* a better acquaintance with *Teshuvot* literature; and not only Halakhah, but also *machshavah,* for Jewish Thought is an essential vessel for Halakhah.

And whatever specialty you pursue within Torah, I urge you to develop your ideas and, if worthy enough, publish them. Disseminating your *chiddushim* is a great spur to your further study and creativity. Remember always this ethical note by the medieval author of *Sefer Hachasidim* (#530):

> Any new idea that comes to you is a divine revelation, and it was granted to you in order that you write it down and share it with others; if you fail to do so, you are in effect stealing from God!

But equally important, Halakhah sets special character criteria for rabbis: there is a more stringent code of *middot tovot* for rabbis than for laymen. On behalf of your distinguished teachers, I insist that you learn well and deeply, and apply carefully and wisely, the fifth chapter of Rambam, *Hilkhot Deiot.* Here Maimonides codifies the law of *yerei shamayim ba-seter,* the Inside Conduct, of a Rav.

For now, let me cite the opening of *halakhah* 1, which is an outline of the details that follow, and the beginning of the last *halakha* (13) to which I recommend that some of you give special attention.

> Just as a wise man (for which read: Rabbi, Rav) is distinguished by his wisdom and his character, and is thereby different from all others, so must he be distinguished in his conduct—in his eating and his drinking, his sexual life and his natural functions, his talking and his walking, his dress and his choice of words, and his way of doing business. All his deeds must be appropriate and refined.

Now we turn to the very end of that chapter, 5:13, where Rambam elaborates on this last item, the higher standard for a Rav in the conduct of his business:

> The business dealings of a *talmid chakham* must be conducted with integrity and faithfulness. His "yes" must be "yes" and his "no" must be "no." He must be strict for himself but generous and forgiving and undemanding towards others. And he must pay his bills immediately.

Your education at our Yeshiva for the last four or more years was the community's and Yeshiva's gift to those who are preparing for a life dedicated to *avodat ha-kodesh*—the rabbinate, Jewish education, Jewish community service, and the like. So, if that is your goal, you are not required to repay us for your learning here all these years. You are asked to remember that *Rabbanim* too must give *tzedakah* and, as your benefactors, we appeal to your sense of fair play to direct your largess to your yeshivah at least as well as to others.

But if, after all, you decide to devote your careers to something other than *avodat ha-kodesh*—to business or accounting or law or medicine or computers (all of which are more lucrative than the rabbinate)—then RIETS asserts a claim on your indebtedness to us for the Torah education you received here. It was our pleasure to provide scholarships and thus allow you to learn without overbearing financial worries. But as soon as you can you must, as *talmidei chakhamim,* abide by this last halakha which we cited: You must pay your bills *le'alter,* "at once!" We will forgo the last requirement of *le'alter* . . . but sooner or later we expect you to support us to the degree that you were supported by us here as a matter of genuine indebtedness, and not as charity; and then you must add to it, as do other *musmakhim,* as an act of *tzedakah* . . .

Do this, and we will know, with pride, that you are *talmidei chakhamim* who are *yerei shamayim ba-seter,* that you are authentic rabbis on the Inside.

Outside

But a Rav must also be a *yerei shamayim ba-galuy,* one whose concern radiates beyond himself, even beyond his congregation and community or classroom and school. And that means, in one word, spiritual leadership. Now, not everyone has the capacity for broad leadership, but everyone has *some* measure of leadership he can exercise—sometimes despite himself. And spiritual leadership, in particular, has many dimensions, some of them quite novel. Let me enumerate but three of them, equivalent in ascending order to the increasing levels and responsibilities of enhanced leadership

First, as mentioned, is the readiness to have your concern embrace *kelal Yisrael* and even the rest of humanity. And I add this important caveat: you must never fall prey to the comfortable but execrable and scandalous notion that the term *Kelal Yisrael* is restricted to only those who do and think as we do . . .

The most elementary level of leadership requires that you step out of "four cubits of the *Bet Midrash*" and venture into the *reshut ha-rabbim,* the public arena; that you turn your face and your concern from the exclusive preoccupation with the Inside to the Outside. To be genuine and effective Torah leaders of our people, you must be ready for the wrenching experience of emerging from the warm and nurturing milieu of the yeshiva and into the tumultuous, frustrating, often false and defiant public arena. I do not mean, *chas ve'shalom,* that you close the door to the *Bet Hamidrash* behind you—as if anyone ever "graduates" from the study of Torah . . . but that to a large extent you must turn outward, that you venture out of yourself to face the rest of the world. And it is cold outside!

I know many rabbis, both young and old, who are wonderful human beings, great Jews, fine scholars—but as rabbis they are incomplete; they are *rabbanim be'seter* but not *be'galuy!* And that simply will not do. The Orthodox community and the Jewish world are yearning for leadership, and they are impatient.

The rabbinate is a blend of priesthood and prophecy. The Outside mission of the rabbi is his prophetic function. Permit me to share with you something I heard from Chief Rabbi Avraham Shapira a few months ago: In the famous passage of Elijah confronting the prophets of the Baal on Mount Carmel, he proclaims: *ani notarti navi la-Shem levadi*—"I remained alone of all the prophets of the Lord" (I Kings 18:22). But this raises a difficult question: how can Elijah say he alone remained of all the prophets when just nine verses earlier, in the same chapter, Obadiah informed Elijah that he personally hid one hundred prophets in a cave?

The answer, says Rabbi Shapira, is that a prophet who stays in a cave is no prophet! A cave is secure and safe and protective—

but one who does not venture out to meet the brutal realities of "real life" to which ordinary Jews are subjected, who prefers safety over risk and caves over vision and his own security over his people's needs—is no prophet!

The same holds true for the rabbinate. A rabbinic leader who refuses to emerge out of the cave of his "shul" or school, who is a *yerei shamayim ba-seter* but not *ba-galuy,* who is satisfied to be a rabbi only Inside and not Outside—may be pious and may be a rabbi, but he is not a full rabbi, and he certainly is not and cannot be a leader.

I recommend to you as role models in this respect those who, in our very own times, were able to lead *shelomei emunei Yisrael* by exercising influence in the Outside world, outside the cave. These include Dr. Bernard Revel, who founded this yeshiva and endowed its ideology; Rabbi Feivel Mendlowitz, who built Torah Vodaath; Rabbi Aaron Kotler, who not only established the Lakewood Yeshiva but also inspired kollelim around the country; Rabbi Bloch who brought Telshe to Cleveland and Rabbi Ruderman who founded Ner Israel in Baltimore; my revered predecessor and Rebbe, Dr. Samuel Belkin, who began in a shtetl as a brilliant *talmid chakham,* grew in both Torah and Madda, and led this institution in its most constructive phase; and, *le'havdil bein chayyim le'chayyim,* our great mentor, "the Rav," whose word and guidance were sought by multitudes of Jews, and even non-Jews; the Lubavitcher Rebbe, who built an empire of Torah and Hasidism—and alumni of RIETS who founded and led Torah Umesorah in its beginnings and at its heights; who founded day schools and *mikva'ot* and synagogues around the country; who built and developed some of the most renowned yeshivot and other institutions in Israel; who rose to head the most prestigious Jewish communal organizations in this country, and who brought glory to the Torah community. These were—and are—*rabbanim* who abide by our definition of *yerei shamayim ba-seter uva-galuy,* rabbis Inside and Out.

The second level and its requirement for true spiritual leadership is: courage, the moral strength and spiritual power to fight a lonely battle, to stand up against great odds and to struggle for what you believe and know is right. I am not championing mavericks who are dissenters just for the fun of it. I refer to the quest for principle, for the stubbornness that comes from seeing and holding fast to a truth when others are blind to it.

The late Satmarer Rav, one of the stubbornest men of principle in our generation, once asked: why the halakhic formulation *yachid ve'rabbim halakhah ke'rabbim* (when there is one authority against the many, the law is with the many); why not simply *halakhah ke'rabbim* (the law is with the majority)? He answered: *yachid* refers (as it often does in rabbinic literature) not to a single human, but to *Yechido Shel Olam,* to the divine One and Only. Thus: follow the majority only when you know that God, the One, is with the many; otherwise, hold out, even against the whole world.

I am not known to be a particularly avid supporter of Satmar. But this particular policy I accept as axiomatic. It is not an especially pleasant position to be in—but it is the right one. Many Yeshiva *musmakhim* of my generation had to fight such lonely battles, and while some succumbed to weakness and gave in, others fought and prevailed. It is relatively easy for you to feel good about your not accepting a "mixed pew" congregation; we hardly have any of those any more . . . But your older colleagues had to battle that, and parking lots, and corrupt community kashruth, and unkempt and unpopular mikvahs, and . . . the list goes on and on.

You undoubtedly will face other kinds of problems. Your leadership will be tested—constantly, and by both extremes. If you are convinced of the rightness of your position, disregard numbers and, if necessary, defy the *rabbim* in the name of the divine *Yachid.* Do it cleverly, do it strategically, but most of all—do it!

There is a third and highest level of leadership, and that is the most demanding of all, even more difficult than standing alone against the world when you know you are right and can clearly see the justice of your own point of view. And that is—the ability to lead even when the horizon is murky instead of bright, the issues muddled instead of clear, positions gray instead of black-and-white; when all the alternatives are flawed instead of perfect; when you can't "look it up," and have nothing but your judgment to consult; when there is no *devar mishnah,* only *shikkul ha-daat.* At such times—and they come often, too often, in the life of a responsible leader—you have to take a position without the comfort of self-righteousness, with nothing more than a prayer to the

One Who knows all human thoughts that your good intentions be acknowledged by Him whose glory you serve, and that they be correct and effective—and that, ultimately, your colleagues and followers and even antagonists appreciate both your integrity and wisdom.

Such leadership requires a broad "Outside" and not only a narrow "Inside" rabbinate; it demands of you that you be a *yerei shamayim ba-galuy,* and not only *yerei shamayim ba-seter.*

Permit me to share with you what I told a convention of the Orthodox Union a year or so ago about this very theme. The Rambam in his *Perush ha-Mishnayot* to *Avot* quotes the Sages: "Whosoever is appointed a leader *(parnas)* by the community here below, is considered wicked *(rasha)* up above."

What a strange thing to say—especially considering that Rambam himself was the preeminent *parnas* or leader of his Egyptian-Jewish community!

I suggest that the intention of our Sages was more than a caution against the *hubris* that often bedevils high position in society. Rather, more subtly, they meant that you cannot attain the highest level of leadership without somehow being tainted as a *rasha,* because such "wickedness" emerges from the very nature of leadership. That is a tragic but inescapable fact. Leadership involves making hard decisions—better: dirty decisions—choosing between unpalatable alternatives, but opting for the one which is least harmful, the least evil. Anyone can make risk-free decisions, clear-cut choices between right and wrong. But it takes leadership to be ready to embrace the risk of being considered a *rasha mi-le'maalah,* less than perfect in the abstract, of being guilty of error and failure, if by so doing you protect the integrity of *tzibbur mi-le'mattah,* of your community—which is the responsibility of an authentic leader.

The Zohar (III, 23a) offers a similar thought. On the verse *asher nasi yecheta* "when a prince shall sin" (Lev. 4:22), the Zohar adds: *vadai yecheta,* "he most certainly will sin!" (The Zohar is intrigued by the word *asher* instead of *im,* "when" instead of "if," as though it is inevitable that the leader of the people sin. It therefore maintains that this is indeed so, and explains this certainty that the prince will sin as the consequence of overconfidence inspired by the readiness of his followers to be led. But the same inevitability can be tied to the essential nature of leadership which results from the need to make impossibly difficult decisions, rather than to the subjective weakness that leaves the leader exposed to the temptation of arrogance.)

You cannot be a *nasi* unless you are prepared to be accused by some—even by the most honorable of people—of being *vadai yecheta.*

No great leadership is possible unless you are ready for such crises of moral ambiguity. If you shrink from it, you can be a fine person, a Rav who is a *yerei shamayim ba'seter*—a "private rabbi"; but you are not a leader, neither a *parnas* nor a *nasi,* certainly not a *navi,* if you cannot become a *yerei shamayim ba-galuy.*

Conclusion

Allow me to summarize.

Rabbanut demands of you that you live on two levels: Inside and Outside, as an individual and as a public persona.

Your *seter,* your inner, private, personal life, was fashioned in our *Bet Midrash.* Your *galuy* will be molded as you encounter an often hostile world and seek to apply the norms of Torah and the values of our sacred tradition in a world that is usually reluctant to learn and impervious to your teaching. The public *galuy* world, unlike the private *seter* one, is an arena of more questions than answers, more problems than solutions, and of tormenting inconsistency, where you must make decisions and take stands where the issues are messy and murky and distasteful.

But face it you must—and do so with gusto, with brio, with zeal and enthusiasm and a bright and lustrous love for Torah and for Israel. And don't let anyone intimidate you!

How will you know that you are on the right path? And if you can't know for a certainty, then at least are there any precautions that you can take so that even an error will be an honest one?

Only one way: by making sure that your *bagaluy* is added to but does not displace your *ba-seter;* that you turn your face to the Outside world without ever turning your back on the Inside one; that you always maintain contact with the *Bet Midrash* and the Torah you learned and will continue to learn in it; that you always test yourself by the loyalty you maintain to your yeshiva.

On the verse, "I considered my ways and turned my feet unto

Thy testimonies" (Psalms 119:59), the Yalkut (*Be'chukotai* 670) comments:

> David said to the Holy One: Master of the Universe! Every day "I consider my ways" and say: I will go to this place, I will go to that abode. But my feet turn me towards synagogues and study halls!

No matter where you go in life, no matter what destiny beckons to you, no matter what other designs you have for yourselves, no matter where you plan to go—let the magnetic attraction of the memory of the years of learning Torah at the feet of masters always pull you back, and let your feet bring you once again here to our *Bet Midrash* of Yeshivat Rabbenu Yitzchak Elchanan, to your home at Yeshiva University.

Your feet will bring you back here, as long as your heart and mind and soul remain here, in the sacred precincts of this *Bet Midrash* where you were nurtured and where you grew as mature *benei Torah* and given *semikhat chakhamim.*

Do that, and you will be in a remarkable position:

- You will face the Outside without relinquishing the Inside
- You will be *yerei shamayim* both *ba-seter uva-galuy*
- You will go without leaving
- You will move on without moving away

In that spirit, we say to you, *tzetkhem le'shalom u-vo'akhem le'shalom.*

On behalf of myself and your distinguished *Rebbeim,* I wish you *kol tuv.* May the Almighty shower all His blessings upon you and grant you every *hatzlachah.*

May all of us, together and individually, be privileged to make immortal contributions *le'hagdil Torah u-le-haadirah.*

~ 43 ~

THE SPIRIT OF ELIJAH RESTS UPON ELISHA

There is a bitter-sweet quality to this celebration. On the one hand, there is a sense of joy when, at this impressive quadrennial *Chag Ha-semikhah,* we initiate a new group of rabbis into their roles as congregational rabbis and educators. On the other hand, this is the first such celebration in my memory, since my student days, at which our two great luminaries, the Rav and Reb Dovid, of blessed memory, did not grace the occasion with their presence.

In a sense, both the joy and the sorrow speak to the same theme—the transferring of spiritual authority from one generation to the next, the passing of responsibility for the entire *mesorah* and Torah leadership from teacher to student.

Permit me, therefore, to refer you back to an incident in the early history of the Jewish monarchy, when the prophet Elijah invested Elisha as his disciple and successor, as related in I Kings, chapter 19. It is a chapter which is itself worthy of study and also serves as a metaphor for your *Semikhah* at this juncture of our history.

Elijah had just gone through a soul-searing experience. Having challenged the prophets of Baal, confronted their royal supporter, Ahab, and therefore earned persecution by the infamous Jezebel, Elijah finds himself distraught, in total despair, having given up hope that his people are ready for their mission as the *am Hashem.* He is so filled with grim forebodings and feelings of inadequacy that he wants to die. God instructs him to stand at the mouth of the cave, where He reveals Himself to him. Elijah learns that God speaks to him not in the howling winds or the raging fires or the savage earthquake, but in the sound of gentle stillness, i.e., in patience and sensitivity. God then gives him three very specific commands: to anoint Hazael as the new king of Syria, Yehu as the new king of Israel, and, last, "Elisha, son of Shaphat, as a prophet in your place."

Delivered at the Chag Ha-semikhah (Ordination ceremony) of the Rabbi Isaac Elchanan Theological Seminary, March 6, 1994.

What does Elijah do? Does he proceed to follow the divine instructions exactly as they were given, namely, to anoint the two kings and then Elisha as his prophet successor? No, he does not. He changes the order. We hear nothing, for a long time, about anointing the new kings of Syria and Israel. Instead, he immediately does the last thing first:

> [Elijah] . . . found Elisha the son of Shaphat who was plowing . . . And Elijah passed by him and threw his mantle upon him. And [Elisha] left the oxen and ran after Elijah and said, "Please let me kiss my father and mother and I will then follow you"—then [Elisha] arose and followed [Elijah] and attended him.

Why the change in order, appointing Elisha first and leaving his diplomatic mission for later? I suggest that this was to teach posterity that, important as political moves and international relations and diplomatic maneuvers are, the single most important task before the Jewish people in every generation is to ensure the continuity of its spiritual leadership! Let kings and heads of state wait; let matters of historic moment bide their time; let the politicians stand aside and let the statesmen cool their heels in the outer offices of our attention. The priority of priorities is that there be prophets of God and teachers of Torah and models of moral conduct and exemplars of Torah ethics to make our people worthy of saving.

And so it is with us. Of all the causes that the Jewish community, including Yeshiva University, espouses, the teaching of Torah and the education of *talmidei chakhamim* and *rabbanim* is the most important. Unless we immediately attend to the future, the past is pointless and the present turns puerile. That is why this *Chag Ha-semikhah* is such a very important occasion. You who have become *musmakhim* these past four years are our Elishas, and your *rebbeim* are your Elijahs. We consider your learning, your *Semikhah*, your future development, as our greatest mission, and it is to that end that we expend every effort in preparing your *shiurim*, counseling you, worrying about your education, and—yes—in the endless and thankless task of raising funds to ensure your ability to learn without worry and distraction—and without tuition fees. Because without Elisha, Elijah's life and prophetic career have no continuity. We need you. And you need us.

And let no one minimize the difficulties we face and which will undoubtedly continue and **intensify** during your careers.

You *musmakhim* who sit before me this day are being formally inducted into the rabbinate during one of the most tumultuous, perilous, and fateful periods in American Jewish history. Since the last *Chag Hasemikkah,* the danger to our continuity as a people has been encapsulated and symbolized in the National Jewish Population Study which showed that over 52% of American Jews are marrying out—a sure sign that the majority of American Jews is unalterably assimilating and, thus, being lost to Jewish posterity.

These shocking statistics are not the end of the story. The problem is not only demographic but spiritual as well: Jews who are marrying out are not only marrying Christians, they are becoming wedded to Christianity! The group which claims to be "the largest denomination in Judaism" has, by virtue of its "outreach to the intermarried," opened the door to the most radical dilution of traditional Judaism in American Jewish history. Even a faculty member at a Reform seminary has complained in an official publication that what began as a welcome to non-Jewish spouses in the temple, and progressed to non-Jews becoming members of the temple (and thence to serve as officers of a Jewish congregation), has now developed to the point that non-Jewish spouses are permitted to participate and lead in "ritual" activities in and on behalf of the congregation. And if Christians are now to conduct Jewish services, can the importing of Christianity itself be far behind? How sad!

If anyone is skeptical about the danger of such *shemad* and the ultimate christianizing of the Jewish community, such doubts dissolve in a Jewish Telegraphic Agency report at the beginning of this past January that **some 20% of the Jewish community—or about a million Jews—attended church services on Christmas.** We are in deep and unprecedented trouble—if even half these figures are true!

And not only are we in trouble in America; the situation in Israel is not much less disturbing. The peace process and the political, diplomatic, and security future of the Jewish state are matters of critical importance—and in the light of recent events doubly so. But in the long run the uncertain **Jewish** future of the state is even more critical. Israel is far more secure Jewishly than the Diaspora—that is why we encourage *aliyah* for our students—but not far enough. Rabbi Adin Steinsaltz said recently, with too much justification, that the great question in Israel is not whether there will be a Palestinian state, **but whether the State of Israel will be a Jewish state.** Under such conditions, we cannot comfortably dismiss any worry about the spiritual as well as demographic destiny of American Jewry by assuming that the prophetic promise of "out of Zion shall go forth Torah" is at hand in these "Messianic times," and that, therefore, we can rely upon Israel to do for us religiously, culturally, and educationally what we cannot or will not do for ourselves.

Moreover, all is not well in our own Orthodox community. To illustrate this point let me refer again to that scene of the old prophet and his young new disciple and this time pose a halakhic question: Elijah is commanded to **anoint** Elisha as a prophet. But since when does a *navi* require *meshicha?* We know that a king and a *kohen gadol* and other "officials" require anointing—but a prophet? A *navi* is always a charismatic individual, an inspired nonconformist, not a formal office-holder, and there is no other case of a prophet being anointed.

The solution—and it is a relevant one—may be found in the Talmud (*Horayot* 11b), which asserts that the son of an anointed king does not require *meshicha,* because he inherits his father's status automatically. But, the Gemara asks, why then was Solomon anointed? Was not his father David anointed, and do we not constantly speak of King David as the Anointed King?

The answer the Talmud gives is that, in a time of *machloket,* of dispute and controversy and rancor, when the social and political consensus has been broken and the legitimacy of the new leader may be challenged, there should be a modified form of anointment—*meshicha be'afarsemei dakhya,* anointing with pure balsam oil; the original kind of oil, the *shemmen ha-mishcha,* was not used, but there was **some** kind of anointment, in order to confirm the new leadership and dampen the polemics. And that is why Elijah anointed Elisha—it was a necessary symbolic confirmation of his mission in stormy times.

For the same reason, your *Semikhah* at this critical crossroads of our history is so very important. Your *Semikhah* is a *meshicha* at a time in which we suffer from a fragmented polity, a lack of consensus, and therefore threats to our very existence. And when radical changes are upon us and the earth is shaking under the entire Jewish community to a degree the Richter scale cannot even contemplate, our own Torah community is split and polarized—and unnecessarily so.

The polemics that infect the body politic of our Orthodox community are not always ideological. In truth, the ideological differences are not unbridgeable and the problems are not insoluble, because all of us aspire to the flourishing of *talmud torah* and *yirat shamayim* and wish to enhance and increase Jewish education and the observance of the *mitzvot*. If only, when your generation comes to power, you could remove the personal and organizational egos, and along with them the inevitable enmity and envy; if you could concentrate on working together instead of proving your credentials by attacking the other; if you could scrap the monumental silliness that so often seeps into the most serious of our dialogues—then you would indeed successfully cooperate with mutual respect, and even love, to enhance the goals we all cherish. If the Chofetz Chayyim and Rav Kook, and the Chazon Ish and Rav Herzog were able, despite their differing views on the communal policy of loyal and observant Jewry, to learn with each other and address each other with *derekh eretz* and affection, why cannot we do the same—without demanding that the "other side" first abandon its own principles? Why do we insist that all *chilukei deiot* must lead to *machloket?* And if there must be ideological or even political *machloket*, why must it always be so uncivil, so destructive, so arrogant and self-righteous? Why must we imitate the *goyim* of our times and insist that there are "politically correct" ways of acting like Orthodox Jews, and that all who do not conform are beyond the pale?

It is not differences of opinion that are troublesome—these can be trying but also very healthy—but unrestrained contempt and verbal aggressiveness that make any kind of dialogue exceedingly difficult and preoccupy all of us with paltry politics and petty polemics, thus distracting us from confronting cooperatively the larger and far more consequential menaces to our common future. Nero fiddled while Rome burned. And we compliment our ancient foe by emulating him in our own circumstances.

All in all, this is not a pretty picture that I have painted for you, but it is unfortunately all too real. It is into this troubled world that you enter as rabbis and educators, and your *Semikhah* is, therefore, a kind of anointment with balsam oil. It confirms our faith and trust in you as you grow in Torah and mature as *rabbanim.*

In order to do so successfully, I recommend five guiding principles, two negative and three positive.

First, despite all that I have said, you who are this day being invested in the rabbinate dare not be discouraged! The *Sefer Chasidim* of R. Yehuda Ha-hasid teaches us that one who composes *chiddushei torah* (Torah writings) and does not publish them is guilty of being *mo'el be'hekdesh,* of illicit use of sacred property, because our intellectual achievements in Torah are the gift of the Almighty and we dare not keep them to ourselves and deny them to our fellow Jews. And if this is true of Torah novellae, which another *talmid chakham* may well be able to disprove, how much more so is it true of creating Torah personalities, of making Jews who will live and support Torah! You have no moral right to be frightened, no right to abandon your fellow Jews, no right to hoard Torah for yourselves and deny it to others—even though you are reluctant and they are unreceptive!

Some of you who are blessed with the gift of leadership may soon rise to be the agents of great, perhaps dramatic, improvements in the relationship between Torah and Israel. But each of you can, if you will it, make at least a dent here and a change there, so that together you will have achieved mighty contributions, together with other *musmakhim* of our Yeshiva and other yeshivot and *benei torah* from all over the country.

The second "negative commandment" is: do not allow yourselves to be sucked into any of the fashionable extremisms that are tearing our people apart. They are tempting, even seductive. Supporting them can make us feel good emotionally without burdening our intellects.

Extremism threatens to rip off the thin membrane of civilization that covers the inner volcano of violence. Violence from the mouth of a gun is a cancer that grows from the verbal violence from the mouth of a careless speaker or the pen of an irresponsible writer. And the oncogene—the cancer's seed—is extremism in dehumanizing your adversary.

There is a special obligation that lies upon all who have influence over the public—especially younger people, who are less prone to make fine distinctions, who are often at the mercy of boiling hormones. You will soon be in such positions in your congregations and classrooms. Remember what King Solomon taught: *ha-chayyim ve'ha-mavet be'yad ha-lashon,* the tongue has the power of life and death; speech has consequences.

The Rabbis of the Mishnah taught:

> Sages, be heedful of your words, lest you incur the penalty of exile and be exiled to a place of evil waters, and the disciples who come after you drink thereof and die, and the Heavenly Name be profaned.
>
> —*Avot 1:11*

In Halakhah, exile is the punishment for manslaughter, unwitting murder, for incurring careless loss of life. The negligent teacher who uses loaded words indiscriminately will thereby arouse the evil waters—the surging waves of hatred—to churn into violence. And younger, impressionable students, bright but still immature young people controlled as much by their glands as their minds, will imbibe these words and cause death and destruction to themselves and others. And the result will be—a terrible, massive *chillul Hashem.*

So I say to you—and to your teachers and faculty and administration and myself—*Hizaharu be'divrekhem,* be heedful of your words!

Beware of carelessly stigmatizing another person. Let no hothead dare call the Prime Minister of Israel a "traitor." Let that same Prime Minister be heedful and think twice before branding all *olim* from the Orthodox community of Brooklyn "a foreign implant." And let all of us be very, very careful not to belittle any adversary as an *"apikores"*—or even as an "extremist"—before thinking carefully two and three times.

Beware of intolerance, and beware of tolerance for the intolerant. There is a fine line that separates passion from violence and zeal from zealotry.

Beware of the tendency to deny that any other position can have merit, that your one concern takes precedence over every other consideration, that the adversary is invariably demonic, that every means is legitimate to achieve your end. Those who passionately take strong positions in Jewish life must know that there are unbalanced people who flock to extremes and who can, with what they consider good intentions, subvert the noblest goals.

Hizaharu be'divrekhem. Let us never forget the lesson of this past week or two of dreadful history: extremism begets fanaticism and fanaticism leads to the worst of evils—bloodshed and the desecration of the Divine Name—the most horrific terms in the lexicon of Judaism—all in the name of high principle and noble ideals and love of one's people.

As you grow and gain influence in the rabbinate, do what you can to bring peace and reconciliation and harmony to our harassed community. Reach out to others in the community to cooperate in bringing Torah to the masses of Jews who are alienated from it, so that they can join you in staving off the insatiable monster of mass assimilation. And, above all, learn not only to speak and speak out, but also to *listen.*

Remember that, as King David put it, "Then did the God-fearing speak *(az nidberu)* to one another, and the Lord listened and He heard." Why, indeed, is the Almighty so attentive to us? Because David writes not *az dibru,* that they spoke, but *nidberu,* in the transitive form, that they let themselves be spoken to by others. This means that, unlike our normal conversations where we are interested only in holding forth and declaiming to others, a truly God-fearing person is genuinely interested in listening to what the other has to say; he is as willing to be spoken to as he is to speak—and he is not anxious to invalidate the other as not God-fearing. That is why the Almighty, as it were, perks up, emulates us, and does likewise: He listens to us—and He hears!

So, be ready to listen, to understand, to be sensitive and civil and respectful of others. But do so without submitting to ideological demands imposed upon you by others.

The third, and positive, item is—to continue to immerse yourselves in Torah study; never stop. Your Torah will be your refuge and your strength, your consolation and your joy, and your inspiration to greater aspiration. And it, above all else, will help you help your people. It is our firm belief that, as the Sages told us, the eternal light of Torah will lead people to the paths of goodness and holiness, and that "the people" in this case refers both to your congregants or your pupils, and to you yourselves as well. It is inevitable that your long immersion in the world of *Gemara* and *Rashi* and *Tosafot* and *Rishonim* will inspire you to devote your lives to spreading Torah and to the Jewish people. It is inconceivable that your adventures in the fascinating universe of *Shakh* and *Taz* and *Peri Megadim,* in arguing with R. Akiva Eger and R. Chaim and the *Minchat Chinukh,* should leave you unready and unwilling to bring these giants of the intellect and the spirit to the loving attention of all your fellow Jews. After having been immersed in Torah in the sacred precincts of our Yeshiva, we expect you to dedicate the best efforts of your life to Torah and *am Yisrael.* For you will one day be the Elijahs who will place your mantles upon the shoulders of yet unborn Elishas.

The next positive thing you will need, and in great abundance, is the love of Israel, *ahavat Yisrael.* Truth to tell, it is a quite difficult *mitzvah* to perform. Not all Jews are lovable, and some are downright unlovable. But we were not commanded to love only those whom we admire or respect or already love. This *mitzvah* applies not only to individual Jews, but also to *Kelal Yisrael,* to us as a people.

Do not be put off by those who are openly antagonistic to Torah. We have accepted the burden of responsibility *(arevut)* for all Jews, regardless of the labels they wear. Save your aggressiveness for the battle against *am haaratzut*—that and the ubiquitous hedonism and rampant materialism which are so pervasive in our society. Be prepared to fight indifference to Jews and Judaism—by showing love for the very Jews who are indifferent. Work for them, befriend them, draw them close, sacrifice for them—and they, or many of them, will respond. Jews today, more than ever before, are attracted by spirituality and authenticity, and that means such things as your *kavanah* in your "davening," your *yirat shamayim,* your genuine commitment to Torah—and true and palpable love of all God's creatures, all humanity. Share these traits with them in true friendship, and you and they together will be prepared to face the greatest odds and wrest victories out of them. Remember what the Baal Shem Tov told a hasid who was broken-hearted because his son had abandoned Torah Judaism: "Love him more" . . .

Finally, and very briefly, what you will need, after learning and love, is gratitude. It is a theme that has been occupying my attention in recent years, probably because it is so rare and I miss it so much. You will be in the position, as a rabbi or a teacher, to do favors for people, to help and guide and support people. Do not expect their gratitude so that you will not be disappointed. But for yourselves, remember that it is a criterion of both your ***yiddishkeit*** and your ***menschlichkeit***.

Your gratitude must be extended to all who deserve it, and I here specifically mean our Yeshiva—yours and mine—which has given us the best of Torah, the only source of Torah Umadda, the warmest climate of intelligent piety and, along with it, intellectual challenges and high ethical standards and, not least, a free Torah education that has put us on the road to becoming Torah scholars. Do this by keeping and nourishing your links to Yeshiva. We will always support you. But soon it will be your turn to help support us—by sending students, by rallying supporters to us, by giving of your own substance. And I am proud to say to you that of all our alumni, it is the rabbinic alumni who are, relative to their ability, the most generous to their alma mater. May you continue in this grand tradition of *hakarat ha-tov.*

The world you are entering as you bear the sublime mission of our holy *mesorah* is more complex, more opaque, more hazardous than that of your teachers. At times, and in time, when you will be called upon to wear the mantle of Elijah, it may seem that the sheer novelty of the problems and volume of the challenges you face are so overwhelming, so vastly different from and much more difficult than those faced by your predecessors and mentors that, like Elisha, you will feel abandoned, and perhaps even resent that "Elijah went up in a storm to heaven," that they live in a Paradise, in heaven, in an ivory tower of the *Bet ha-Midrash,* while you must man the front lines, whether in your community or your classroom.

But do not lose courage. Because with the help of the Almighty, you will be granted the request for a double portion of his spirit—*pi shenayim be-ruchakha*—that Elisha made of Elijah as he bade him farewell; a double portion of your teachers' spirit will rest upon you. For our efforts, invested in you, will come to full fruition, and you will add to them your own internal resources of love of God and Torah and Israel, of courage and spiritedness.

And then your contemporaries will say of you, as the onlooking fellow disciples of Elijah—the *benei haneviim*—said of Elisha, "the spirit of Elijah now rests upon Elisha."

So may it be His divine will.

~ 44 ~

THE WHO, WHAT, AND WHERE OF THE RABBINATE

In greeting you on our last Chag ha-semikha of this troubled century, and on the 50th anniversary of the State of Israel, permit me to share with you some thoughts as to your role in a future that is, at one and the same time, both frightening and beckoning. To help you in your transition from a relatively cloistered existence in the Bet Midrash and college classroom to that varied and oft fearsome "outside world," allow me to turn practical and offer you some thoughts on the "who," "what," and "where" of your developing careers. (The "when" is obvious—Now—and requires no elaboration.) And while I address you as pulpit rabbis, those of you going into education or allied fields, simply apply my words to your own context.

The "who" consists of your relationships with your "baalebatim," your lay people, whether congregants, pupils, parents, board members, etc.

Many of you have expressed apprehension, during the sessions I have had with you as Semikha I and Semikha IV students, as to how to deal with the myriad of problems a rabbi has to contend with. I sympathize with you. We at Yeshiva hardly expect you to be full-fledged *posekim* and accomplished experts in human relations from the moment that you are placed in your first or even second position. But your "baalebatim" do not know and perhaps do not *want* to know this, and so you must be prepared with some guidelines even as you expect to learn much "on the job."

Of the many things that ought to be on your agenda regarding your "baalebatim," let me mention three.

The first obligation of a Rabbi is *chessed*—loving-kindness, care, generosity. I must repeat what the Rav, of blessed memory, would always caution us about. He would tell us what his grandfather, R. Hayyim Brisker, told his son—the Rav's father and predecessor here at Yeshiva, R. Moshe Soloveitchik—when

---

Delivered at the Chag Ha-semikhah (Ordination ceremony) of the Rabbi Isaac Elchanan Theological Seminary, March 22, 1998.

the latter was about to leave for his first "shtelle": "Listen to me, Moshe: a Rabbi must not only know 'how to learn'; the test of a Rabbi is if he practices *chessed.*" So, you will be judged by your "mentschlichkeit" as much or more than by your "lomdus."

You are not only going to sit in your synagogue office or classroom and dispense wisdom or offer a fine analysis of a halakhic text. You will also have to take care of the poor and the single parent and the latch-key child. You will have to hear people's problems and counsel them and find help for them. And that is a state of mind, a spiritual mission, and an art—all rolled into one. It will take time, but you will learn it. The Rav quotes R. Hayyim as saying, "I am basically a cruel person and I am also stingy, but I worked on myself and turned my cruelty into kindness and miserliness into generosity." So, work on yourselves! Both you and your people will benefit.

The second thing you must learn is courage—the courage to resist and to stand alone.

You are entering a world that is crazy (from the French *ecrassé*—split or cracked), confronted by new problems even while still wrestling with stubborn old problems, full of paradoxes and antinomies and contradictions and absurdities—especially those thrown up by science and technology, such as the potential for humans to direct the future evolution of the species. You will have to consult your *Rebbeim* and older colleagues, and some day you may be called upon to make such fateful decisions. You will confront a Jewish world disappearing at the margins, with an entrenched secularism that refuses to budge from old and tired formulas. You will be faced by young Jews who have suddenly become enamored of Eastern religions, spawning assorted forms of spurious spirituality. You are already in a Jewish community of sharp denominational divides where virulent anti-Orthodox sentiment has reached unparalleled proportions. You will have to work in an Orthodox community riven by internecine conflicts and burning animosity—and in our own part of the Orthodox community, a lack of dialogue, an unwillingness to treat those who differ with even a modicum of respect, a spiraling intolerance, a hardening of confrontational postures.

That is the kind of world you are entering—*and you will have to have the courage to change it!*

There will come a time or many times in your careers when

you will have to make unpopular decisions—unpopular with your laymen, with your colleagues, with the media. But your conscience as men of Torah will allow you no other recourse. You may even, sometimes, have to risk your very livelihood because of principle. True, leadership means you must get your people to trust and follow you, but you must also have the courage to go out front, by yourselves, and show what you stand for. You may be reviled, you may be attacked. But you must develop the backbone to resist and withstand.

Remember that the courage to go it alone when necessary is the mark of authenticity. The playwright Brecht puts into the mouth of Galileo the following sentences: "Good philosophers . . . fly alone, like eagles, not in flocks like starlings. A single Arabian steed can outrun a hundred plow-horses."

And centuries before him, a good—very good—philosopher named Maimonides or Rambam wrote to a student, in a letter preserved to this day in the *Guide for the Perplexed,* "I'd rather please one intelligent man, even if it means displeasing ten thousand fools."

Moreover the same Rambam codified it as a *halakha* when he established this prerequisite for a *dayyan* or for a Rabbi and for any principled Jewish leader:

> Learn from Moses, the teacher of all prophets: when the Holy One sent him to Egypt . . . tradition tells us that He said to Moses and Aaron, "[you must accept leadership] on condition that [you are prepared] that they will curse you and stone you."

So you must brave the imprecations and the insults and even the stones hurled at you. If you speak out on the important issues of the day which demand the voice of Torah authority, you will be criticized—no matter what you will say. And if you will say nothing, you will be criticized for that too. Even a deliberate decision to keep silent requires courage.

And third is an even greater challenge: the special code of conduct of a Rav. The first part of the same *halakha* in the Rambam shows how a Jewish leader must comport himself:

> One must not act with officiousness or vulgarity over the community, but with modesty and piety. A community official who intim-

> idates the community excessively will be punished . . . And one must not treat people with contempt even if they are ignorant . . . Even if they be common and lowly, they still are the children of Abraham, Isaac, and Jacob; they are the hosts of the Lord whom He took out of Egypt with great strength and a mighty hand. So must he bear patiently the bother and the burden of the community as did Moses . . .

This is a difficult standard, but there is no excuse for violating it. You must feel a basic compassion for your people and treat them with dignity—even if you feel they are undeserving. Follow the example of Moses who, even if he didn't particularly *like* his Jews, he did *love* them . . .

So much for the "who."

The "what" of your callings as congregational rabbis or educators is one word: *Torah.* Without it, your sermons will consist of insipid strings of pious platitudes, your counseling will be bereft of the wisdom of the ages, and you will reduced to the level of pastoral entertainers or, at best, social workers in rabbinic garb. There is nothing wrong with social work, but a Rav must be a Rav before and above all else.

What gives you your authenticity as *Rabbanim,* as *Orthodox Rabbis,* is your study of and commitment to Torah—and that means all of Torah but primarily Halakha.

Take it from someone with some experience in being busy: your communal and professional obligations, if you are sincere, will be overwhelming. They will make it seem forgivable to you to neglect your setting aside time to study Torah, and before long you will forget more and more.

But if you keep up with your learning, your professional experience will become a source of edification; it will lead you to a form of Torah study of a different order. You will be learning with your usual halakhic acumen which you acquired under the tutelage of your distinguished *Rebbeim,* but the very act of living with people and their intimate problems—experiences far beyond those you were exposed to during your years at Yeshiva—will endow you with the ability to find in other branches of Torah marvelous secrets or dimensions you never knew existed. The Torah—both Halakha and Agada, Shas and Midrash—will enrich your ability to deal with people, and will become, if you are wise and sensitive, a source not only of *derashot* but for the wisdom of life itself.

One of the greatest and still under-appreciated giants of Hasidic thought, R. Zadok Hakohen of Lublin, tells us that there are two traditions about the number of facets Torah possesses. According to one Midrash, there are 49; another passage puts the number at 70 (Mid.Psalms, 119, and Nu.R. 13). How explain the difference? R. Zadok says that it depends upon the nature of the Torah studied, for there are two kinds, each with a different provenance. Torah which has 49 aspects stems from the Tree of Knowledge of Good and Evil. But the other famous tree in Gan Eden, the Tree of Life, has an even greater efflorescence; it has 70 faces or facets, as opposed to the 49 of the Tree of Knowledge.

Thus, the learning of Torah that issues from the Tree of Knowledge is more restricted: 49 aspects are the maximum one can attain by the pure exercise of intellect in the pursuit of knowledge. But when you study Torah that derives from the Tree of Life—the fruit of a life of holiness in the here-and-now, experience in the hustle and bustle of the daily struggles of existence, there you will uncover and discover not only 49 but 70 aspects of Torah! And those extra 21 faces of Torah will be yours as you move from the Tree of Knowledge to the Tree of Life.

So—learn from your experience, and learn to find your guidance someplace in the 70 dimensions of Torah. Don't separate Torah from life. Each enriches and expands the other.

Finally, we come to the "where" of your future lives.

You are now, as I indicated earlier, in a state of transition—between school and career, yeshiva and the rabbinate, absorbing and giving, being led and leading. Some of you are prepared to go to the ends of the earth (one of you is here from Hong Kong and another from Turkey!) to teach Torah. But many of you, alas, feel that you must stay close to home, i.e., New York, or at most Israel—and even then, only Jerusalem; that everything in America west of the Hudson is the equivalent of beyond the mythical River Sambatyon, and everything north of Rockland County is the remote area of the Hills of Darkness. The Rav used to say that he never met anyone as parochial and provincial as the typical New Yorker. How right he was!

I can understand your reluctance at leaving the environs that have served you so well for so many years. Even a fetus, psychologists tell us, experiences trauma upon being expelled from its mother's womb. But it must happen. To you the Psalmist says, "I have today—*today!*—given birth to you" (Psalms 2:7). You must leave and must make your way to wherever there are Jews who need you, Jews who need to be taught and instructed and counseled and loved, and you must do so as authentic *benei Torah,* filled with *ahavat Yisrael.* Yes, despite phones and fax machines and e-mail and the Web, you will be distant from your *Rebbeim,* your colleagues, your family. But even a chick must be pushed out of the nest at some point. And you too must learn to fly—and to soar on the wings of learning and love, to heights you never expected and to satisfactions you never imagined—along with frustrations and longing and loneliness.

Some of you will question what I say on the basis of a *Beraita.* Let me bring it into the open, because it speaks to your and our situation.

> R. Yosi b. Kisma said: I once was walking on my way when I was accosted by a man who greeted me, and I returned his greeting. He said to me, "Rabbi, what place are you from?" I said to him, "From a great city of scholars and scribes." He said to me, "Rabbi, would you be willing to live with us, in our place, and I will give you thousands upon thousands of golden dinarim and jewels and pearls?" I said to him, "Son, even if you gave me all the silver and gold in the world, and all the precious stones and pearls in the world, I would not live in any place other than a place of Torah" (*Avot* 6:9).

I can imagine that scene: the forward, aggressive shul president accosting the holy R. Yosi: "Hi, Rabbi, I heard your lecture last night. It was terrific! Listen, I'm the president of a shul and the head of the Search Committee for a rabbi. Come to our *shtelle* and I'll guarantee you an enormous salary, terrific benefits, retirement package, insurance, car, apartment, trip to Israel—the works . . ." The man must have been shocked at R. Yosi's response.

Apparently this *Beraita* argues for your remaining in this, the largest Jewish community in the world, and not venturing to the hinterland where gold and silver rather than the discourses of "scholars and scribes" are the tokens of success.

And yet I tell you that go you must, if you are to be true to the mission towards which you have been educated. And that is so for two reasons.

First, the view of R. Yosi b. Kisma is not the only authentic voice of our tradition. There are other views, other than that of R. Yosi b. Kisma. Thus, Resh Lakesh, in the Talmud (*Sukkah 20a),* tells us that several times Torah was all but forgotten in Eretz Israel, and only the infusion of strength in Torah learning by *individuals*—such as Ezra, then Hillel, then R. Hiyya and his sons—who were willing to struggle in a new environment for the sake of Torah, leaving behind the secure walls of Babylonian *batei midrash,* was able to restore Palestinian Jewry to its former eminence.

Imagine if the elite of Polish Jewry—the Babylon of this historical epoch—would have gone on aliyah to Israel. How different the State of Israel would be and look now, 50 years after its founding!

Imagine if some of the greatest *gedolim* at the end of the 1800's and early years of this century had decided to come with ordinary Jews to the United States to introduce Torah learning here on a grander scale. R. Jacob Joseph would not have been a voice in the wilderness and it would not have taken 80–90 years for Orthodoxy to mature to where it feels it has a chance in this country.

Imagine if Dr. Revel and his early predecessors as well as Dr. Belkin and the Rav had decided to nestle in the warm and supportive environment of Eastern Europe—or the lush oil-fields of Oklahoma—and not ventured here to build Torah and our yeshiva. Where would we be today?

Imagine if R. Aaron Kotler had preferred to stay in Brooklyn, where he had all the comforts and support that an admiring Orthodoxy could give him, and not gone to Lakewood to build a great yeshiva.

So, R. Yosi b. Kisma offers a legitimate view of the role of the rabbi and his preference for the "great city of scholars and scribes," but others offer competing visions. And I submit to you, freshly minted *musmakhim,* that your obligation lies first with the small, outlying communities where you may well struggle financially, be disappointed at the absence of intellectual and Torah companionship, nurse your dreams in loneliness. *But*—you will be working out your mistakes while making a supreme effort to do what Ezra and Hillel and R. Hiyya and his sons did for Eretz Israel Jewry in their generations. You will be building reputations at the same time that you will be participating in the renaissance of Torah even in the hinterlands. Remember that they too are Jews, they are as deserving of our attention and sacrifice as are the Jews of Boro Park or Spring Valley or Teaneck or the Upper West Side.

And then there is a second reason for urging you to be more adventurous geographically: perhaps R. Yosi b. Kisma didn't at all mean what most people assume he meant. Rather, he meant something totally different—something that I believe is of supreme importance to you as you leave the sacred precincts of the yeshiva.

Note the recurrence of the term "*makom*"—place, not town or city—in this whole passage. The discerning but materialistic and somewhat brash shul president asked the Rabbi, "what *place* are you from?" Every man and woman has a *makom*—a place or locus, spiritual-psychological rather than geographical, a rootedness that determines and fixes his character and his aspirations, his dreams and ambitions and orientations. Mr. President wanted this talented and famous rabbi not only to move to his town—that would have been quite appropriate—but to change his *makom,* his locus, to transform his very identity from a scholar of Torah to a clerical professional, from a perpetual student to an efficient administrator, from a spiritual to a social persona. Rabbi, you've got to be like one of us, one of the boys, "to live with us in our *makom,*" to adjust to our self-identification, and then you can aspire to all the wealth and social prominence that goes with it. And the answer of R. Yosi b. Kisma is loud and clear: all the money and fame in the world will not move me to change my *makom* from one of Torah to one of vulgarity—rich, comfortable, well-meaning, kindly, benevolent vulgarity, but vulgarity nonetheless. I'm ready to go anyplace to teach Torah, but I am never going to transform my very identity from *ben Torah* to anything other than that. That is my *makom*—that and no other.

So perhaps, after all, R. Yosi b. Kisma was not speaking against moving to a smaller and remote community, but against transmuting his locus, his *makom,* his very identity.

Therefore, when we urge you to raise your eyes and look beyond the confines of neighborhood and city, to broaden your horizons and expand your scope, it is purely a matter of geography, not identity and spirituality. Indeed, wherever you go and whatever you may eventually do professionally, inside the rabbinate or outside, your *makom* must always be here, firmly fixed within the walls of our Bet Midrash forever and ever, for this is the *makom* which nourished your souls and sharpened your wits and fostered your dreams, where dedicated and brilliant *Rebbeim* taught you how to learn, shepherded you through abstruse texts and educated you in the art of applying the light of Torah to illuminate the most dark and difficult of human situations. It is this *makom* to which each of you must always return to refresh your *neshamah* and reenergize your mind and reconfirm your commitment.

Do so, and you will find that your *makom* is very, very crowded. You will find there, with you, your *Rebbeim,* and our giants of yesteryear—the Rav and Dr. Belkin and Dr. Revel and "the Meitchiter Iluy" and all the *Gedolei Yisrael* who graced our yeshiva with their learning and their teaching. They will always be with you.

It is in this spirit that I conclude with one of the pearls of wisdom of the great Tanna, R. Meir:

> R. Meir had a favorite saying: [God says:] Learn with all your heart and soul to know My ways and to be energetic when approaching the doors of My Torah. Keep My Torah in your heart, and may the fear of Heaven always be before your eyes—then I will be with you in every *makom,* for wherever your destiny takes you, your *makom* will always be in My precincts, the *makom* of Torah and fear of Heaven (*Berakhot* 17a).

Indeed, may He be with you for years without end, years of accomplishments for Torah, for yourselves and for your families, for all of us at Yeshiva and for all our people wherever they may be.

~ 45 ~

CAVES AND ENCLAVES

When our Father Jacob was having problems with his father-in-law and employer, Laban, he turned to him in frustration and said:

> I have been with you for twenty years . . . and I have not eaten any of the animals of your flock . . . In the daytime I was consumed by drought, and with frost by night. And sleep fled from my eyes (Gen. 31:38–40)

I can sympathize with some though not all of Jacob's complaints. No one ever accused me of eating any members of Yeshiva's flocks, although various interesting and imaginative rumors have come to my attention during these past two decades . . . I have not suffered the radical changes of temperature that afflicted our shepherd forefather; instead, I made up for that with varied kinds of headaches. But I have worked—and worried—quite hard these twenty years, and indeed, often, too often, "sleep fled from my eyes." But unlike Jacob, I have no complaints; instead, I offer thanks to my colleagues, trustees, supporters, alumni, students, my very devoted wife and family who have borne with grace so much of the burden I carried and, most of all, to the Almighty, for having given me the privilege of serving a cause I consider sacred and an institution that I believe in and love with all my heart and all my soul and all my might. And I pray that God will give me the strength to continue such service into the future.

Twenty years is not unusual for a presidency of Yeshiva, but quite rare for the stewardship of an American university. It calls to mind the story of a couple celebrating their 60th wedding anniversary. A local reporter approached them and asked one of them, "How does it feel to have lived 60 years with one person?"

This centennial address was delivered in May 28, 1997 at the celebration of the 100th anniversary of the Rabbi Isaac Elchanan Theological Seminary.

The answer: "Oh, it was like two days." Why two days, the reporter asked. The reply: "Like Yom Kippur and Tisha Be'Av!"

In my case, the answer would be that twenty years passed like only *one* day—Simchat Torah. Not all was song and dance, but there was always the joy of serving a great, transcendent cause with which I fully identify.

Our celebration today is in honor of the foresight of our founders in renaming Yeshiva Eitz Chaim for the Kovner Rav, R. Yitzchak Elchanan Spektor, who died the year before.

It is not generally recognized that this Gaon in many ways adumbrated—explicitly but mostly implicitly, in the way he behaved—the ideals which inspire this Yeshiva and make it unique. Together with the Netziv and R. Shmuel Mohliver, he identified publicly with the Hovevei Zion movement—the precursor of Zionism. He believed in the unity of the Jewish community, and did not hesitate to attend conferences with assimilationist Jews. He wrote letters on behalf of cooperating with non-observant Jews in responding to challenges to what was precious to all Jews. Despite his apprehensions about America and its corrosive effects on Jewish loyalties, he permitted many of the students of his Kollel to emigrate to the United States. His attitude stemmed not from some liberal religious or political doctrine, but from a sophisticated *ahavat Yisrael*—the same source for his historic attitude to helping *agunot* reestablish normal lives. His approach thus finds a home with us after a whole, violent, historic century.

What, indeed, is it that we stand for now, at the brink of a new century and new millennium on the secular calendar? Let me respond by means of a story told in the Talmud (*Shabbat* 33b) which is a powerful metaphor for our own RIETS (Rabbi Isaac Elchanan Theological Seminary). It concerns the great R. Simeon bar Yochai and his son R. Elazar:

A few of the great Tannaim of that generation were discussing the occupying government, the Romans. R. Simeon bar Yochai made a sarcastic comment about them, and the information soon reached the Roman authorities who condemned him to death. He fled, together with his son R. Elazar, and eventually the two found refuge in a bare cave, with nothing but a carob tree and a fresh well to sustain them. There they stayed for twelve years, growing intensely in their learning and their spiritual development, until the Prophet Elijah announced that Caesar was dead, and hence they were free to leave. They left, and the first scene they encountered was that of a farmer plowing and planting his field. They were outraged by the apparent "normalcy" they beheld, and commented, "They abandon life eternal (i.e., the study of Torah) for ephemeral life!" They could not bear the thought of such normalcy. And, wherever they cast their eyes, it was burnt to a cinder, i.e., they reduced such pretenses to ashes. Whereupon a Divine Voice issued from Heaven and exclaimed, "Have you left your cave in order to destroy My world? Go back to your cave!" They returned and stayed there for another twelve months. At the end of that period, another Divine Voice commanded them, "Leave your cave." They did so, and wherever R. Elazar wounded (i.e., he kept up his radical dissatisfaction with mundane life) R. Simeon bar Yochai healed (i.e., he was reconciled to "normal" life). On the eve of the Sabbath they saw an old man hurrying, with a pair of myrtle twigs in his hand. "What are these for?" they asked. "In honor of the Sabbath," the old man answered. Whereupon the father said to the son, "See how the people of Israel love the *mitzvot*." Thus, they were pacified.

At this point, both older and younger man understood that sincere devotion of even a layman, a non-scholar in Torah, is precious, and should not be deprecated.

What do we learn from this? We learn that caves are important, that they are critical if we are to create *talmidei chakhamim* and nourish people of great spiritual capacity. But it is not the norm for Jewish society and community or, for that matter, for *talmidei chakhamim*. Any attempt to impose the discipline of the cave on the "real world" is destructive, and those who advocate it are told: *go back to your cave!* . . . The Divine Voice favors the newfound maturity of R. Simeon bar Yochai, not the radical view of his son; hence, the command to us is clear: *leave the cave* . . . The regular Jewish community that remains loyal to Yiddishkeit is a precious one and should be valued, even as is an old and apparently uneducated man who does what he can with love. "See how the people of Israel love the *mitzvot!*"

We too, then, must include every Jew who cherishes his Jewishness, even though he may be ignorant of the correct way of doing so, in the circle of our deepest spiritual concern and personal regard and friendship and love, and never seek to exclude him.

We who study and teach at Yeshiva essentially live in a private community—a marvelous enclave, one of study and thought and research, of vibrant ideas and creative concepts and novel interpretations and spiritual growth, all on the very highest levels. But it is an *enclave,* not a *cave;* we are not hermetically sealed off from the world. Yes, the "cave experience" can be, and indeed is, a vital element in one's Torah development, and that is why we recommend a year of intensive immersion in Torah in Israel and, for Semikha students, at our Gruss Institute in Jerusalem. But the cave is not the natural habitat of Torah; a "house of study"—a *bet ha-midrash*—is where Torah flourishes, not a "cave" of study. We do not and should not aspire to educate our students to live in caves once they have left the Yeshiva. We have and should have higher and more demanding standards than the rest of society and Jewish community, but not so high that *we* look upon *them* with withering contempt—"wherever they cast their eyes it was burnt"—and not so demanding that *others* look upon *us* as out of reach and irrelevant.

Unquestionably, the great mission and prime emphasis of RIETS is *Torah lishmah*—"the study of Torah for its own sake": not for professional achievement, not for adornment or prestige, not for the glory of any individual or any institution. In the context of Yeshiva University's Torah Umadda education, this goal is in the tradition of R. Simeon bar Yochai when he emerged from his cave the second time. Our credo is and must remain that Torah is the highest and most sublime ideal of *am Yisrael,* that study of Torah is the noblest occupation, that the Torah way of life is worthy of the most demanding sacrifice. But Torah is not incompatible with a creative life in the enormous variety of pursuits open to us in modern life: in the arts and sciences and business and crafts and professions.

The second emphasis of RIETS, as the premier institution of Modern Orthodoxy, is therefore on service to the Jewish community. The adjective "Modern" should not fool anyone. Our commitment to and celebration of *Torah lishmah* is no less than that of any other advanced yeshiva; but unlike others, our confrontation with modernity is more nuanced, more subtle, and more balanced. We neither accept it uncritically nor reject it unthinkingly. We believe, as the Rav taught us, that Torah can be lived and implemented in every time and circumstance, and that includes modernity and post-modernity. We stand firmly in the world of Halakha, but we shall not turn our backs on the world of *Madda*—of culture and science. We shall ever heed the Voice that bids us "leave the cave!" That dialectic between the Cave and the World is the source of our glory—as well as of our dilemmas, our tensions, and our perplexing inconsistencies. Our commitment is to Torah, to this community of Modern/Centrist Orthodox Jews, and to this ideology. And it is a commitment, not a compromise or concession.

On this centennial of the naming of RIETS we are summoned to reaffirm our commitment to that historic vision, for it is our truth. And, as the Hasidic Zaddik R. Hirsh Rimanover taught, in a playful but profound comment on the verse *lo tonu ish et amito* ("you shall not deceive your fellow man"—Lev. 25:17): The word *amito,* friend or fellow man, is spelled with an *ayin;* with hardly any change in pronunciation it can be read as if it were spelled with an *aleph,* thus: "do not deceive your [very own] truth." In other words: *Be true to your own ideals!*

This restatement of our institutional mission should be self-evident. It should also be evident to all that this is not an easy task educationally, for our ideological balance is always precarious, and we are constantly called upon to exercise careful judgment. Younger people, especially, incline to idealistic perfectionism and are less tolerant of the foibles of an imperfect humanity and an inconsistent community—much like R. Elazar, son of R. Simeon bar Yochai. That is the way of the world, and we should be proud of our students. And if they sometimes tend to relatively extreme views, it is because of the purity of their ideals and their quest for absolute consistency, aspirations which are inspiring and admirable. It is true that such over-demanding youthful idealism can lead them and us astray, and thus prove quite dangerous. But we are adults, and so must be confident that they will mature; and we who are older must be wiser and teach them how to bank the fires of youthful zeal and sublimate their passionate idealistic yearnings in a manner that will enhance and not destroy the community of *kelal yisrael;* that will heal and not hurt, following the more mature R. Simeon bar Yochai rather than his son R. Elazar—and yet keep their idealistic ambitions alive and active for the rest of their lives.

And we must look with love and appreciation upon the non-

Yeshiva lay community, encouraging their observance of *mitzvot* at whatever level they have attained—"See how the people of Israel love the *mitzvot*"—inspiring them to greater love of *mitzvot,* to deeper study of Torah, to a more intense passion for our people and land, to increased support for Torah and its schools, and urging upon them a nobler degree of ethical and moral conduct.

As I consider our alumni and our current students, I can tell you that the overwhelming majority live up to and exceed our expectations. They are aflame with dedication, but they are more mature than their years. They are idealistic, and among their great ideals are their love of their fellow Jews, their love of Eretz Israel, as well as their love of Torah. Be proud of them! They deserve it. And we deserve them. R. Isaac Elchanan too would have been proud of them.

It is fitting and proper that at a celebration of this sort we invoke the memories of my two illustrious predecessors, to whom Yeshiva owes its success, indeed, its very existence. Dr. Bernard Revel and Dr. Samuel Belkin, *zekher tzaddikim liverakhah,* sacrificed their lives and careers for the sake of this institution and we should always remember them in gratitude and love.

The one who shaped RIETS and put the stamp of his genius on it was the Rav, Rabbi Joseph Soloveitchik, *zekher tzaddik liverakhah,* and it is his legacy that must be preserved, expanded, and continued as a living tradition at Yeshiva University and RIETS. But—it must be his *true* legacy. No one-sided distortion of this complex intellectual and spiritual giant should be countenanced. Let it be stated clearly and unequivocally: his attitude to "the wisdom of the nations," to Torah Umadda, to the broader Jewish community, was not cavalier; it was *le'khat'chilah,* not *bidiavad.* Any contrary assertion diminishes the *Gestalt* of this unconventional Rosh Yeshiva and *gaon she'bi-geonim.* The Rav was an integrated human being whose thinking was complicated and deep, and we should be suspicious of any effort to cut him down to fit the size of our own minds, minds so much less capacious, less bold, less profound than his. We here stand by the man he was, as the highest instance of our ideals and our aspirations. And the Rav was a man of the broadest vision, intellectually and spiritually; he was not an advocate of life-long voluntary incarceration in the cave . . .

After his cave-experience, the Talmud tells us, R. Simeon bar

Yochai wanted to offer thanks to the Almighty for the miracle of his survival. He said, "let me go and accomplish something" practical and useful for my people. The Talmud tells us that he learned this from our Father Jacob, the same Jacob who labored for twenty years for Laban and then survived his encounter with Esau. In a comment on a verse, the Talmud relates that Jacob arrived *shalem*, "whole—physically, economically, and spiritually," and that in gratitude he instituted several important contributions to the welfare of Salem, the place he came to.

I pray that I, together with all of you, be privileged to follow the example of both R. Simeon bar Yochai and Jacob and accomplish great things for RIETS and YU and, through them, for all our people, for *kelal yisrael*. And I believe that the greatest contributions that remain to be made as I conclude 20 years of service is to put our beloved Yeshiva in the condition in which Jacob arrived in Salem: improved physically, financially, and spiritually on the ever higher levels of Torah to which we all aspire.

The future beckons, and we must respond, all of us, with the determination of which R. Simeon bar Yochai spoke: to accomplish great, practical, real things on behalf of Yeshiva.

In that way, each of us individually and all of us collectively, can attain the wholeness which is worthy of our greatest sacrifices and most cherished aspirations.

So may it be His will.

Chapter 9

ISRAEL AND ZIONISM

The first two articles in this chapter discuss two movements in the Orthodox community, each one at another end of the political spectrum: Mizrachi and the Neturei Karta or Satmarer.

The two pieces that follow are ruminations about the Six-Day War and its aftermath, and the period of the Yom Kippur War—two decisive events in the history of modern Israel.

Following that are three entries revolving about the late Prime Minister Yitzchak Rabin. The first is the eulogy I delivered upon learning of the assassination, the second was offered at the sheloshim *(thirtieth day after his death), and the third consists of my reflections on the effects his death had on subsequent developments in Israel and the Diaspora, with special attention to the Oslo "peace process" and an evaluation of the halakhic arguments that were forcefully presented in opposition to the process.*

Following that is an article I wrote upon returning from a visit to Latvia, which gave rise to reflections on the relations of Israel and the Diaspora.

The final two articles concern Israel on its fiftieth anniversary, and an attempt to discern a direction for the next half-century.

~ 46 ~

RELIGIOUS ZIONISM

The Mizrachi

Religious Zionism is in disarray. Underneath the thin veneer of "normalcy" lies a reservoir of sadness, tension, worry, and foreboding apprehension. There is *angst* and melancholy in the air generally in Israel because of events that do not require repetition by me. For Mizrachi, there is the awareness that it is today at a critical point in its history. Politically it has lost half of its parliamentary seats—at least, as of this writing; the next Knesset may deplete even that. Organizationally, it is in decline throughout the world. Some of us have begun to feel like vestiges of the past instead of harbingers of the future.

Some may think I am overstating the case, yet others that I am understating it. Whatever, the situation is an unhappy one. And yet, our historic challenge and duty is to resist being gripped and paralyzed by a psychology of defeatism. As Hasidism taught us, despair is the greatest sin. Greatness is achieved only in calm confrontation with great challenges.

This means that our generation can no longer look upon itself as a *dor ha-hemshekh,* as those who continue the past, but as those who must rescue that past by reconstituting and reformulating it in the face of adversity. We have an unparalleled opportunity to leave our mark upon history. This is the time neither to ignore the difficulties nor to despair of them and lose heart, but to rise to the occasion with a clear mind, a firm spine, and a fierce visceral determination to change the course of events and prevail.

Indeed, this challenge is greater than that faced by our predecessors over 80 years ago. They founded Mizrachi in the growth phase of the Zionist movement. Zionism was new, the ideal of the Return to Zion had a certain freshness about it, and thus was born Mizrachi, the *Merkaz Ruchani,* the "Spiritual Center." It is far more difficult, more painful, and more arduous to rebuild than to

---

Published in Morasha: *A Journal of Religious Zionism, Fall 1984, this essay is based upon an address,* "Towards the Renewal of Mizrachi," *delivered in Jerusalem, December 1982, on the 80th anniversary of Mizrachi.*

build. As the Talmud taught us: *Kasheh attika me-chaddeta,* the old is far more impervious to the creative gesture than the new. But for the same reason it is more admirable and praiseworthy.

I have often wondered at the fact that we do not celebrate Rosh Chodesh Nisan as the day that the *Mishkan* was erected. Similarly, we have no observance to commemorate the building of the first or second *Bet ha-Mikdash.* The only holiday we do celebrate with regard to the *Bet ha-Mikdash* is Chanukkah—which commemorates not the *building* but the *rebuilding* of the Temple. Why so? Because rebuilding is more taxing, less glorious, more demanding, and less personally satisfying than building—and therefore more creative and more laudable.

It is time to resurrect Mizrachi, to breathe into it new life and energy and passion and thus bring blessing not only to religious Jews, but to all Israel—people and State. "Every generation in which the Temple was not (re)built, it is considered as if [members of that generation] destroyed it" (J.T., *Yoma* 1:1).

The organizational renewal of Mizrachi must be based upon a clear distinction between *Tenuah* and *Miflagah,* between Movement and Party—for the ultimate good of both. This is something a number of elder statesmen of Mizrachi have been advocating for some time now. For the very health and security of Mafdal, the (the National Religions) Party, we must ensure that Mizrachi, the Movement, will not be its handmaiden. Indeed, it is Mizrachi which must be the sanctuary of the values and ideals of our cause, and to do so it must have an independent existence and identity. Only thus can the two, Tenuah and Miflagah, fructify each other creatively.

Only Mafdal may endorse political candidates or engage in partisan negotiations. The Tenuah must never do so. Its responsibilities must be much broader: the welfare, both spiritual and organizational, of Jews and Judaism throughout the world. Indeed, members of other political parties should be encouraged to affiliate with the Mizrachi if it is their natural spiritual and ideological home.

The Miflagah must remind us that the State is crucial, pivotal, and central to Jewish concerns. The Tenuah must teach us that it is not absolute.

The Movement *embodies* an idea; a Party is only a *means* to achieve and enhance it in the political forum. If there is to be only

Mafdal without a Mizrachi, or with a Mizrachi so weak and ineffectual that it is devoid of significance, then one may question whether in the long run such a party serves the higher purpose to which we are dedicated, and one must undertake a cost-benefit analysis to determine whether its existence is justified. No such calculus is relevant to a national religious movement. Indeed, the Tenuah alone can vindicate the Miflagah.

Political parties must respond to the flux of events, the vicissitudes of government policy and public opinion and political trends. Its fortunes are linked to external events rather than to internal processes. The Movement must transcend such concerns. As the expression of overarching spiritual and ideological commitments, it has the power to abide all such conditions and endure all such changes, because it is focused on ideas and ideals rather than on persons and structures.

Thus, it is conceivable that a two-party system will emerge in Israel and that Mafdal will attach itself to one of them. I am by no means advocating that. But as an illustration, even if that should occur, Mizrachi as a Movement will and must survive, its integrity uncompromised and its mission undiminished.

Similarly, if the opposite should occur, and the Miflagah will divide, amoeba-like, into two or three or four political parties, the natural spiritual and ideological home of all of them remains Mizrachi.

To effectuate the *chanukkat ha-Mizrachi,* let it seek out a leadership that is preferably uninvolved in the daily rough and tumble of partisan political activity. Its leaders should be the finest and the best of its spiritual and intellectual elite throughout the world—the most able of the Yeshiva world (provided that they not only attend or teach in Hesder Yeshivot, but truly represent and are committed to its ideas); the most appealing of the religious academic world; businessmen and professionals whose lives and activities are reflections of the Mizrachi ideology concerning Torah, Eretz Yisrael, Kelal Yisrael, and the modern world. Above all, Mizrachi must shun mediocrity.

There is a place for party functionaries—in the Party. There is a need for politics—in Mafdal. The Party must confront and deal with the jagged edges of a stubborn and unmalleable reality. The Movement must stand a bit apart, beyond, and hold aloft the ideals for which the men of the Party work and struggle.

There need not, perhaps ought not, be unanimity of opinion between the two. But the dialogue will be constructive and creative and benefit all Israel.

THIS LEADS ME to the second renewal—that of fraternity, a reassertion of our friendship, our mutual trust, our cohesiveness. Most regretfully, Mafdal politics has been too rough, too truculent, too *ad hominem* for too long. It is true that Mafdal is blessed with highly competent leaders, men of competence, personal integrity, and probity. But God knows how many people were lost to the cause because of the unseemly infighting, the slurs, the disrespect, and the lack of self-restraint we have allowed to go unchecked.

I am not naive—I know that politics is politics is politics. Indeed, the involvement with personalities rather than issues is more characteristic of a Party than a Movement, and a good argument for the revival of Mizrachi as a Tenuah. But certainly a religious party—and most certainly a religious Zionist party—should be more elegant, more civilized and tolerant and forgiving, less jugular and brutal in its politics—and always aware of the fact that politics must serve the cause, for otherwise it is bankrupt.

There has been too little *shalom bayit* in our ranks. If in America we were for a while too tolerant, even of those unworthy of our trust, in Israel we have been too critical, even of those deserving of leadership roles.

I recall the story of a Jewish professor in Western Europe who spent 15 years researching humor in the Talmud, and could come up with only one joke in all of the Talmud: "*Talmidei chakhamim marbim shalom be'olam,* scholars (of Torah) increase peace in the world."

As a relative outsider to the inside politics in Mafdal, I can only plead with its leadership—all of whom I admire and for whom I bear personal affection and esteem—to heal the breaches of the past, both because of enlightened self-interest and a desire to avoid the desecration of the divine Name. The times call for statesmanship rather than politics.

Former Secretary of Health, Education and Welfare of the

United States, Dr. Gardner, once said that one must be neither an uncritical lover nor an unloving critic. Of course we must be critical—but also loving.

This advice is useful not only for Mafdal, but equally—indeed, much more so—for the other political parties in Israel. The ferocious partisanship, especially in the course of the Lebanon campaign, has left American Jews embarrassed, deflated, and angry. One recalls the words of Pogo, a famous American comic-strip character: "We have met the enemy and he is us."

Divided opinion in a country is good for its soul. It ensures vigorous debate of great issues that enhances the democratic character of a nation. But when the polemics are so ferocious that they go beyond politics to fratricide, then the controversies are convulsions of a feverish and sick people.

When extremist fringe groups like the Neturei Karta publish ads in the American press excoriating Israel, we are indignant at this instance of religious fanaticism. But what excuse is there for a leftist politician to commit the same unpatriotic act? Here there is not even the fig leaf of a venerable religious tradition of quietism, though grievously misread. There is only the nakedness of unrestrained ambition and the self-pity of political powerlessness. With such "leaders," who needs enemies?!

Irresponsible political rhetoric, even if it is only by one individual and meant not literally but only as an expression of frustration, is not only politically counter-productive, but is a threat to the security of the State and the Nation.

So renewal of what Rav Kook used to call *ahavat chinam* is the second element in the *chanukkat ha-Mizrachi,* important for our group and important for the whole State and all the people of Israel.

THE SPIRITUAL RENEWAL of Religious Zionism will take place only when we appreciate the real need there is for us—whether or not it is yet perceived.

Wise leaders of Israel, men of vision, even if they are not of our camp, recognize this. Towards the end of his last trip to America, the late President Shazar asked me to see him just prior to his leaving for the airport. I shall never forget his brief but moving request. He said, while holding my hand,

> You know, Rabbi Lamm, that I have been a Laborite and not a Mizrachist all my life. Yet I must plead with you and your colleagues to make a special, heroic effort to save Bnei Akiva from its state of deterioration in America. Bnei Akiva is a precious national treasure and we are morally forbidden to stand aside and see the movement go down the tube and do nothing about it.

A man of Labor, President Shazar appreciated the value of Bnei Akiva—and what is this youth-group if not the spawning grounds of the future of the Movement?

Indeed, without Mizrachi, all Torah would be identified as anti-Zionist and anti-State, isolated and inward-looking. Without Mizrachi, how long would Israel remain a *Jewish* State, instead of just a State of Jews, an independent Birobidzhan in the Middle East?

The same need for Mizrachi that led it to its historic contribution in the past remains relevant and potent today. And the less others realize this, the more cogent is the need!

Hence a source for spiritual renaissance lies in the awareness that we are needed and have a purpose, a mission, a role to play. In this we are more fortunate than a number of other groups which, while they may be more viable financially, more active organizationally, and more numerous electorally, have lost their raison d'etre and have begun to rot within.

In Lithuania it used to be the custom of the *chevra kadisha* that during or before the *taharah,* the Gabbai would address the corpse of the deceased and say, "So-and-so son of so-and-so, know that you are dead!"

There are, unhappily, a number of organizations to whom that applies: They are dead and do not know it. Fortunately, that cannot be said of Mizrachi. Even if many of the twigs are brittle and dry and its branches bent, the trunk is healthy and the roots vital. Such an organism is capable of regeneration and rebirth.

In that case, the pessimistic note with which I began has to be reevaluated. Maybe our potential is far greater than our sorry present reality would indicate. Maybe the substance is quite different from the perception.

There is a need for Mizrachi—a need to speak to the State and its citizens today and to call them back to their roots, to assist the State to fulfill its true stature.

Mizrachi must teach that if Israel will strive to be America or England or France, it will be neither America nor England nor France—nor Israel. If Israel will try to be Israel, then it will be Israel, and not need to be America or England or France.

There is no one else who can say that quite as clearly, with as much conviction, and with as much spiritual authority as Mizrachi.

Mizrachi must affirm for the rest of Jewry that our people are peaceful but not pacifist, that the State must be powerful and must defend its borders and vital interests with all the means at its disposal. But arms are a means, not an end. An army is a necessity, not as desideratum. We have already proven that a Jew can fight to defend himself, and there is no longer any reason to posture and to stage military parades on *Yom Haatzmaut*—even to think of it. We can use weapons and even produce them and make them technologically better than many a Western country. We are proud that a young Israeli can use a gun if necessary, but our emblem is not the Uzi but rather *Ha-shem uzi u-ma'uzi*—a faith in and commitment to a transcendent vision and higher Being who summons us to peace and construction and human felicity and spiritual excellence.

Israel is now going through an agonizing period because of what happened in Lebanon and its aftermath. It constitutes a small demon in our recent past, an aberration, totally out of character with what we are, what we purport to be, what we strive to be. At great pain and with much chagrin, we are exorcising it. At the same time, there is a giant, ugly demon in Arab circles that no one really seems to care about. There are other, equally ugly demons in the chancelries of Western capitals, in the editorial rooms of great newspapers and in television news studios—demons of overstatement and gleeful rhetorical mugging of Israel—and no one talks of exorcising them.

So be it. "The House of Israel is not like unto other nations." In our very chagrin and dilemma we have much to be proud of. If we have a guilty conscience, at least we have a conscience. That is a mark of the Jewishness of the Jewish State. I am proud of the leadership of Mafdal for having insisted upon the trial that aired all this and brought this catharsis about. I am confident that Mizrachi leadership will be equally forthcoming in meeting other such challenges as they may arise, and that it will be as vigilant in self-criticism as in the criticism of others.

What Mizrachi has to tell Israel, a message that makes it vital for us to survive and thrive and speak out, is perhaps best exemplified by a nightmare in the novel, *Temol Shilshom*, by Israel's Nobel Laureate Sh.Y. Agnon.

Yitzchak, the young *Oleh* who is the hero of the story, has a bad dream. He is at the seashore at Jaffa and forgets his shoes. The wind blows off his hat. So he remains barefoot and bareheaded. He hears the sound of prayer in a *shul* on a second floor that can be reached only by a ladder. He climbs up and enters, when the window slams shut, his head is within the synagogue and his body outside it.

Shoes represent the satisfaction of physical needs, material comforts. The head-covering symbolizes spiritual felicity, religious authenticity. Our fate, if we are not extremely careful and thoughtful, may yet be that we remain without shoes *or* hat, material *or* spiritual well being—and, *davka,* with our uncovered heads *in* the shul and unshod feet outside it. That is the nightmare Israel must avoid—a country poor in natural *and* spiritual resources, a population that cannot find its *kipah* in its sanctuaries and its shoes where it ought to tread proudly.

Mizrachi—with its teaching of Torah *and* Zion, of a productive and prosperous state *and* a vital flowering of Torah—can avoid this nightmare and return to the State both its *kipah and* its shoes, its material well-being *and* its spiritual dignity.

I propose that in its ideological stock-taking as it prepares for renewal, Mizrachi affirm its essential moderation, long a hallmark of the Movement.

By moderation I do not mean an ideological evasiveness that leads to compromise. That is what is today called a "cop-out." I refer rather to what I recently termed "radical moderation," a moderation that is achieved through clear thinking and which has the power to summon up the passion of commitment even though it is not extremist.

Mizrachi has long battled against extremism in Jewish life, and it must be wary as well of extremism in its own ranks. While the Movement must have place for all who profess allegiance to its fundamental ideals, I would not want to see it wedded to any extremist position. It may seem attractive to tap the sources of passion by opting for an extreme political course. But that will turn away more people than it will attract. The Mizrachi must be a nesting-place for both hawks and doves, but never for terrorism.

We must always bear in mind the warning of the Sages that one must not respect even a Rav when *chillul ha-Shem* is involved. There is no such thing as acceptable terrorism for the sake of Torah or for the sake of Israel.

But the spiritual renewal cannot be achieved, either by intellectuals or by *hoi polloi,* unless Mizrachi as a Movement returns to what was and should always have remained its priority: education.

By "education" I mean primarily *talmud torah.*

There was a time when Mizrachi was the prime mover for Torah education in the Diaspora. In America it founded a number of important institutions, and its leaders were all educationally oriented.

It is imperative that every member of Mizrachi, wherever he or she is, be active in Jewish education. Mizrachi as a Movement must use its power and influence to persuade the World Zionist Congress and the Jewish Agency to place more emphasis on education.

In the long run, education is more important for the future of the State than Aliyah. Aliyah will not necessarily produce educated Jews. But education will improve and enhance Aliyah. Consider the Yeshiva University experience: despite (or maybe because of) no formal Aliyah propaganda or *shelichim* for Aliyah, we have some 10% of our alumni living in Israel—some 1500 families, may they increase!

In Israel, Mizrachi must continue to improve and expand its primary and secondary schools—and encourage its Hesder graduates to make careers in teaching in these schools.

Mizrachi has done magnificently in creating the Yeshivot Hesder. It must now, as part of its spiritual renewal, undertake:

1) to strengthen them and increase their number.
2) to tap them for leadership in the Movement.
3) to reorient them to the basic ideals of Mizrachi.
4) to give them the prominence and prestige in our circles that will not make them seek approbation and authentication from other Yeshivot who claim for themselves and for another movement exclusive hegemony over Torah.
5) to make it possible for the best and most talented of Hesder students and graduates to receive an advanced secular education as well.

But in educating and striving for the realization of the ideals of religious Zionism, Mizrachi must consider problems of broader scope and impact, beyond that of Israel. And that is, the whole question of how the Jewish tradition relates to the contemporary world. Of course, the educational expression of that concern by Mizrachi is Bar-Ilan University.

This is an issue with which we in America are vitally concerned. Yeshiva University stands for a certain interpretation of that relationship. It expresses a *Weltanschauung* of which religious Zionism is only one aspect, albeit an important one.

While Mizrachi must be primarily involved with Israel, it most certainly should see itself as part of, or related to, that movement which maintains that Torah must neither retreat from nor capitulate to the secular Western world.

What I am saying is that the fortunes of Modern or Centrist Orthodoxy in the United States and elsewhere in the Golah and those of Mizrachi are linked to each other—not organizationally, but fraternally. While our constituencies are not and need not be identical in all respects, it is clear that we are closely related, and that relationship should be encouraged, elaborated, and developed.

With self-confidence in our cause we can turn to the historic task of self-renewal, the *chanukkat ha-Mizrachi.*

~ 47 ~

THE NETUREI KARTA

The obscure but highly vocal group known as the Neturei Karta was born in 1935 when a few hundred members of Agudat Israel considered the Agudah too lenient to Zionist groups, and generally too moderate, and under Amram Blau seceded and formed the Neturei Karta. They number today several hundred families in Israel, and have followers and adherents in Brooklyn and several other centers throughout the Diaspora.

Neturei Karta means "Guardians of the City." The term appears in the Jerusalem Talmud (*Chag.* 1:7), which relates that three sages, under instructions from R. Judah the Prince, traveled through the land to make sure that every town had sufficient teachers of Bible and Mishnah. They came upon one town that had none, and said to the townsfolk: Show us your *Neturei Karta*, i.e., the guardians of the city. Thereupon they produced police (*Sentorei Karta*—sentries of the city). No, said the Rabbis, these are destroyers of the city. Who then are the Neturei Karta? They are the teachers and scribes, for without them a city is fated to destruction. Neturei Karta, therefore, are teachers of Torah by virtue of whom, despite their small number, the rest of the population survives.

The Neturei Karta come to our attention usually through acts of dramatic protest or minor violence, rarely serious. Their publication is restricted largely to shrill posters, polemical pamphlets, and strident banners. The only serious works of any real consequence are by the aging "Satmarer Rebbe," R. Yoel Moshe Teitelbaum, a Romanian Hasidic leader in the United States since the end of World War II.

It is true that the Neturei Karta is fragmentized around different personalities, and that—like all other groups—it contains elements that are more radical and some that are more conservative; some more pacific and "responsible," and some more militant

---

Published in Tradition, *Fall 1971, as* "The Ideology of the Neturei Karta: According to the Satmarer Version." *This paper was first delivered at the Ideological Seminar of the World Union of Jewish Students in Kiljava, Finland, in 1969.*

and "reckless." There are differences between many of the Jerusalem group and the Rebbe from the Williamsburg section in Brooklyn. Occasionally their inner dissensions have been exposed to public scrutiny and have proved most fascinating or bizarre—depending on one's perspective. However, all these internecine conflicts are not fundamentally ideological in nature but tactical; and whatever ideological differentia one can discern are not of sufficient significance to warrant detailed analysis by those not committed to its major premises. This article, therefore, will be confined to an exposition of the views of the Satmarer Rebbe as detailed in his three volumes published in the last ten years: *Va-yoel Mosheh* (Vol. I—1959; II—1961)* and *Kuntres al ha-Geulah Ve'al ha-Temurah* (1967).** Their orientation is, in essence, the continuation of the strongly held views of the Hasidic dynasty of Muncacz and their Hungarian-Romanian followers.

Now, these views are, by any current standards, extreme. Most Orthodox Jews—even non-Zionists and anti-Zionists—reject them, and many of them consider them reprehensible. Yet they represent a consistent ideology of Jewish life, and they are not without some basis in the classical Jewish sources. The Satmarer, of course, claims far more than this for his views. He sets out to demonstrate that his ideology is what we might call "mainstream" Judaism, and that his formulations flow naturally and logically from the classical sources of the Jewish tradition: Bible, Talmud, medieval scholars, etc. The author does not hesitate to offer a program of action which includes extremely radical suggestions. It is a major achievement, although I am convinced that the arguments are often contrived, always one-sided, and decidedly extravagant.

The context in which the discourses proceed is that of the Jewish theology of history, which revolves around the two poles of *galut* (exile) and *geulah* (redemption). We are now in a major exile which will ultimately result in the final Redemption, ushered in by the Messiah, descendant of David, the original *Mashiach* or King anointed by the Lord.

The Messianic concept is subject to a vast variety of interpretations and is one of the most fertile ideas in Judaism. Mainly, he is

---

**Hereinafter to be referred to as* VM; citations and references to Vol. 1 only.

***Hereinafter to be referred to as* GT.

conceived of as the divine instrument of the redemption of the Jewish people, leading to their independence, their restoration to the Land of Israel, and the building of the Third Temple; and through the renaissance of Israel, to the redemption of all mankind, ushering in an era of universal peace and justice.

Now, Messianism is a highly corruptible idea—the whole sad history of pseudo-Messiahs, from Jesus through Sabbatai Zevi, amply demonstrates its vulnerability. But it bespeaks an optimistic view of life, an imperishable hope for a happy ending to history, a powerful faith in the divine promise of redemption for His exiled people.

Within this rubric, there are large gaps. Normative Judaism itself has a tremendous history of Messianic speculation, some of it more authoritative, some less so. How we treat this literature, how "normative" we consider it, will determine, to a large extent, our view of current events.

Against this background, sketched in all too briefly, we may discern four major premises in the Neturei Karta ideology as formulated by the Satmarer.

A. Divine Redemption and Human Passivity

God alone will redeem Israel in a supernatural, miraculous manner (*VM* 126, 7), making His power manifest. Israel will remain passive as history comes to an end without human intervention. All Israel must do is submit to the yoke of exile while it waits faithfully and lives in accordance with the divine will, i.e., Torah (*ib.* 10). The Neturei Karta do not accept the view that Messiah will have primarily a political function—ensuring Israel's restoration and independence—and insist instead upon seeing his advent as the occasion for cosmic changes and indisputable miraculous events. Man's contribution is purely spiritual; his "waiting" is, politically speaking, utterly passive.

The Satmarer acknowledges that in other areas, such as earning a livelihood and promoting health, divine governance of human affairs does not contradict human initiative; but he asserts, without adequate distinction, that this does not apply to the redemption of Israel—here only God can act, not man (*VM*, 137). In effect, he seizes upon one strand in the complex Jewish tradition, that of religious quietism, and transforms it into the very fountainhead of Judaism; what we might call "quietistic apoliticism" becomes for him the fundamental expression of Jewish faith. Hence, he considers the very idea of an independent Jewish State, before or without Messiah, as heretical. Political initiative is a gesture of defiance of the divine Redeemer (*VM*, 7); it is an act of arrogance, and is "cynical" or dog-like (*VM*, 113).

The major source for the Satmarer is the passage in the Talmud (*Ket.* 111a) which raises halakhic problems as to whether husband and wife can legally compel each other to change residence from the Land of Israel to Babylon and vice-versa. Appended to this is a lengthy discourse, based on Scriptural verses, in which a tradition is recorded that at the destruction of the Temple and the beginning of exile, God administered a number of oaths; four of them are especially relevant. God made Israel swear that they will not use force in a massive return to the Land of Israel; that they will remain loyal to the countries of their dispersion; and that they will not take the initiative in hastening the advent of Messiah prematurely. Also, he adjured the gentile nations that they not oppress Israel in exile more than is necessary or bearable. Now, everyone agrees that the other nations violated their oath; about this there can be no argument. Some Talmudists, such as R. Meir Simchah of Dvinsk, maintain that the oaths are all interdependent, they constitute one package-deal; and since the gentiles violated their oath, Israel is released from its oaths which are now null and void. The Satmarer, however, considers this interpretation as both heresy and nonsense (*VM*, 135).

Now, the key here is the distinction between Halakhah (law) and Agadah (the non-legal portions of the Talmud—such as legend, ethics, general wisdom, etc.). Halakhah is normative, decisive, and follows a systematic form. Agadah, though possessing mines of Jewish teaching, is non-legal, and hence does not require any decision between competing points of view. It is given to hyperbole and is non-normative.

The Satmarer insists that our passage concerning the oaths, despite its obvious non-legal style and form, is not Agadah but Halakhah (*VM* 12), and he proceeds to apply to it the whole, complex, systematic halakhic methodology of analysis and decision. The results are often grotesque. For instance, this involves him in a number of immediate difficulties—such as Maimonides' omission of the whole passage of "oaths" from his legal code in the Laws of Kings, where he discusses Messiah. The author's response is fanciful, to say the least. He asserts that the "oaths" are not technically oaths but—far more than oaths! They are fundamentals of Judaism, the essence of the faith, and hence not classifiable as ordinary *halakhot* (*VM* 67).

In order to overcome Maimonides' rational, non-miraculous interpretation of Messianism, he resorts to a rather modernistic point. In a famous passage, Maimonides (Laws of Kings, Chap. XII) declares:

> (1) Let no one think that in the days of the Messiah any of the laws of nature will be set aside, or any innovation be introduced into creation. The world will follow its normal course. The words of Isaiah: "And the wolf shall dwell with the lamb, and the leopard shall lie down with the kid" (Isa. 11:6) are to be understood figuratively, meaning that Israel will live securely among the wicked of the heathens who are likened to wolves and leopards, as it is written: "A wolf of the deserts doth spoil them, a leopard watcheth over their cities" (Jer. 5) . . .
>
> (2) Said the Rabbis: "The sole difference between the present and the Messianic days is delivery from servitude to foreign powers" (B. *San.* 91b). Taking the words of the Prophets in their literal sense, it appears that the inauguration of the Messianic era will be marked by the war of Gog and Magog; that prior to that war, a prophet will arise to guide Israel and set their hearts aright, as it is written: "Behold, I will send you Elijah the Prophet" (Mal. 3:23). He (Elijah) will come neither to declare the clean unclean, nor the unclean clean; neither to disqualify those who are presumed to be of legitimate descent, nor to pronounce qualified those who are presumed to be of illegitimate descent, but to bring peace in the world, as it is said: "And he shall turn the hearts of the fathers to the children" (Mal. 3:24).
>
> Some of our Sages say that the coming of Elijah will precede the advent of the Messiah. But no one is in a position to know the details of this and similar things until they have come to pass. They are not explicitly stated by the Prophets. Nor have the Rabbis any tradition with regard to these matters. They are guided solely by what the scriptural texts seem to imply. Hence there is a divergence of opinion on the subject. But be that as it may, neither the exact sequence of those events nor the details thereof constitute religious dogmas. No one should ever occupy himself with the legendary themes or spend much time on midrashic statements

> bearing on this and like subjects. He should not deem them of prime importance, since they lead neither to the fear of God nor to the love of Him. Nor should one strive to predict the End by calculations. Said the Rabbis: "Blasted be those who reckon out the end" (B. *San.* 97b). One should wait (for his coming) and accept in principle this article of faith, as we have stated before.
>
> (3) In the days of King Messiah, when his kingdom will be established and all Israel will gather around him, their pedigrees will be determined by him through the Holy Spirit which wil rest upon him, as it is written: "And he shall sit as a refiner and purifier . . ." (Mal. 3:3). First he will purify the descendants of Levi, declaring: "This one, of good birth, is a priest; this one, of good birth, is a Levite." Those who are not of good birth will be demoted to the rank of (lay) Israelites, for it is written: "And the Tirshatha said unto them that they should not eat of the most holy things, till there stood up a priest with Urim and Tummim" (Ezra 2:62). It is inferred therefrom that the genealogy of those considered to be of good lineage will be traced by means of the Holy Spirit, and those found to be of good birth will be made known. The descent of the Israelites will be recorded according to their tribes. He will announce: "This one is of such-and-such a tribe, and this one of such-and-such a tribe." But he will not say concerning those who are presumed to be of pure descent: "This is a bastard; this is a slave." For the rule is: once a family has been intermingled with others, it retains its [legitimate] status.
>
> (4) The Sages and Prophets did not long for the days of the Messiah that Israel might exercise dominion over the world, or rule over the heathens, or be exalted by the nations, or that it might eat and drink and rejoice. Their aspiration was that Israel be free to devote itself to the Law and its wisdom, with no one to oppress or disturb it, and thus be worthy of life in the world to come.
>
> (5) In that era there will be neither famine nor war, neither jealousy nor strife. Blessings will be abundant, comforts within the reach of all. The one preoccupation of the whole world will be to know the Lord . . .

Such sentiments, which Maimonides considers Halakhah, cannot by any stretch of the imagination be reconciled with the whole temper, let alone the details, of the Neturei Karta view of the Messiah. The Satmarer, however, points to the Messianic speculations in the famous "Epistle to Yemen" where Maimonides' thinking is considerably closer to the traditional views. The reason for the change, according to the Satmarer, is that Maimonides wrote the Epistle *after* he wrote the Code, and this indicated that he changed his mind (*VM* 71ff, 146). This solution might be considered acceptable if not for the fact that his great Code was concluded in 1180, and the Epistle to Yemen was written in 1172. But all this is really irrelevant. What the Satmarer refuses to consider is that in the Code Maimonides writes Halakhah, whereas in his correspondence he permits himself much greater latitude, especially when addressing a pious, Messiah-intoxicated community which if not restrained, might well be misled (by an unfortunate madman who proclaimed himself the Messiah) into the most terrible consequences, including persecution by the Yemeni non-Jews.

There are other issues which the Satmarer dismisses quite unconvincingly. Thus, the logic of his own argument should lead us to agree that the Balfour Declaration and United Nations vote on establishing the State of Israel cancel out the assertion that Zionism violates the oaths of rebellion against the gentile governments and forcible immigration to Palestine. Yet the author gives this compelling notion short shrift, despite important authority *(Avnei Nezzer)* to the contrary (*VM* 149).

His most important post-Talmudic source is a remarkable statement by the MaHaRaL (R. Loewe) of Prague that forbids the transgression of the above-mentioned oaths even if the nations insist that the Jews return to Israel, even if they physically force the Jews to redemption—even under pain of torture and death! A critic of the Satmarer, the renowned Talmudic scholar, R. Menachem M. Kasher, takes up this citation in his encyclopedic (and, in some ways, rather strange) and massive work on the interpretation of contemporary Jewish history, *Hatekufah ha-Gedolah* ("The Great Epoch"), a kind of traditional *Heilsgeschichte* of modern times. R. Kasher shows that the MaHaRaL has been misread and misinterpreted by the Satmarer. Further, the statement is patently absurd, for to resist efforts by Gentiles to force us to return to the Land of Israel, because we are bound by the oaths, would entail in itself violating the oath of not rebelling against the Gentile governments! Nevertheless, this becomes a *locus classicus* for the Satmarer, and a major source for him to elevate the precipitate return to the Land of

Israel to the rank of a most solemn sin, legally obligating us to resist it even unto death, equal in severity to idolatry, unchastity, and murder.

From the above, the Satmarer concludes that "forcing the End," human initiative in precipitating the redemption, is the vilest sin available to Jews today. Zionism is thus the archheresy of our times—and, of course, Theodor Herzl is the heresiarch of modern Jewish history. For only God can redeem, and any endeavor by man to hasten the process is a breach of faith and an intolerable and perfidious act of arrogance.

B. Sequence of Redemption

Torah and the Jewish tradition speak of eschatology, the End of Days, as including both national restoration and spiritual renaissance—*geulah* and *teshuvah,* Redemption and Repentance. The Neturei Karta hold that there can be no *geulah* without prior *teshuvah,* and that this sequence is crucial to the Jewish belief in redemption. Even if Messiah were to come before the mass repentance of Jewish people, the actual redemption would be delayed until such collective religious return to God took place (*VM* 81–83). One who denies this necessary sequence is no different from one who denies belief in the Messiah himself (*ib.* 84). But Zionism is a prime source of denial, atheism, and heresy (*VM* 14). The whole movement of Jewish nationalism is but an imitation of the gentiles (*VM* 124). Obviously, then, the attrition of religion caused by Zionism vitiates any claim by Zionism to be a precursor or agent of redemption.

C. Only the Pious Can Be the Agents of Redemption

It is inconceivable and absurd that God should bring on redemption by means of those who deny and hate Him. Hence, Zionists and the State of Israel are in effect obstacles to the true redemption (*VM* 9, 216; *GT* 6) because they are a source of irreligion. The Satmarer thus implicitly and uncompromisingly rejects the well-known view of Rav Kook that the irreligious, by virtue of their zeal and sacrifice for national goals, are unconscious agents of the divine redemption.

D. The Messianic State—a Complete Theocracy.

The Satmarer holds that democracy is valid for non-Jewish political communities. For Jews, however, democracy is utterly unacceptable. Only the laws of the Torah, as interpreted by its authorized expositors, are obligatory for Jews (*VM* 164). The Zionist state, a majority of which is non-religious, and of which even the religious Zionist faction accepts democracy, is untenable and reprehensible.

THE FOUR MAJOR elements we have discerned are: there can be only divine, not human political initiative; spiritual return must precede political redemption; the agents of redemption must be the pious, those committed to God and Torah; and the Jewish State must be a thorough theocracy, not a democracy.

Hence, any cooperation with the Zionists or the government of the State of Israel is a major sin (*VM* 14); this would be true even if the whole government were composed of saints and sages (*ib.* 139). One should rather submit to martyrdom than become a member of the Knesset (*ib.* 152). Those who cooperate with the government of Israel—such as the Agudath Israel—do so because of unworthy motives: they are bribed by power, and other important principles are compromised (*ib.* 220). The evil king of Biblical times, Ahab, had the halakhic status of a king; but the Zionist government, because its very inception is in defiance of Torah, cannot be accorded the status of even a *de facto* legitimate government (*ib.* 208).

The ideology so far delineated serves as the criterion by which to judge and evaluate the climactic events of current Jewish history. That such an evaluation is necessary is evident from the triumph of just those forces condemned by this ideology. Zionism, execrated as heresy, has the allegiance of the majority of the Jewish people. Its political aspirations have been realized in the establishment of the State of Israel. The very groups so deplored by the Neturei Karta have scored phenomenal military successes. The great majority of religious Jews identify with the State and with those organizations that believe in full cooperation—while the Neturei Karta dwindle into more and more precarious marginality, and must resort to futile gestures of violence in order to make their presence felt. Under such conditions, a rather extreme philosophy of history is called for.

The Rabbi of Satmar, as the chief theoretician of the Neturei Karta, does indeed offer such a philosophy of history. He sees the events of modern Jewish history, from Herzl to the Six-Day War, not as secular history, certainly not as sacred history—rather, as an elaborate, diabolical scheme to ensnare Israel by dangling before it the wicked temptation of Zionism. In a word, the Neturei Karta's reading of this history is: *demonological*. The State of Israel is a satanic kingdom that has unloosed dark powers upon the Jewish people. The Satmarer even names the demon in charge of this unholy intervention in human affairs: Samael. Samael is frequently mentioned in the Zohar and Kabbalistic literature and occasionally in the Talmud and Midrash. (The Satmarer does not consider a symbolic interpretation of demons.) Samael, general of the profane legions, is charged by God with ensuring the success of Zionism and the State of Israel (*VM* 10). God permits this because Zionism is a *nisayon,* a trial or test for Jews: will they succumb to the evil illusion of their own autonomous initiative in effecting redemption, or will they faithfully refrain from interfering in the course of the divinely preordained destiny of Israel (*VM* 8)? Such demonic intrusions into Jewish history occurred before, in the form of pseudo-Messianic movements. Zionism is just the latest such manifestation; its precursors are the Messianic pretenders, such as Bar Cozeba (Bar Kokhba), those of medieval Yemen, and, of course, Sabbatai Zevi (*VM* 13). It has happened before our times that Samael triumphed, and the majority of the Jewish people were misled: our people succumbed to paganism during the First Commonwealth. In the days of Gideon, only 300 people were left who did not kneel to the idol (*VM* 8, 89). We who dissent, the Neturei Karta assert, are the ones who will save the entire people from the Satanic ensnarement of Zionism. The picture is two-tone: black and white. The Zionists are defiled, *reshaim* (wicked); we are *tzaddikim*. It is as simple as all that.

The demonology of history focuses, of course, on the most demonically apocalyptic event in all of human history: the Holocaust. Politically, this is interpreted by the Satmarer as a response to the incitement by Zionists when they challenged Hitler and declared war on Germany. This vain but provocative gesture aroused the fury of the tyrant (*GT 11*). Spiritually, the Holocaust is divine punishment for transgressing the three oaths and yielding to Samael (*VM* 5, 182). It was only the prayer of the righteous (i.e., the Neturei Karta) which effected the rescue of the remnants of Jewry (*GT* 18).

But the question arises: did not the Zionists attempt to save the pitiful few survivors of the Holocaust? Did not the State of Israel become the haven and refuge for the Displaced Persons? The Satmarer refuses to give the State any moral credit: since the Zionists were responsible for the original massacre, they are not to be lauded for opening their national home to the straggling survivors. In a parable, he refers to the Zionists as criminal arsonists who stay for the fire and then enthusiastically help to save a few survivors (*VM* 185, 6).

The Zionists are responsible not only for the Holocaust, but for the three wars from 1948–1967 (*GT* 171). Were it not for their political ambitions, England would have permitted an unlimited number of refugees to Palestine (*VM* 184). Their policies are to be blamed as well for causing the expulsion of the Jews from the Arab countries (*VM* 183).

The Sinai invasion of 1956 was morally unjust. The use of the Suez Canal was not worth jeopardizing human lives in battle and the difficulties that ensued for Egyptian Jewry (*GT* 88). Any war carried out not in accordance with the opinion of Torah authorities is not a war but simple murder (*VM* 112). This military action of 1956 led to the war of 1967. The Arab threats of genocide against Israel were the direct result of Israeli intransigence (*GT* 11). The Zionists were the aggressors, for aggression is in character with their over-reaching in forcing the redemption (*GT* 10, 89).

The Satmarer is of two minds as to why Israel won the Six-Day War. At one point he attributes it to the prayers of the righteous (i.e., the Neturei Karta), for which he feels he must apologize, since both Arabs and Zionists are *reshaim* (wicked) (*GT* 12, 13, 88). Elsewhere, he reverts to his demonological theory: Samael was at work again (*GT* 7).

But was not the dramatic Israeli victory a true miracle, as religious Zionists and even non-Zionists—indeed, even some secularists—declared? First, answers the Satmarer in an almost rationalistic vein, a true believer is unimpressed with miracles; his faith cannot be shaken even by supernatural attacks against it (*GT* 7). Second, as we have said, if there were miracles, they were part of Samael's satanic designs further to ensnare unsuspecting Jews *(ib.)*. Third, it was just extraordinary success, but no miracle at all (*GT* 8). All of what occurred was perfectly natural, and largely the end product of Arab technological backwardness and military inferiority (*GT* 36). Reports that the war brought in its wake a renewal of religious feeling are discounted by the Satmarer, who compares it to the religious enthusiasm that swept over many Jews in the days of Sabbatai Zevi, and thus must be considered illusory at best, satanic at worst (*GT* 100). Donning the mantle of prophecy, the Satmarer expects more apparently miraculous victories for Israel. But this does not gladden his heart, for it will be the work of Samael and will thus further delay the true redemption (*GT* 137).

As a result of this approach to contemporary history, the Satmarer lays down the following guide-lines of policy.

A. The policy most in accord with the divine will is that the State now be dissolved. It should be emphasized that this does not by any means imply the advocacy of a permanent exile in the Diaspora. Paradoxically, the Neturei Karta favor giving up Statehood now so that, by this gesture of renunciation of human initiative and overreaching, the Messiah may come and usher in the complete redemption and restore Israel to its ancient eminence. Meanwhile, the United Nations will see to it that the Jewish population is protected (*GT* 10).

B. Until such time that the State is dismantled (and the Messiah will have to undo the entire State and rebuild it on sacred rather than demonic foundations—*GT* 133), the Satmarer strongly disapproves of visiting the Western Wall, and other shrines and holy places. The possession of the Wall by the evil, corrupt, and unclean Zionists is an unmitigated disaster (*GT* 153). They have desecrated the shrines by assembling at them frivolously and immodestly (*GT* 142). To visit them, even with the right motives, implies support of the Zionist State (*GT* 139, 142). Since the United Nations is opposed to Israeli rule over the Old City of Jerusalem, therefore residing there is a violation of the oath of rebelling against the nations and is to be discouraged unless one is a true saint (*GT* 160). At times his logic is piquant: if

God had wanted Jews to return to the Old City, He would have arranged for them to return to it legitimately, under proper aegis, and not in violation of the oath (*GT* 162). He uses similar reasoning—perhaps even more astonishing—in counseling against visiting the Cave of Machpelah (*GT* 165).

C. Consistent to the end, the Satmarer declares that the commandment of *Yishuv Ha-aretz* (settling the Holy Land) is applicable only to the period of the Temple and is not in force today (*VM* 37f). And the ingathering of the exiles too is therefore contrary to Judaism (*VM* 55).

D. Finally, the Neturei Karta are not disturbed, at least ideologically, by the successes of their Zionist adversaries. The Satmarer does not subscribe to triumphalism, the idea that political triumph validates the ideology of the victors (*GT* 92)—an idea that used to be part of Catholicism's self-justification. Numbers are no guarantee of truth. In a charming homily, he asks: Why does the Talmudic formula read *Yachid Ve'rabbim Halakhah Ke'rabbim* (when one individual opinion is opposed to the majority, the Halakhah is in accordance with the majority); would not the more economical expression *Halakhah Ke'rabbim* be a sufficient legal maxim? He answers: We are to follow the majority only when the One—the One God, the *Yachid*—is with the *rabbim* (the majority). Without God, no majority can prevail. Indeed, he tells us in a psychologically revealing aside, the Neturei Karta are the only real Jews left. All the others possess the souls of the multitude of non-Jews—the riff-raff or rabble—that accompanied the Israelites out of Egypt in the days of Moses (*VM* 229).

Clearly, we are dealing here with a fringe group that, in its extremism, its hyperbolic language, its extravagance and simplicism, reveals a psychological pattern of defensiveness. Yet its fierce independence of thought, its refusal to be outvoted on matters of principle, the courage of its convictions, and the coherence of its ideology, cannot but elicit our admiration. Courage, especially idealistic courage, expressed at great personal sacrifice, is so rare that even if we disagree with its thesis, it deserves our respect.

However, the Neturei Karta's uncompromising ideological integrity is not matched by an equal intellectual honesty. R. Menachem M. Kasher and others have pointed out the careless manner in which the sources are treated so as to yield a predetermined conclusion. The Talmudic passage of the oaths, for instance, can be easily disputed. Most objectionable is the Satmarer's misapplication of legal, halakhic methodology to nonlegal, agadic texts. Classical talmudists often did this, but only as a kind of academic playfulness, never imagining it to be a *bona fide* avenue for determining practical issues. There are many other instances where the Satmarer tries to fit a square peg in a circle; his intellectual gymnastics are a tribute to his mental agility, not to scholarly objectivity. The Jewish tradition certainly does possess, here and there, a quietistic element, one that was most noticeable in Hasidism. But it certainly does not predominate. Similarly, his simplistic, demonological interpretation of Jewish history would be amusing were it not frightening.

The Neturei Karta are incapable of appreciating that the Jewish tradition often embraces divergent views, and that it is neither necessary nor desirable to reconcile them. The Neturei Karta thus emerge with an awesomely consistent ideology. But its very coherence and consistency is itself an indication of its vulnerability. One need not return to the philosophic criticisms of ideology to feel that the ideology here discussed ignores much of Jewish tradition and literature—which, reflecting life itself, possesses ambiguities, ambivalences, paradoxes. Thus, his simplistic view of Messiah, while it may long have been popular, ignores the element of absurdity that must of necessity participate in the Messianic process. Of course it is absurd to view one who denies the Messiah as his very agent for redemption. But then, the survival of Israel, its restoration, indeed the very notion of an eventual vindication of the divine promise to Abraham—these too are by nature absurd. No wonder that Maimonides counseled against any extravagant speculations about Messianic days. But such ideas are anathema to superconsistent ideologues who will not allow facts to jeopardize consistency.

Finally, with all the aversion of most Jews to this outrageously anti-Israel stance, two things ought to be remembered. First, while the Neturei Karta, theoretically and practically, are totally opposed to the State of Israel, they are not opposed to Israel as a people. On the contrary, they oppose the State because they favor the people. We may deplore them, but we must not indiscriminatingly condemn them (as has been done) as religious anti-Semites.

Second, the existence of this group, scandalous as it sometimes may seem, can prove a much-needed corrective. There may be a time when Israel will incline to an inflated view of its own power and prowess. Its triumphs may, in the nature of things, go to its head, and militarism may some day turn from an unwanted necessity to a way of life. Moses already warned us against boasting that "my power and my might have wrought all this." Modern Israel must scrupulously avoid this fallacy, a fallacy which is dangerous not only morally and spiritually but also politically. The Neturei Karta are irritating reminders that activism can lead to the illusion of total self-sufficiency, and self-sufficiency to arrogance, and arrogance to presumptuousness.

Granted that the medicine of the Neturei Karta is too strong for the illness it seeks to cure, and the patient shows no real symptoms of the disease, it is a medicine nonetheless. It need not and should not be swallowed, but its presence on the shelf serves a purpose of sorts.

~ 48 ~

THE SIX DAY WAR

At the recent World Conference of Orthodox Ashkenazi and Sephardi Synagogues in Jerusalem, there emerged two centers of concern, which we might designate by two Hebrew words which have one common origin: *aliyah* and *hitalut*, both of which come from the Hebrew root, *a-l-h*, which means: "to go up." By this we mean, that the dual concerns of the Conference were Aliyah, the problem of literally emigrating to Israel from all over the world, and Hitalut, the act of self-improvement, self-transcendence, self-elevation in Jewish commitment and in loyalty to Torah.

IT IS INTERESTING that both these concepts, of Aliyah and Hitalut, are discovered by one commentator, Abarbanel, in one word of the Biblical narrative about Israel in the infancy of its history. When the Pharaohs of Egypt became anxious about the growth of the Jewish community and its prosperity, they decided to scheme against the Israelites for fear that they were growing too strong, and because of the suspicion that in case of war they would join the enemy and *ve'alah min ha-aretz,* which literally means: "And he will go up from the land." Normally, this is taken to mean that the Pharaohs feared that in case of crisis the Jews would leave Egypt and go on Aliyah to the Land of Israel, much in the same way that the Communist commissars of Soviet Russia are today worried that if they open the doors and allow the Iron Curtain to part, most of the Jewish community of Russia might emigrate to the State of Israel. Abarbanel, while agreeing with this interpretation, adds one other insight. He maintains that the phrase can also be interpreted as "they will rise beyond the rest of the land." He interprets the word *min* not as derivative, "from," but comparative, "than." The concern of the Pharaohs was not only that the Jews would perform Aliyah and

---

Originally entitled "Up and Over," this was published in Jewish Life, *March–April 1968.*

go up *from* the land of Egypt, but that they would experience *hitalut* and that they would rise in their stature and in their quality *beyond* the rest of the population, they would become greater *than* the rest of the Egyptian population.

What bothered the Pharaohs, bothered us: the twin problems of Aliyah and Hitalut. At the risk of sounding frivolous, we might say that our attention was directed to the question of Jews going "over" to Israel, and of growing "up" in the quality of their commitment—"up and over" being the antidote to "down and out."

The foremost impression that one takes away from even a brief tour of the State of Israel, provided that one has paid attention not only to seeing places but also to meeting people, is the seriousness with which Israelis take the entire question of Aliyah. There is little doubt in my mind that we have paid far too little attention to it, assuming unconsciously that when the Israelis speak of Aliyah they are engaged in a kind of ritualistic rain dance in which they do not really mean for us to take them with any earnestness. But that is clearly not the case. The Israelis desperately need us; and we need them even more.

Only 17% of world Jewry now lives in the State of Israel; yet it is there, to use the current colloquialism, "where the action is." Chief Rabbi Unterman was quite right when he told the Conference that whereas the *rov minyan* of world Jewry is in America, the *rov binyan* is in Israel; that is, that while the majority quantitatively resides in the United States, the qualitatively weightiest group, which will decide the destiny of our people, is the Jewish community of the State of Israel. Jewish history will be written, and is being written, primarily there, not here. And no one should be so self-effacing and modest as to confine himself forever to the margins and periphery of the arena where history is being forged and molded.

I have no solution to offer on the Aliyah question; our best minds have not yet devised a proper answer to the question. I know that if the tables were reversed, and we would be in Israel and demand of the people now in Israel to come on Aliyah, they would have the same hesitation and reluctance that we experience because of practical matters. But that does not and should not allow us to escape confronting the problem squarely and acknowledging that we must give great weight to the challenge, especially as Orthodox Jews. We dare not cut down our ideology to conform to the limitations of current circumstances. We dare not develop a theory of Jewish life which will do away with Aliyah in order to satisfy practical considerations—for then we will have abandoned Orthodoxy. Great deeds are demanded; deep thinking is the challenge of the hour. We must no longer treat Aliyah as a pipe dream or as a piece of perfunctory Israeli propaganda not deserving of our serious attention. It may be true that it is unlikely that the generation now ensconced in the business and professional life of this country will perform this mitzvah. But this does not excuse us from so raising the next generation that it will be possible for them to perform Aliyah without the difficulties that face us.

FROM THE FIRST problem, that of Aliyah, we proceed to the second center of concern, Hitalut. The most dramatic case of Hitalut, or Jewish improvement, I find in Israel itself.

I confess: there was a time when I all but despaired of the secular majority in the State of Israel. Religion had been so subject to the extreme politicization that is endemic to the country; anti-religiousness was rampant to such an extent; the belligerence against Torah was so doctrinaire; the machinery of Israel's religious establishment was so antiquated—that there was little reason at all for optimism or encouragement. I saw the major, if not the exclusive, hope for a Jewish renaissance in the United States.

I have now revised my opinion. I know that all is not well. Those in Israel who are spiritually insensitive will probably remain obtuse and coarse. The religious establishment is, unfortunately, still largely ineffective in reaching out to the great majority of the alienated Jews of Israel. But I detect a new spirit since last June, a sense of apocalyptic fulfillment, a feeling of the imminence of Messianic days, an awareness that we have passed a threshold in Jewish history, that we have crossed a watershed in the story of our people.

Great opportunities are ripening for a mature and enthusiastic approach—by an Orthodox Jewry which does not want to segregate itself but wants to live in this world—to the heretofore alienated Israelis.

Permit me to share with you an experience which, in a manner of speaking, was even more moving than that fabulous Friday night *Kabbalat Shabbat* at the Western Wall.

Quite by accident, we took advantage of the opportunity to pay a visit to a kibbutz, which is one of the northernmost outposts of the State of Israel, on the Lebanese and not far from the Syrian border. The terrain is mountainous and rough, and the members of this agricultural commune must work hard and long hours in order to prosper. Our conversations for these several hours were held with a few people, especially one who was "the old man" of the kibbutz, who had celebrated his 40th birthday only two days earlier. All members of this settlement, which was founded only eighteen years ago by young men and women in their late teens and early twenties, were the children of anti-religious socialist idealists of the Kibbutz movement. But in this particular kibbutz, the children had moved beyond the sterile positions of their parents.

For instance, this kibbutz is non-kosher; but they use only kosher meat. Only recently they had introduced a kind of *Kabbalat Shabbat* service, which included the recitation of *va-yekhulu* and the communal reading of the Sidra of the week. At this time we tried to persuade them to include the *Kiddush* as well; I believe they will accept this recommendation. The members of the kibbutz encourage only religious ceremonies for their weddings. Their thirteen-year-old boys are now taken, as a matter of course, to nearby Safed for their Bar Mitzvah, and they have developed the charming custom of informing each child on his Bar Mitzvah day of his whole family history, as far back as it can be traced into the glories of the Jewish past.

Perhaps most interesting, though tragic to relate, is the following illustration of the difference between the two generations: Several months ago one of their members was killed by accident by a guard who mistook him for a Syrian infiltrator. He was the first person to be buried in their cemetery. The father of the slain kibbutznik, himself a member of an older, well-established, thoroughly anti-religious kibbutz, refused on principle to recite the *Kaddish* at his son's funeral. However, his younger son, who was likewise a member of the younger kibbutz, as well as his friends, did recite the *Kaddish!*

THE FINEST INDICATION of the truly religious mood of this young generation is the attitude they evinced in the conversations. A question they persistently directed at us was, "How is it that we were privileged to achieve such a victory?" That question deserves to be studied well. Usually, when Jews turn to a rabbi with a question of this sort, it is just the reverse: "Rabbi, why did God punish me so much?" But these young and brave men and women put the question the other way around: "Rabbi, why was God so good to us?" This is clearly indicative of a profoundly religious stirring that deserves our utmost attention. There is a gracious humility and spiritual sensitivity under the tough Sabra exterior.

There was, however, one jarring note during this visit that bothered me especially much because of its symbolic significance. It is, I believe, instructive and worthy of pondering. Two of the kibbutzniks produced for us a Mezuzah each, birthday gifts from their wives. They were anxious to affix them properly, with the appropriate blessings, for they would be the first to be seen there. Both of us—the Israeli rabbi who accompanied us, and I—were delighted by the opportunity, and I had the sense of participating in a historic act. My Israeli colleague had the presence of mind to examine the Mezuzah scrolls within the metal tubes before proceeding. They were, alas, completely *pasul,* invalid; they did not even bear the proper Biblical passage, the *Shema!*

It is a frightening symbolic portent of what may come to pass if we are not sufficiently alert and active. The new thirst for Judaism may be slaked by impure waters. There is no guarantee that a genuine quest for God and Torah and tradition will be satisfied by authentic Judaism. The generation that may shortly be returning to Judaism is long on integrity and short on knowledge. Unless we and our colleagues in Israel are there to fill the spiritual void with the Torah tradition, others may rush in from all over the Diaspora to fill it with the truncated and distorted versions of Judaism that have plagued us in America. If we do not provide a kosher scroll for the Israeli who seeks a Mezuzah, someone will surely provide him with one that is *pa-*

sul—and much less expensive, less taxing, and less inconvenient. Whether we are currently geared to reach out to such individuals, to engage them in meaningful dialogues, to convince them of the integrity of the religious tradition we represent—that I do not know. I do know that it will be futile to use force or legislation or pressure to prevent our competitors from making their sales-pitch. We shall have to make a convincing case of our own—although I wonder which groups within the religious community in Israel are both willing and able to execute this task and do it well.

So there is an incipient Hitalut in Israel, and it is obvious in this small portion of the population, those who live on the kibbutzim, who are the most sensitive idealists and the pace-setters for the rest of Israel. And despite the dangers, this is a wonderful and encouraging development for which we ought to be grateful.

DOES THIS MEAN that we should give up on the *Golah?* No. I disagree with those Israelis who have despaired of the future of Judaism in the Diaspora. I do not believe that love for Israel and the encouragement of Aliyah to Israel should be dependent upon a negative view of Jewish life in the Diaspora. On the contrary, only if there is true Hitalut amongst Jews in the Diaspora, can we ever expect a substantial Aliyah of these Jews to Israel. If our contacts with the Israelis at the World Conference showed *their* Hitalut, the very fact of the World Conference was an indication of *our* Hitalut. Organized Orthodoxy in the United States has come of age, in that it has finally seen fit to meet with Orthodox Jews of similar disposition throughout the world, despite all the opposition which was quite inane and at times ugly. We broadened our horizons. We learned to appreciate the different circumstances in different Jewish communities. The element of Hitalut was evident to anyone who saw the impression that was made upon the large and influential French delegation, or the encouragement that was given, for instance, to that lonely young rabbi of the dwindling Jewish community of Athens.

There is a great need for further such contacts and more such meetings, without fear and always with dedication. Without ever neglecting our local needs, we must strengthen our bonds with Jews all over the world, and they are the bonds of Torah. But especially important is the continuing interplay and interaction between American and Israeli Orthodox Jews. Together we must strive for spiritual Hitalut and for actual Aliyah.

IN THE INTERESTING debate between God and Moses, when Moses is reluctant to accept his prophetic mission, God tells Moses that his brother Aaron is coming towards him. "And he will see you and he will be happy in his heart." Aaron will experience inner joy upon meeting his beloved brother Moses. Yet the Rabbis found an oblique source for criticism of Aaron in this verse. They say, if only Aaron had known that the Torah would record for all posterity his emotional reaction upon meeting Moses, then he would not have been satisfied with experiencing joy in his heart, but he would have greeted Moses with a whole band of drums and fifes.

We live in a time of *ha-katuv makhtivo,* of Biblical proportions and Scriptural dimensions. The challenge to us is historic and will be recorded for all times. Good will and fine intentions about Israel and Judaism are simply inadequate. To be "happy in the heart" simply will not do.

There are times when history turns a telescope upon a particular period. At such times, our actions, our movements, our achievements, are meaningful only in the perspective of the great flux of world events which have their origin in the dim past and their climax in the remote future; but our actions by themselves, in a small segment of time, are fairly inconsequential and meaningless.

But here are other times when history turns not a telescope but a microscope upon a particular epoch. At such times, every action, every gesture, every deed, almost every word, assumes gigantic proportions. In a period of this kind, whatever we do is invested with enormous significance by itself for all of history.

Today is a period of history's microscope. *Ha-katuv makhtivo*—it is almost a period of Biblical magnificence, when all that we say and do and achieve is of the greatest significance, when our failures are catastrophic and our successes are enduringly illustrious.

ONE CAN HARDLY blame us, in this first year of *Yisrael Hashelemah,* the "Whole Israel" of historic dimensions, for experiencing great joy in our hearts. But this joy must not remain in our hearts. It must rise up out of the heart, and pull us up with it. It must *rise* to the occasion.

We must take counsel on how our community can achieve "up and over," how we can literally rise to Israel in Aliyah, and at the same time rise to a life of Torah and Mitzvot and Jewish spirituality in ever increasing Hitalut.

~ 49 ~

THE YOM KIPPUR WAR

The events of the Yom Kippur War and its aftermath are so traumatic, that we do not yet have the mental equanimity to assess the situation in the psychological calm requisite for such judgments. Perhaps an halakhic analogy is apt: the *avel* (mourner after the deceased has been buried) is expected to grieve over a situation which he then begins to perceive and perhaps even understand. But the *onen* (mourner before interment) is released from all religious obligations to mourn because he is assumed to be so stunned that he has not absorbed the gravity of his predicament and its implications. Nevertheless, certain moods have already made themselves felt.

Israel's Image

The Yom Kippur War was for Jews a trauma of the order that Vietnam was for most Americans. This psychological, and perhaps spiritual, issue revolves around the question of image and the values that feed it and flow from it. I do not believe that this is the only or even the most important issue, but it is so significant that to ignore it would be irresponsible.

Heretofore, many friends of Israel of all faiths have had a somewhat ambivalent attitude to the State. On a conscious level, there was delight in Jewish self-assertion and pride, and admiration for the tough Israel-born sabra. People took vicarious pleasure in his self-confidence, brashness, even his rudeness. The *galut* mentality with its timidity, self-abnegation, and passion for invisibility, had for so long been a burden and a shame, that the successful effort of Zionists deliberately to change that image and that reality was applauded.

On a more unconscious level, however, things were not always quite that clear. In an occasional article, in a snatch of intimate

---

This article appeared in a book of the same name, edited by Moshe Davis, and based upon a lecture in 1974 as a response to questions posed to participants in a symposium about the effect of the Yom Kippur War on different segments of the Jewish community.

conversation, one could sense a pervasive uneasiness, particularly on the part of certain Jews. Was it merely that the *galut* mentality was causing mental pain as it was being extracted and replaced by the image of the new *Homo Israeli?* Perhaps, and perhaps something more than that. A number of factors seem to have contributed to this inner malaise. There was an unexpressed fear that the bubble would burst, and the inexorable numerical superiority of the Arabs and the underlying anti-Semitism of the Christian West would eventually join forces, rise, and take revenge. There was apprehension that Israeli braggadocio was too extravagant and would unnecessarily provoke resentment. There was an uncomfortable feeling that the Jews, who had always protested militarism in American politics, who had always been hypersensitive to the influence of the military in government, were now passively accepting a situation in Israel in which military officers were taking command in the highest levels of government and industry. This discomfort was not allayed by the knowledge that Israel's was largely a civilian army, that many of its most distinguished leaders were scholars, that, in Israel's awkward and ponderous bureaucracy, the army was perhaps the most efficient organization. There was, too, an annoyance at the inversion of traditional Jewish values such as the abhorrence of bloodshed, the reluctance to rely on force alone, or at the very least, the aversion to glorifying the arms and weapons instead of the achievements of the mind, the heart, and the spirit.

It is these diverse and yet related feelings that emerged almost angrily when the Arab surprise attack "demythologized" the popular image of Israel. The later successful counterattack by the Israelis, no matter how brilliant, did not make up for the sudden feeling that we had all been "taken." Jews began to look back wistfully to their youth, ended just a month or two earlier, when it seemed that everything was so certain, so clear, so secure. Dying illusions are painful, and also enraging.

Suddenly on Yom Kippur more than one American Jew became sharply aware of these and related questions. What was all that rhetoric about relying on "our own strength?" Had independence for Israel become not merely a non-negotiable national value, worth every sacrifice, but an ideological fixation and a theological absolute, in an age when even great powers have to depend upon each other for survival, when mighty nations are often reduced to diplomatic sycophancy? This resentment—focused as much on oneself and one's own gullibility as on Israel—of course exaggerated matters, overlooked the pressure of historical circumstances, generalized too much, and lacked intellectual sophistication and analytic depth. But it was real—it still is—and may be a major psychological underpinning for the standoffishness of many intellectuals, and for the distress of even those who rallied to the flag and labored zealously with other Jews for Israel.

One can, of course, interpret these originally inchoate feelings less charitably and more cynically, and discover in American Jews, particularly intellectuals, an inner resentment of Israeli assertiveness and pride. This would attribute to American Jews, still entangled in the tentacles of their old *galut* complex, a subconscious jealousy of the martial components of the Israeli charisma. Such an assertion may have a measure of validity; but it is no less a fact for being psychological and irrational.

This erroneous and unrealistic image projected by Israel represents not only a public-relations failure (which it is because the one-sided view neglects so many of the human and constructive features of the State), but also an educational disaster of vast proportions. What is needed is a profound reordering of priorities in creating a new conception of what the Israeli would like to be, a model for his own future development. The answer, I believe, lies in the direction of a synthesis of the new Israeli dignity of regained nationhood with the pioneering spirit and moral commitment of early Zionism, and these, above all, integrated into the continuum of the historic spiritual values of the Jewish tradition.

We can afford nothing less, because the present image can only bring us grief—witness the ludicrous "imperialism" charge so seriously and solemnly hurled at us by otherwise intelligent people. Daniel Elazar has observed that many Diaspora Jews, having lost faith in God and Torah, have begun to apotheosize the State of Israel. I subscribe to his assertion of the existence of this "Israelolatry." We have contributed to this dangerous attitude which has made the State an end in itself. In true religious fashion, its worshipers have attributed to their idol the qualities of power, wisdom, and benevolence to an absolute degree. Like all objects of faith, Israel has been exalted beyond criticism. The danger is that, ultimately, the idol will be found to have clay feet. And when that happens, the devotees will blame not their own gullibility but the limitations and inadequacy of the idol.

The figure of David has often been conjured up as the historical model or metaphor for the new Jew of Israel. It is a good symbol, provided it takes David in the fullness in which he appears both in the Bible and in the Jewish oral tradition. Little David confronting Goliath is not an incorrect image. But it is inadequate. David was the fighter and the king, but also the composer of psalms. David had not only a slingshot, but a harp. He was a soldier and poet, fighter and musician, a sinner who was manly enough to accept criticism and change his ways, a brave warrior who was not ashamed to be afraid and who trusted in a Higher Force, a general who prayed, a student of Torah and of political sophistication, and a man of firmness and moral magnanimity.

It is this traditional image which inspired Orthodox Jewry in all its sub-groupings. Their response to the crisis may help illuminate the wider spectrum of American Jewish feelings.

Positions in American Orthodoxy

Orthodox circles in the United States experienced a remarkable identification with Israel no matter what disagreements individual religious groups or individuals may have had with Israeli policy or society, and no matter how bitter their previous frustrations. On Yom Kippur day, political and religious differences with regard to Israel faded and all religious Jews, whether Agudah, Mizrachi, or unaffiliated, showed genuinely deep concern, worry, and a desire to help in every way possible.

Yet, despite this feeling of solidarity with Israel in its time of crisis, almost all religious groups experienced a reaction similar to the disaffection of the intellectuals. It might be called an alliance of the religious right and the political left in decrying the excessive pride that has come to be associated with Israeli statehood. The attitude is one against which Moses warned at the threshold of Israel's entry into Canaan:

> Then thy heart be lifted up, and thou forget the Lord thy God, who brought thee forth out of the land of Egypt, out of the house of bondage. . . . And thou say in they heart: *"My power and the*

> *might of my hand have gotten me this wealth."* But thou shalt remember the Lord thy God, for it is He that giveth thee power to get wealth, that He may establish His covenant which He swore unto thy fathers. . . . (Deut., 8:14, 17, 18).

It is this Biblical exhortation—and it is surely a fundamental of the whole religious *Weltanschauung* of Judaism—that makes the oft-repeated assertions that "we can rely only on our own strength" sound so abrasive and sacrilegious, even blasphemous. Traditional Judaism is by no means pacifist, but it rejects arrogance and self-assertion which ascribe power and success to arms alone.

Religious Jews were upset when the Declaration of Independence of Israel gave only begrudging acknowledgment to the Deity in veiled reference to Him as the "Rock of Israel" *(Tzur Yisrael)*, but it was forgiven, or at least accepted, in the turmoil of those difficult days. The Six-Day War inspired the whole people, and religious Jews saw the hand of Providence at work. In those heady days, the issues were clear, the victory astounding, and the return to Jerusalem certainly lifted events out of the stream of ordinary, every day history. Secularists who could not bring themselves to speak of "miracles," except metaphorically, testified to at least the uniqueness of the events of 1967.

Unfortunately, the sense of national joy and thanksgiving quickly evaporated. Maybe it is in the nature of things that such levels of religious exultation or exquisite historic awareness must soon fade as the routines of life take over and clamor for attention. But even before the Yom Kippur War, some of the poetry and mystical charm began to vanish. Not all of it was the result of natural attrition. Humble gratitude gave way to a much less noble interpretation of the events of the war. Israeli military men who came to speak to American Jews reveled in "demythologizing" the victory and reserving full credit to *Zahal* for all the accomplishments of the 1967 war. Not Providence, not faith, not luck, not accident, but *Zahal's* superiority in power and generalship gained the victory. There was also the shameless public polemic of the generals, some of whom declared there never was a threat of massacre prior to June 1967, that all fears of another Holocaust by the Arab armies were propaganda, that the Army was in control of the situation all along. Not only the poetry and the magic, the miracle and the exultation, but even the sense of relief (and perhaps even justice of our cause) were stolen from us retroactively. Israel's power and the might of its hand have begotten for us not wealth, but confusion and resentment—and an image as unattractive as it is unrealistic. It was unattractive both to intellectuals and to religious Jews, although no one really bothered to talk about it. But when the Yom Kippur War showed it to be unrealistic—as well as highly dangerous—these simmering sentiments came to the fore in both disparate circles. Perhaps a good lesson for the future when, with the help of God, peace and security return to Israel, is for Israel to keep its generals and colonels and majors at home or in service, and send other kinds of spokesmen for Israel to the communities of the Diaspora.

Theological Responses

In the attempts at formulating an interpretation of these events and integrating them into a theological framework, several divergent tendencies in the Orthodox community are beginning to appear. It must be stressed that, as of this time, some six months after the outbreak of hostilities, the situation is still fluid and no crystallization of approaches has yet taken place. Our listing of theological responses must therefore be taken as tentative and provisional.

Three major reactions may be discerned: that of the non-Zionist Orthodox community, the one usually associated with the yeshivot; that of the religious Zionist community and its sympathizers; and that of Orthodox Jews who, despite associations with one or both of the above, take an independent approach. The writer belongs to this third group and will speak from that vantage.

The "right-wing" groups of the yeshiva and Hasidic worlds have never endowed the State with Messianic or pre-Messianic significance. The exception is the *Neturei Karta* group, whose major spokesman is Rabbi Joel Teitelbaum, the Satmarer Rebbe of Brooklyn. His demonological interpretation of Zionist and Israeli history paradoxically does invest the State with a perverse negative Messianic function: the State, as the creation of the Zionists, is an arrogant usurpation of the divine prerogative, for God alone can usher in the redemption; the State is thus a diabolical invention tempting the people of Israel away from true faith, hence impeding the coming of the Messiah. (See my article on the *Neturei Karta* earlier in this chapter, no. 47.) Nevertheless, the stunning events of both 1967 and 1973 have engendered a considerable amount of Messianic speculation, more evident in the general community than in its official leadership.

There are groping efforts to explain the events of 1973—especially the superpower confrontation—as the beginning of the apocalyptic cataclysm that tradition predicts as the prelude to the coming of the Messiah. There was much talk abroad in these circles of "The War of Gog and Magog" being at hand, and not only *Ezekiel* and *Daniel* but a number of kabbalistic texts were found to contain prophetic hints of current events.

Several works elaborating these "signs" have recently been published in Israel and have had a rather wide currency. The two most notable are by Shabbatai Shilo and Chaim Shevili. In 1970, Shilo published a short book with a long title, *The Redemption and Eternity—Happy is He Who Waits for and Reaches the Days of 1973.* The outbreak of the Yom Kippur War in October 1973 was considered little short of amazing, confirming his designation of 1973 as the decisive year in the Messianic drama centering around Israel's refusal to surrender Jerusalem, thus provoking an international military expedition against the Holy City. The invading army, composed of Russians and Arabs, was to conquer Jerusalem. Then the miracle, precipitated by an earthquake, was to have occurred—the divine intervention on behalf of Israel and the appearance of the Messiah. Shilo designated Hanukkah, December 1973, as the height of the war against Jerusalem. (In his defense one must cite the "tolerance of error" of one year that he reserves for himself.)

Chaim Shevili long ago predicted that 1948 would be a fateful year in the process of redemption. In 1935 he published his *Vision of Life,* in which he calculated that the Temple would be rebuilt in 1948–49. The founding of the State in 1948 was sufficient to establish his credentials. In 1964, his *Book of Calculations of the Redemption According to the Book of Daniel and the Writings of the Gaon of Vilna and Rabbi Isaac Luria and Chapters on the Dates of the Creation* pointed to 1967 as the pivotal date in the Messianic redemption. Naturally, the Six-Day War lent his thesis considerable credibility.

While most leading rabbis and heads of yeshivot have refused to endorse such Messianic speculations, at least publicly, the sense of crisis and frustration has kept these issues alive, anxiety giving rise to anticipation. The eruption of the recent war on the holy day of Yom Kippur itself has understandably underscored the Messianic nature of the war to those predisposed to such interpretations. I do not know, however, if such a tendency will develop further, for the following reasons. First, there has always been an inclination to identify the vicissitudes of contemporary Jewish life as the catastrophic fulfillment of prophecies of pre-Messianic agonies. In our own lifetime there have been several major confrontations that have evoked similar theological speculations—from World War I through World War II, to the Cold War between the nuclear powers. Second, the nuclear war that is part of the contemporary version of the Gog-and-Magog scenario, may, one prays, not take place. Third, such an ascription of pre-Messianic cataclysm to events concerning the State paradoxically invests the State of Israel with at least some element of Messianic redemption which these groups themselves vehemently deny. Sooner or later the contradiction must become apparent.

The above approach and the one following have one thing in their favor, and that is the advantage of a ready-made pattern, exegetically elaborated, into which historic events can be integrated. The ability to relate the twists and turns of an impulsive and sometimes convulsive history to a foreordained process, by imposing a rational structure on otherwise reckless and chaotic events, decreases the anxiety of the unknown future.

The second response to Israel in Orthodox circles is that of the religious Zionists, who subscribe to the thesis that the State of Israel represents a definite and crucial stage in the Messianic process. This is identified as the *at'chalta di'geulah,* the "Beginning of the Redemption." The term first appears in the Talmud, *Megillah* 17b, where, however, it clearly refers to personal salvation rather than to the collective political redemption of Israel (see Rashi, *ad loc.*) The notion of the beginning of the Messianic redemption is more accurately called *ha-ketz ha-meguleh,* the "revealed end (of days)," referring to *Sanhedrin* 98a.

More accurately, the founding of the State is considered a key event *within* the *at'chalta di'geulah,* the genesis of which is located in the first agricultural resettlement of the Yishuv (Rabbi A.I. Kook, *Iggerot Hareiyah,* Part III, in a letter dated 1918.) Rabbi Akiva

Yosef Shlesinger had already expressed his consciousness of living in *at'chalta di'geulah* in 1873 (*Kollel Ha'ivrim,* ed. 1955, p. 19.); and thirteen years earlier Rabbi M.N. Kahanow, noticing prosperous Jewish orchards in the vicinity of Jaffa, declared this a sign of the "Beginning of the Redemption" (*Sha'alu Shelom Yerushalayim,* Odessa, 1861.) For those inclined to interpret the early Zionist movement in such redemptive terms, the establishment of the State was embraced as a political validation and vindication of the Messianism implicit in Zionism. The remarkable conjunction of the declaration of statehood and the Holocaust that immediately preceded it without doubt lent credence to such exuberance. The survival of the fledgling state and its growing prosperity were further confirmation of the new plateau that had been reached in *at'chalta di'geulah,* and the events of the Six-Day War were the miraculous revelation of what the believers had known all along: the State of Israel was the herald of the Messianic Kingdom.

The setbacks of 1973 now become quite problematical for those who persisted in ascribing a Messianic dimension to the State. It is clear that the traditional Jewish view insists upon empirical criteria by which Messianic claims may be tested. Maimonides codified these criteria in his *Yad, Hilkhot Melakhim,* and Nahmanides made ample use of these empirical standards in his polemics against Pablo Christiani. If, therefore, one affirms a Messianic role for the State, he must explain the reverses of the Yom Kippur War. It is reasonable to assume that if success proves the truth of a proposition—if 1948 and 1967 are the validations of the Messianic claims for the State of Israel—then failures prove the opposite.

Not many of the advocates of this school have responded to the challenge of the Yom Kippur War to clarify their thinking. In the United States there appear to be two contradictory assessments of the Israeli performance in the 1973 war. The first reaction is one that has an air of unreality about it: despite the setbacks, the military performance of *Zahal* was so brilliant as to keep intact its reputation for invincibility. The contemporary Messianic calculus has its own logic: losses become gains and reversals become triumphs. At a time when leaders of the military themselves rue the day they allowed the myth of Israeli military invincibility to gain currency, the Messianists will not allow "invincibility" to give up the ghost, fearing, as well they might, that even a minor defeat invalidates the evidence they had previously adduced from earlier victories for the Messianic nature of the State.

The second reaction is more compelling in its reasonableness by subjecting the theory to logical criticism. The Messiah will not come suddenly, the Talmud states, but *kimah kimah,* bit by bit, like the rising of dawn. So the State, as the political harbinger of the Messianic redemption, cannot be expected to score an unbroken string of triumphs without occasional slackening or discomfiture. There is a commendable modesty to this answer, and it allays somewhat the uneasy feeling that the *at'chalta di'geulah* theory is a form of triumphalism. This may be one of the theologically salutary results of the Yom Kippur War. But while it may be acceptable to those who seek a more naturalistic and rationalistic interpretation of the belief in the Messiah, it does not any longer allow one to use successes, when they arise, as evidence of the imminence of the Messiah's arrival. To do so would be to make the whole theory of the "Beginning of Redemption" an unfalsifiable thesis and hence of questionable validity. We are then thrown back upon faith—in itself no tragedy—rather than history, in supporting our feeling of experiencing the "Beginning of the Redemption."

A third approach, with which this writer identifies, takes exception to the apocalyptic-salvific versions of current history as illustrated by the two theories described, especially the second. Some criticisms have already been mentioned and more can be added. Most important, while searching for Messianic clues has been a psychologically understandable and spiritually justifiable endeavor, the development of a formal ideology that asserts dogmatically that we are in a specific stage of the Messianic redemption may well be an act of presumption. Are those of us who are devoid of the gift of prophecy privy to divine secrets?

Even to Moses, the greatest of all prophets, it was told, "Thou shalt see My back, but My face shall not be seen" (Exodus, 33:23.) God's plans may be known to man in all their magnificent detail and moral fullness only retrospectively. We may, at best, "see My back." But we have no clairvoyance into the future and even the present is concealed from us if it is considered as part of a continuum whose culmination lies in the future. The assertion that the State is *reshit tzemichat geulatenu*—another term for *at'chalta di'geulah*—as so many Israelis and Diaspora Jews declare in their "Prayer for the Peace of the State of Israel," entails a certain spiritual arrogance, as if we have lifted the veil into the mysterious *eschaton* and wrested from the Messiah his deepest secret: the time of his arrival. To read the present as a historian of the future, instead of as a journalist, is the prerogative of the prophet, provided God has shared His secrets with him. Ordinary humans tread on dangerous ground when they purport to view events from a divine perspective.

I wish to make it clear that I do not *deny* the Messianic character of our times or of the State. To do so with any conviction would be to commit the same sin of presumption. What I am saying is that I *do not know,* and that I believe this form of skepticism or Messianic agnosticism is the only valid spiritual position under the present circumstances. Since the Messianic quality of present-day events is not empirically demonstrable or verifiable, the wisest way for one who is committed to the traditional belief (or, more accurately, any of the various traditional beliefs) in the Messiah is to "bracket" the question, as phenomenologists would say.

History bears eloquent testimony to the grief that comes in the wake of premature Messianic expectations and unchecked eschatological ferver. Professor Gershom Scholem makes the point that of all the cornerstones of traditional Jewish theology, only the belief in redemption continues in full force. All the more reason for treating the supposed Messianic dimension of the State with a great deal of caution, there being no guarantees that secular pseudo-messianism is any less dangerous than the religious kind.

It must be granted that the coming of the Messiah is, by its nature, the kind of event that raises doubts, especially in the light of the history of false Messiahs, and that such skepticism can congeal into an automatic denial of any and all Messianic claims even where they might be legitimate. There is a certain amount of risk-taking that cannot be avoided. But mistakes, even honest ones, can be made—witness Rabbi Akiva and his sponsorship of Bar Kokhba as the Messiah.

I prefer to view the events of our time as providential and not (necessarily) Messianic. I accept that the rebirth of the national homeland, after the vicissitudes of our history, and especially on the heels of the Holocaust was a "miracle," in that it defied all predictability and probability.

I accept the State as an act of redemption, but not every redemption is necessarily Messianic. The terms here associated—*at'chalta,* Messianic, pre-Messianic—must be reserved for that specific period of history which will culminate in the fulfillment of all the visions of the past—political autonomy, economic welfare, intellectual advancement, spiritual flowering, religious renaissance—climaxed by the leadership of a unique individual who will create these conditions and possess the leadership capacity to enable them to be enjoyed by the people of Israel, ushering in an era of peace and justice in the world. I am not trying to summarize the traditional Messianic beliefs as much as to isolate such a period from the normal, run-of-the-mill, historical epoch. If we understand this, then what is to prevent us from experiencing non-Messianic redemptions, of various extents and scopes, in the course of Jewish history?

Neither *aliyah* nor solidarity of the Diaspora with Israel requires the apocalyptic-salvific hypothesis of the *at'chalta di'geulah* advocates. On the contrary, the attribution of Messianic importance to the State leads, paradoxically, to two opposite and unfortunate conclusions: one, that the State, as a Messianic instrument, is beyond criticism, and hence its leaders can do no wrong; and two, that the State of Israel is disastrously delinquent in not living up to the high moral and religious standards one would expect of a Messianic state.

The Jewish commitment to the State of Israel does not require Messianic presuppositions. That commitment was forged in the fires of the crematoria; in the hatred of and indifference to Jews by the civilized countries of both West and East; in the Covenant, which has paradoxically allowed us to live without Eretz Israel for 2000 years—and for 2000 years has not let us give up our longing for it; in the knowledge that the realization of the Torah and the fulfillment of the Word of God are more likely to be found in Israel than anywhere else on this globe. The State of Israel is the guarantee of Jewish survival today, whether or not it is a Messianic state.

For the Future

The suggested "bracketing" of the Messianic element by no means implies an abandonment of the belief in the coming of the Messiah. It asserts that the role of Israel in history is not exclusively linked at every point with the Messianic element. The Covenant speaks of God's *hester panim*—His turning away of His face from us—and *he'arat panim,* His smiling upon us. These Biblical categories, while less emotionally charged, may ultimately be more fruitful than exclusively Messianic terms in interpreting the great events of our times. *Hester panim* and *he'arat panim* are relational ideas, implying the absence or presence of mutuality and reciprocity between God and Israel, the two partners in the Covenant. While a fuller development of this theme cannot be given here, I do suggest that these concepts will serve better than *at'chalta di'geulah* as the parameters for a contemporary theological evaluation of Jewish history.

The Messiah is only the messenger of God. It is He, and He alone, who redeems. If He has chosen to redeem us and to restore us to the Land promised in the Covenant, it is a divine redemption. And a divine redemption is not that far inferior to a Messianic redemption.

As I mentioned, the common religious reaction to Israel's national psychology, precipitated by the Yom Kippur War, does not end in the criticism of "my strength and the might of my hand." Religious groups, especially the religious right, so long critical of Israel's illusion of self-sufficiency and its rhetoric of national self-assertion, have already begun to articulate a constructive criticism of the prevailing mood of the country: its sadness, depression, and pessimism. They are consistent with their premises: just as national bluster was a symptom of lack of *emunah* (faith) when the news was good, so the despair and depression and sense of foreboding today are equally inconsistent with *emunah.* If our previous error was an unwarranted trust in our "power and might of our hand," our present mistake is forgetting that "Behold, the Guardian of Israel neither slumbers nor sleeps" (Psalms, 121:4.) Both arrogance and despair have the same provenance: a lack of faith.

What the religious groups are saying, then, is that it is time to get on with the people's business, to do what has to be done whether pleasant or not, but to do it in the humble confidence that, God willing, we will prevail.

It is a consoling and comforting summons, and one that makes good sense.

~ 50 ~

"WITH HANDS NOT BOUND AND FEET UNCHAINED"

The victim was a general, a celebrated hero of his people, deeply involved in the diplomatic and political issues of government. He came to this rendez-vous unsuspecting, in peace, wanting peace, expecting peace. Followed by the assassin, he knew nothing of what lay in store for him.

But then the stalking assassin struck and, within a moment, the leader lay dead—laid low not by an enemy of Israel, but by the hand of a fellow Jew.

Thus was Avner ben Ner killed by Yoav (II Samuel 3:26–27).

When King David heard the news he was horrified, and at the funeral he pronounced the following immortal words:

> "Your hands were not bound, nor your feet put in chains."

One would have expected Avner to die a hero's death—gloriously, on the field of battle, slain by an enemy in the course of combat on behalf of his people. Instead, he was done in by one of his own who came silently, in stealth.

We assemble here today to mourn and honor a modern Avner ben Ner. And we are filled with grief and apprehension.

Direct yet thoughtful, tough but introspective, unceremonious, even humble, always tense and nervous—which he had every reason to be—Yitzhak Rabin was an unusual leader of his country.

Yeshiva gave him an honorary degree, and he spoke before Yeshiva University audiences on a number of occasions since. Personally, I knew him since his days as Ambassador to the United States. At all times I found him to be respectful, deferential, courteous, and with the highest regard for this institution. Losing him is much like losing an eminent and respected authority figure in one's family. The assassination of Yitzhak Rabin may

---

A eulogy upon the assassination of Prime Minister Yitzchak Rabin, delivered at Yeshiva University on November 6, 1995.

leave in its wake consequences as disastrous as they are unforeseen and unforeseeable.

Mourning, in the Jewish tradition, contains within it an element of repentance. It is therefore appropriate for us to examine ourselves and learn if we can in any way improve what we are doing and how we are acting, so as to avoid such catastrophes in the future.

In addition to shock and grief, I for one experienced a vital element of repentance and that is: shame. I am chagrined that it was a Jew who murdered the Prime Minister. I was always proud that Jews do not behave in this way . . . And I am deeply embarrassed that it was a religious university student who did it—even if he is a madman. Yigal Amir and Baruch Goldstein were, otherwise, fine representatives of what we stand for. So we have a lot of thinking and pondering to do.

Most everyone possesses within himself a seething cauldron of passions, noxious energies that, if released, can destroy recklessly and with abandon. But we have been civilized—by Torah, by social sanctions, by parental training, by moral conscience. That constraining inhibition is powerful in most people, often as powerful as steel. With others, the lid that holds down the boiling pot of emotions is made of weaker stuff, the psychological equivalent of plastic and glue. But in a few unfortunate individuals, that cover is no more than paper. The inner curbs against blood-lust, violence, rape, and murder are no stronger than tissue paper, tied down with gossamer threads spun by a weary and ineffective spider. A person so poorly endowed can lead an otherwise normal life for a long time, but place him in an environment which is permissive of violence, which exposes him to harsh talk, to hype, to unrestrained overstatement, to irrational and undisciplined expression—and anti-social urges buried deep within his sick psyche will explode in an unspeakably ugly display of hostility that turns men into monsters, society into a jungle, and civilization into chaos.

Our responsibility is to avoid such an environment, never to be guilty of having, knowingly or unknowingly, directly or indirectly encouraged such bestiality.

Our responsibility is to be responsible, to recognize that violent rhetoric invariably leads to violent deeds. In the absence of such awareness, we stand accused of having prepared the ground for the explosion of such malevolence by people of weak restraint, like a sewer blowing its cover and uncontrollably spewing forth its odious and miasmic gases.

Let us say it: we should never have permitted ourselves the luxury of escalating political differences to such heights of hatred—and such depths of depravity.

Let us never again, in Jerusalem or in New York or elsewhere, call a respected leader of Israel a "traitor." Let no one tolerate irresponsible individuals who dare to refer to the Prime Minister of Israel, no matter of what party, as a Nazi. And let us silence those raucous voices of vicious discord who declare that it is a *mitzvah* to assassinate a Prime Minister of the State of Israel!

Remember what King Solomon taught: *mavet va'chayyim be'yad lashon*—"Death and life are in the power of the tongue" (Prov. 18:21). Words can bring joy and enhance life; and words—oral or written—can also hurt and maim and destroy and kill.

I want to make it clear: *Nothing in what I say should be construed as approving or disapproving of the Rabin policies, condemning or condoning statements he may have made.* That is precisely the point that I wish to make: We may deplore what a man says—we may even find it deceitful and hateful—but never may we denigrate his divine Image which confers upon him his basic human dignity. We may oppose, however strongly, the policy, but not savage the personality. That is not the way of any morally mature and responsible, sensitive human being, and certainly not the way of people who study Torah.

The murder of Yitzhak Rabin should put all of us on notice:

Tone down irresponsible rhetoric, which creates the ambience for irresponsible deeds, even the foulest of them.

Beware of even lightly cloaking political views, no matter how much you believe in them, in the mantle of Halakha, because that is an instance of *megalleh panim be'Torah she'lo ke'halakha,* of improper manipulation of the Law. These are issues of such historic import that only a Sanhedrin can decide them *on the basis of Halakha,* or whose decision has the status of Halakha. No one in this generation may arrogate that prerogative to himself.

And keep far away from excessive self-confidence that leads to arrogant self-righteousness that, in turn, persuades us that our ideals are greater and better than those of the other fellow; that we are sincere and he is not; that we are unquestionably right and he is indubitably wrong; that we are therefore entitled to force our views on him—by "eliminating" him if need be, in order to have our "truth" prevail.

Such arrogance and such invitation to violence and such rhetorical extremism must come to an end—whether in the Knesset or in party precincts, whether of the Left (the extremists of which demonized Menachem Begin) or the Right, the Religious or the Secular, whether in Merkaz Harav or in Yeshiva University. Yes, Yeshiva University . . .

We must develop a new sensitivity to extremism of all kinds. When I argue against uncivil speech, it is not a matter of taste or a preference for bourgeois manners. *Le style c'est l'homme.* Style often reveals character. We have allowed ourselves too often the luxury of intemperate, extremist expression, and we must all band together to learn how to avoid it—whether by young or by old. We must no longer be as tolerant as we have been of strident invective and ugly epithets and hurtful hype.

Neither the Right nor the Left have been careful enough in gauging the temperature of debate. All of us must rethink not our positions as much as our methods. And we must develop a new respect for simple civility.

At the creation of man, the Torah tells that the Almighty exclaimed: *ve'hinei tov me'od,* "Behold, it is very good." The Midrash offers a startling commentary on this verse, *tov me'od—zeh ha-mavet*—"very good" refers to . . . death!

The great Rabbi Yosef Engel of pre-war Galicia explains tersely: *kol me'odiyut zeh mavet*—all "very-ness," all extremism—*even "very" good*—is deadly!

I return to the object of our grief, to Yitzhak Rabin. He was not, it is true, an observant Jew. Perhaps if we had his upbringing, we would be no different—and if he had ours, he might easily outshine us . . . But he was a great man—whether or not you agreed with him—and his place in Jewish history is assured.

The famous Kabbalist R.Hayyim Vital teaches that there are within humans two different levels of soul—one is *nefesh* and the other is *ruach*—and that one may possess one or both or neither. If one is helpful to his fellow humans and devoted to his people and his land, if he is motivated by genuine moral considerations, he possesses a higher degree of *nefesh* than one who spends his life in Torah and mitzvot but fails to serve his fellow

Jews and his country, whereas the latter possess *ruach* which the former does not.

I am in no position to judge the quality of Yitzhak Rabin's *ruach.* But I can tell you this: he had a noble *nefesh.* His entire life was spent on behalf of his people and his country. His *nefesh* was one of indomitable courage, of bravery in war and in peace, of genuine heroism on the battle front and in the chancelleries of the world. He laid down his life on the altar of peace. And *shalom* is a Name of the Creator—not a political policy convenient for the agendas of the Left or one that the Right implies we must look upon with suspicion . . .

In Iran there was yesterday and is today celebration. In Lebanon there is dancing. In Gaza there is joyous shooting in the air. On the lips of some incredibly foolish Jews there forms a smirk of shameful satisfaction. But for us, for the majority of sane Jews all over the world, and in the hearts of good men and women of all peoples, there is profound sadness, for we have lost the general who fought for Jerusalem in the War of Independence, who as Chief of Staff of the armed forces of Israel in 1967 liberated Jerusalem, who served his country gallantly as Ambassador, as Minister of Labor and of Defense and twice as Prime Minister and who, above all, was a man of great *nefesh,* of a courage that will inspire generations to come of our people.

May his *nefesh* and *ruach* and *neshamah* be bound up in the bond of immortal life:

~ 51 ~

THIRTY DAYS LATER—RABIN AND THE "PEACE PROCESS"

The Midrash (Lam.R., *Petichot*) describes, in its characteristically picturesque style, what went on in Heaven on the day the First Temple was destroyed:

> The Holy One said to Jeremiah: I am this day like unto a man who had an only son, and prepared for him a wedding canopy—and the son died under the canopy [as he was being married]. Do you not feel pain for Me and for My son? Go, then, and call upon Abraham, Isaac, Jacob, and Moses to rise from their sepulchers, for they know how to lament . . . Jeremiah said to the patriarchs, "Arise! for the time has come that you are summoned before the Holy One." They said to him: "But why?" He answered, "I do not know" [even though he really did] for he was afraid they would say to him, "In your days this [disaster] happened to our children!"
>
> R. Samuel b. Nachman said: When the Temple was destroyed, Abraham came weeping before the Holy One . . . rending his garments, ashes upon his head . . . lamenting and crying: "Why am I different from every other people that I have come to this shame and disgrace?!"

Yitzhak Rabin was killed as he neared the climax of his career, almost like the son who died at the moment of his great joy, his wedding. He was cut down at a rally celebrating his historic achievements. And so we experienced a sense of disaster—both for the assassination of a Prime Minister and for the enormity of the *chilul Hashem*—the desecration of the divine Name—and the devaluation of the kind of "Yiddishkeit" that we and our educational institutions represent, because the murderer was "one of our own." It is a "pain for Me and for My son"—suffering for the man, Rabin, and for our Father in Heaven whose Name has been profaned by this foul act.

And, despite all the eulogies that have been spoken, we are all in the category of Jeremiah who, despite his authorship of the

---

A eulogy for the Prime Minister on the occasion of the Sheloshim (30th day commemoration) of his assassination, delivered in December 1995.

Book of Lamentations, was "unable to lament," incapable of giving adequate expression to the vastness of the misfortune that had befallen his people. And, again like Jeremiah, *our* efforts have fallen short for the same special reason: because we are just too embarrassed to admit that "in your days this [disaster] happened to our children!"—it represents a failure that is peculiarly ours, and it hurts to admit it. We feel deeply, even those who won't admit it publicly, the *bushah u-khelimah;* it is *our* shame and *our* disgrace. It happened on *our* watch, the magnificent age of Yeshivot Hesder, of religious Zionism and religious universities, of the growth of Torah along with openness to the broader culture in which we live.

But if our situation bears remarkable parallels to that of Jeremiah, it is in certain important ways remarkably different from that of Abraham, as portrayed in the Midrash. Both he and we have learned to bewail our situation as best we can, and we experience *bushah u-khelimah*—shame and disgrace. But unlike Abraham, however, our *bushah u-khelimah* is not that we are *different* from all the nations, "Why am I different from every other people that I have come to this shame and disgrace?," but that we are so much *like them!*—like every banana republic where political killing is a way of life, and even like America, which saw political assassinations of its greatest and finest, its best and its brightest.

And perhaps our greatest chagrin is that the Arab world now sees us *as being just like them!* Here are a few choice morsels from a front-page article in the (11/27) *Wall Street Journal;* a similar article appeared a bit later in the *New York Times:*

> A strange thing is happening to many Arabs—they are starting to see Israelis as more like themselves.
>
> The assassination of Prime Minister Yitzhak Rabin by a fellow Jew destroyed a basic element of many Arabs' understanding—and awe—of the Jewish state: that Israel was somehow above the social maelstrom that afflicts the rest of the Mideast.
>
> Post-Rabin Israel . . . is at least an Israel that its neighbors can relate to.
>
> The average person has a stereotype of Israel as unified and democratic; the murder of Rabin reverses that . . . Some Arabs are seeing Israelis as human for the first time.

Now, thanks to our murderous friend, we can achieve peace with our murderous adversaries because they realize that we are as unbalanced and murderous as they are. We too are "human," finally, a "normal people . . . Thank you, Yigal Amir.

Father Abraham would have experienced much greater "shame and disgrace" over this than over the disgrace of the destruction of the Temple. The zealotry of young, immature, arrogant, know-it-alls has made the world—and especially our adversaries—lose all their respect for us. Indeed, "the House of Israel is like unto all the nations" (Ezek. 25:8)!

Of course, this has nothing to do with how one stands on the Peace Process. I must make it crystal-clear: *I am not taking sides on the basic political issues. I by no means disqualify those who are for peace but are against the way the present government is going about it.* I am referring *only* to the way we articulate and propagate and teach certain opinions—and how we treat those who disagree with us.

It would be immoral as well as undemocratic for the pro-government people to exploit the tragedy by demonizing the legitimate and loyal opposition and blaming them, directly or indirectly, for the assassination. We should not and must not tolerate a witch-hunt, an inquisition into what rabbis think—and that is what seems to be taking place—or engage in self-abnegation. Indeed, *no one is entirely guiltless,* the halls of the Knesset least of all.

The entire political culture of Israel is too loud, too intemperate. It was no one less than Ben-Gurion who referred to his political enemy Jabotinsky as "Vladimir Hitler." It was the Left that, during the Lebanon war, taunted Begin to distraction with the epithet "baby killer"—which they adapted from the anti-Vietnam activists in America who proclaimed, "Hey Hey, LBJ, How many babies did you kill today?" It was the late Prime Minister himself who said that the settlers are "enemies of peace" and "collaborators of Hamas."

Nor can the action of a few misguided violence-prone zealots be legitimately used to discredit an entire population that has proven its loyalty to Israel over and over again. No sane, intellectually honest person will hold all Bar-Ilan responsible for Yigal Amir, or all Yeshiva University for Baruch Goldstein. Let it be said openly and clearly: We Orthodox American Jews will not, as Jews, permit extreme secularists in Israel to excommunicate from Israeli society its most Jewishly learned and committed segment. And, as Americans committed to democracy, we will protest vigorously and, in every forum, expose the hypocrisy of so-called "liberals" who use undemocratic and racist demagoguery to delegitimate us. We will stand united in sustained and sharp opposition to the vicious, malicious efforts by the Assistant Minister of Defense who, according to a recent issue of *Haaretz,* threatened to investigate and close all Yeshivot Hesder and Nachal. We will not accept a situation whereby, according to a recent report in *Yediot Acharonot,* it costs 40 shekels in Israel to "buy a stigma"—20 shekalim for a *kippah serugah* and another 20 for a *tallit katan* . . . Remember, we Orthodox Jews have much to be proud of: our rate of Aliyah is disproportionate to our numbers; we send our children to study in Israel in far greater numbers than do others; and we visit and provide political and financial support for the Jewish State. The exercise of introspection and the assumption of a degree of moral responsibility should by no means diminish the value of these achievements.

Indeed, Mr. Peres should be congratulated for taking steps to avoid such group libel and for exploring ways of reconciliation. It is both politically astute and statesman like. That is precisely what is needed at this time. But those in lower positions in government and elsewhere, including the academy, are less scrupulous and must cease exploiting the situation to discredit the political Right and all religious Jews. And the police must learn to be more cautious of civil rights; there are simply too many cases of blatant police malfeasance. I am confident that when Israelis will get their rage and frustration out of their system, the situation will turn tolerable again. All of us pray that soon, very soon, cooler heads and warmer hearts will prevail.

But that does not mean that we can avoid any responsibility by dividing it up amongst many others. What we must aim at is self-criticism as a way of reacting to our *bushah u-khelimah,* even while we refuse to grant to others the right to use that commendable exercise of honest introspection to cast aspersions—and worse—upon us. Too many of us are in a state of denial that we can ill afford. If we will not be realistic, if we will be blind to the gathering storm and deaf to the nearing thunder, we will be defeated by our own defensiveness. Putting your head in the sand is most tempting to an enemy who wants to decapitate you . . .

It appears exceedingly difficult to attempt public stock-taking, even self-criticism, without providing grist for the mill of our adversaries. But it can and must be done. For instance, as the Rav (Rabbi Joseph B. Soloveitchik), *zekher tzaddik li'verakhah,* points out in one of his great *derashot,* the laws of mourning involve self-judgment, the experience of deep guilt, and repentance; that is why the Laws of Mourning are in so many ways similar to those of Yom Kippur, which is the day of guilt-feeling *par excellence.*

But would that justify an "outsider" who visits the mourners to berate them, blame them for their grief, and enumerate their sins? So, such self-critical experiences as we are undertaking are exercises in moral and spiritual growth, and no non-participant may use them to point a finger and cast aspersions upon those who indulge in such commendable self-criticism. Would that they undertake a similar course of introspection.

In a sense, this communal self-judgment is based upon the assumption that we affirm a "double standard." We Jews have grown up through the centuries to know that we are and must be different; that for us there are certain things that, as the Yiddish expression goes, *"es past nisht far a Yid"*—that are not appropriate, not suitable, even unthinkable for a Jew. Indeed, that is the essential content of the concept of Jews as "the Chosen People."

> R. Chananiah b. Akashya said: The Holy One desired to grant merit *(le'zakkot)* to Israel, therefore He gave them a copious Torah and many mitzvot. (Mishnah *Makkot* 3:16)

Note that the word *le'zakkot* means not only to give merit or privilege *(zekhut),* but also purification (from *zakh*). Moral purity and probity in Judaism are incompatible with thoughtlessness, insensitivity, and careless language—let alone murder—even if such conduct is tolerated or expected in other cultures or subcultures.

Hence, *even if the assassination had never taken place,* we should still learn some enduring lessons from the excessive rhetoric that we have too patiently tolerated in the past. But certainly must we do so now that this insufferable and unspeakable crime has been committed.

> Raba (some say, R. Chisda) says: If a man sees that painful sufferings visit him, let him examine his conduct . . . If he examines and finds nothing [objectionable], let him attribute it to the neglect of the study of the Torah. (*Berakhot* 5a)

And what is it that our painful self-examination has discovered? That indeed we sinned in neglecting the study of Torah. And the Torah we failed to learn is in two areas: one, in Tanakh itself, namely, "The words of the wise [are] spoken in quiet" (Eccl. 9:27—and that, therefore, people—whether laymen or rabbis—who shout and clamor forfeit their claim to wisdom . . .) and second, in the Mishnah (*Avot* 1:11):

> Avtalion used to say: Sages, be careful with your words, lest you be condemned to exile and you be exiled to a place of evil waters, and the disciples who follow you drink and die, with the result that the Name of Heaven becomes profaned.

Let us speak the truth: the Amirs and the Goldsteins did not invent their depraved justifications for murder out of thin air. It is true that they were *weeds* in our garden; but they were weeds in *our* garden. The atmosphere in certain quarters was heavy with viciousness and intolerance. There were rabbis who took it upon themselves to speculate aloud and carelessly on life-and-death issues for a whole state, a whole people. They proclaimed that any other opinions are a violation of Torah. They arrogated to themselves the right to throw around, casually, carelessly, and with abandon, such terms as *rodef* and *moser* ("pursuer" and "informer"—both capital offenses) without the hoary, traditional disclaimer *le'fi aniyut daati*, "in my *humble* opinion," or *ilulei de'mistafina*, a phrase of modest hesitation which is standard fare in halakhic responsa of any kind. Is it a wonder that young people, barely out of adolescence and at the mercy of their boiling hormones, extrapolated from it and acted out the consequences?

I know, I know—it has been argued that words are only words, and you cannot blame criminal action upon mere rhetoric. Well, legally you can't, but morally you can! Because if you cannot *blame* words for maiming and humiliating and degrading, then you also cannot *credit* words with encouraging noble actions, expressing love, and promoting heroic achievement. And if that is so, all speech is but static, all communication mere clamor and without consequence, and we humans had best learn to shut our mouths and teach and say nothing at all—and thus be no better or wiser than dumb animals . . .

If our experience of *teshuvah* is to be real and effective, we must ask ourselves a series of exceedingly important questions. They have been teasing and troubling me for a long time, but since the assassination they have assumed more ominous proportions. I offer six questions, and either leave it at that or sketch some preliminary thoughts on the way to a fuller treatment. These include:

1. Is the territorial integrity of "Greater Israel" one of those commandments which must be observed even under pain of death? The last I heard, there were only three such, and the territorial integrity of Israel, or "Greater Israel," was not one of them . . .

Furthermore: There has been much talk of the prohibition of turning over even a square inch of "Greater Israel" to the Palestinians. But this contradicts an explicit teaching of the Torah. In I Kings 9:11 we read of Solomon turning over twenty towns to Hiram, King of Tyre, as a gift to the pagan king; thus: "then king Solomon gave Hiram twenty cities in the land of Galilee"—and not a whisper in the Bible or in the Talmud or Midrash criticizing him for it! Moreover, Hiram wasn't pleased by this gift because the twenty cities were sandy and sterile! In II Chronicles 8:2 we read that Hiram gave Solomon twenty towns—and of the commentators, only Ralbag complains that it was improper for King Solomon to give away territory of Eretz Israel, but he concedes that an *exchange* of territory was quite kosher. The other commentators, such as Malbim, say that Solomon sent in Jewish labor to make the land fertile and then gave the produce to Hiram; but no protest against giving away an inch of "Greater Israel!"

Let us assume one will make every effort to answer the question in some sophisticated way. Is such abstract, theoretical discourse enough to warrant attacking the government with such truculent speeches and savage rhetoric? As the Rav taught us, *pulling any one mitzvah out of context and absolutizing it beyond all others is "avodah zarah,"* sheer idolatry!

2. Who has the right to *"pasken"* halakhic decisions for *kelal Yisrael,* all the Jewish people?—a Chief Rabbi? a community Rabbi? a pulpit Rabbi or a Rosh Yeshiva or a High School Rebbe? Which one of the above would offer a firm halakhic decision *(pesak)* on a microwave oven without expert advice on its physics? And which of the above, therefore, is so proficient in *Realpolitik* and international affairs and military strategy that he can *"pasken"* such issues without hesitation from the comfort of his office or classroom? Clearly, someone who is unqualified and yet passes judgment on such fateful issues must stand accused of endangering all of Israel by a wrongful and arrogant assumption of infallibility, and he will have to answer for the consequences before the Almighty Himself in the Heavenly Court, where every person is forced to confront his own conscience.

3. Indeed, do we have the material with which to issue halakhic judgments affecting the whole of our people, considering the paucity of halakhic literature on such subjects? There are hundreds, thousands, of halakhic tomes on subjects such as the mixture of milk and meat, non-kosher foods, divorces, judicial and other such matters, but hardly anything on the conduct of war according to Halakha—or even the question of "territories" in contemporary times . . .

I am deeply convinced that the attempt to *over-apply* Halakha to situations where our ignorance exceeds our commitment can only damage the reputation of Torah and cause a desecration of Torah and the good name of Judaism—*chilul shem Shamayim.*

4. Do halakhic precepts that obtain for normal, individual or communal life, also apply, in the same way, to national life?

Let me offer one example of misapplied Halakha: the Halakha of *ein dochin nefesh mi-penei nefesh,* that one may not give preference to one life above another (but must follow the natural sequence) is an expression of the Torah's law and ethics regarding a birth which threatens the life of the mother (Mishnah *Ohalot* 7:6). If a woman is in difficult labor such that a choice must be made between her life and the life of the child, then the rule applies: one may not set aside one life for another. Thus, if the baby is yet unborn, it may be killed, dismembered, and withdrawn.

But if most of the baby has emerged from the womb, the same principle applies, and then result is the reverse—the child's life may not be sacrificed for that of the mother.

Now, a distinguished rabbi has applied this principle to the political situation, namely, we may not jeopardize anyone's life now in order to save many lives later. Hence, we may not put the lives of citizens at risk of being murdered by Hamas, or endanger the lives of the settlers, now in order to avoid a nuclear confrontation with Iran or Iraq later on; such a policy is "anti-Torah," and therefore such risk-taking is tantamount to complicity in murder.

Is that really so? Yes, that is correct *only* when deciding a medical question before us. It does not apply to the laws of *war and peace*. Proof comes to us from the Talmud (*Shevuot* 35b): Samuel said: A government which kills only one out of six is not punished. And the *Hatam Sofer* (Responsa, to *Orach Chaim*, I, 208) adds that this refers not only to a *milchemet reshut*, a "permissible war" for which approval was granted by the Sanhedrin, but even to a war which the king or government considered important for reasons of prestige and standing. Without such permission, a general could probably be punished for sending out a reconnaissance group on a dangerous mission; and a democratic government certainly has the right to take risks now in order to save the entire people later. The law of *ein dochin nefesh mi-penei nefesh* simply does not apply to a government.

5. Further, which *halakhot* that we do have clearly apply only in Messianic times? Are we so sure that all halakhot that deal with borders and national and international affairs are meant for our contemporary, non-Messianic reality?

6. Which brings us to the next step: is Religious Zionism inextricably tied to the Messianic assumption, that of *at'chalta di-geulah*, the "beginning of the redemption?" Or can it function, perhaps more successfully, without the benefits of Messianic fervor, but also without its negative consequences?

Such a reassessment involves more than style or civility or even proper halakhic methodology. Our current ideology is based upon the assumption that we are living in Messianic or pre-Messianic times, and that halakhically and politically that must be a major factor in our thinking and attitude. Hence we must seriously confront *the* axiom of the nationalist right of our national-religious camp, and we must ask deep, probing questions about the nature of Religious Zionism.

My feeling is that classical Religious Zionism was tragically sidetracked after the euphoria of 1967 and linked to an extreme form of nationalism (i.e., territorialism) of which the elder Rav Kook would not have approved. I was disturbed by Gush Emunim from the very beginning. I admired them—and still do—but their ideology and self-certainty scared me. I should have talked up more. When I did talk and write (in a *Tradition* symposium shortly after the Six-Day War), about my "Messianic agnosticism"—by which I mean that we can't, as mere humans, identify our exact location in the grand divine plan of redemption, that it may or may not be *at'chalta di-geulah*—many of my colleagues and friends were dismayed. But I should not have been dissuaded.

Look at what we have lost as a result of our smug certainty that we are experiencing, as the phrase in our Prayer for the State of Israel goes, *reshit tzemichat geulatenu*—"the beginning of the flowering of redemption": we have become wedded to the concept of "Greater Israel," and consequently lost control of the Ministries of Education and of Religion, so that these two highly critical portfolios are now held by people who either know little about the subject or are inimical to Judaism. We have lost influence in government, in society, and in the world at large. And we are looked upon—unfairly, it is true—as wild-eyed fanatics who are anti-democratic and a danger to the future of the State. And the settlers—idealistic, self-sacrificing pioneers, the flower of our people—are now suffering a cognitive dissonance as their Messianic ideals unravel before their eyes. I maintain that it was not and is not worth it.

It is because I so identify with Religious Zionism and am so proud of its brilliant record of achievement on behalf of the People and Land and Torah of Israel, that I believe that it is time to reassess the tendency to evaluate all current events through the Messianic prism—*without* at all yielding a single iota of the belief in *biat ha-mashiach be'khol yom she'yavo,* for the latter phrase means, quite literally, *whenever* Messiah comes, and not necessarily that all that is happening this very day is related to his imminent arrival.

The Talmud relates:

> R. Zera, whenever he chanced upon scholars engaged in calculating the time of the Messiah's coming, would say to them: I beg of you, do not postpone it (i.e., Messiah's coming) for it has been taught: Three come unawares: Messiah, a found article, and a scorpion. (*Sanhedrin* 97a)

The best way to have the Messiah come is—by not talking about him overmuch, by not forcing his hand, as it were, by not transforming faith into hysteria, by not assuming that our impatience will influence him to come before the time that the Creator has set for him—but by proceeding with normal life while entertaining the quiet but powerful hope that he come soon.

Too many of us find it easy to scoff at the runaway Messianism of Lubavitch, but turn a deaf ear and blind eye to our own romantic notions of incipient Messianism; and both types of over-eager anticipation of the "end of days" can lead us—has led us—into deep crisis. And we are sufficiently sophisticated to know the tragic historic events which confirm my fears for the future.

These are some of the serious questions that beg to be discussed—seriously, soberly, softly, and without sloganeering. And if the answers offered are concise, clear, crisp, and uncomplicated—you may be quite sure they are crude and misguided, just plain wrong. *Do not trust them!* Life is complex. It is filled with paradox, riddled with ambiguity, suffused with subtlety and nuance, and simplistic answers are dangerously misleading. Never must we entrust our national lives or treasure in the hands of people with primitive perspectives.

Until we are much, much surer of ourselves in correctly interpreting the Halakha, I would prefer that the political debate on Oslo I and II proceed *without* involving Halakha. Bring "proof" to your point of view, if you wish, from interpreting a Biblical verse, or citing a Midrash, or a *"gut vort"*—all of which represent a rather free and non-coercive use of sacred sources and speak of Jewish values in a general sense, but do not invoke the decision-making authority of Halakha. To use Halakha to buttress a political "line" skirts the very dangerous area of *megaleh panim be'Torah she'lo ke'halakhah,* of improper manipulation of the Halakha.

So, at the occasion of this memorial for the late Yitzhak Rabin, we experience regret, deep and soul-shattering and painful regret, at the murder of this Jewish leader whom some of us knew and admired personally; and deep dejection and aching sorrow at the *chilul Hashem,* at our special chagrin that this shameful and blasphemous act was committed and abetted by products of our kind of education.

The time is right for us to begin talking in our schools about tolerance and *derekh eretz* and extremism and respect for dissent and xenophobia and genuine love of Israel and love of humanity and democracy—yes, democracy. I deny utterly the dogmatic assertion by the Kahane followers that Judaism and democracy are irreconcilable—and the announcement by a Labor Party Member of Knesset, equally undistinguished, to the same effect, from the opposite vantage point.

Now the time has come for peace and reconciliation. After almost every terrorist attack in Israel, the government said that it must not be allowed to stop the peace process between Israel and the Arabs. The same reasoning must apply to our situation. This damnable act must not be allowed to ignite, Heaven forbid, a civil war, an uncontrollable *Kulturkampf,* and hatred between Jew and Jew. There must be a *berit shalom,* a covenant of peace, in the corpus of world Jewry, and the leitmotif must be: "[The Torah's] ways are the ways of pleasantness, and all her paths are peace" (Proverbs 3:17).

We have spoken about Israel, about the Diaspora, about Judaism and Orthodoxy and education. But at bottom lies the tragedy of one single man, one distinctive, special, brave soldier and visionary statesman who, whether you agreed with his policies or not, whether you liked him or not, was a living, breathing, sentient, father and husband and grandfather as well as a dynamic and historic leader of Israel. It is a personal tragedy as well as a collective one.

We bow our heads in commiseration with Yitzhak Rabin's family. Perhaps most appropriate, and with only minor paraphrasing, are the eloquent words Abraham Lincoln wrote to Mrs. Lydia Bixby, a grieving mother who lost five sons on the field of battle:

> I feel how weak and fruitless must be any words of mine which should attempt to beguile you from the grief of a loss so over-

> whelming. But I cannot refrain from tendering to you the consolation that may be found in the thanks of the Republic they died to save.
>
> I pray that our Heavenly Father may assuage the anguish of your bereavement, and leave you only the cherished memory of the loved and lost, and the solemn pride that must be yours, to have laid so costly a sacrifice upon the altar of freedom.

Tehei nishmato tzerurah bi'tzeror ha-chayyim.

"May his soul be bound up in the bond of eternal life."

~ 52 ~

AFTER THE RABIN ASSASSINATION

Where Do We Go from Here?

The Questions:

1. Given the divisions within the Jewish people today, what is there that can serve as the basis for Jewish peoplehood? What can be done to strengthen the sense of a common Jewish destiny?

2. The assassination demonstrates that incendiary words can lead to even more incendiary deeds. What can the Jewish community do—both in Israel and the Diaspora—to ensure that freedom of expression stops short of the demonization of the opposition?

3. There are those who believe that Jewish religious teachings at times conflict with the principles of democracy in a Jewish state. If so, what steps can be taken to prevent each from seeking to delegitimate the other?

1. From the very beginning of Jewish history, with the emergence of Abraham, three elements were intertwined: an Idea, a People, and a Land. The Idea was ethical monotheism, later incorporated in Torah; the People was the "seed of Abraham"; and the Land was Eretz Israel. We were able to survive without the third, but only so long as we recognized that we were in "exile" in every place outside the Land.

Our situation today is unprecedented. Israelis have a Land, but very little of a common Idea, and increasingly tenuous connections with a People. Diaspora Jewry, especially American Jewry, is highly ambivalent about the Land as well. This means that our fragmentation is far advanced. I am therefore not at all sanguine about the future cohesiveness of *am yisrael*. Nevertheless, we must exert every effort to get a maximum number of Jews to share a sense of peoplehood and common destiny.

The following are my responses to questions posed at a symposium organized by the American Jewish Committee and published by the Committee in January 1996

The unraveling of the fabric of Jewish identity began with the Emancipation and has accelerated since. When there was at least a minimal standard for Jewishness (the halakhic norm that a Jew is one born to a Jewish mother) that was accepted by almost all groups, religious or secular, one could hope to unite the People around an identity rooted in reality, in this case a biological one—not dissimilar to the statement that a Frenchman is one born in or who lives in France, a geographical reality. However, with the current abandonment of this "reality rooted" identity in favor of a completely, or almost completely, voluntaristic one, as advanced by the adoption of patrilinealism by the Reform movement and by certain decisions of the Israeli judiciary, the common basis for Jewish peoplehood becomes more and more remote.

Can some compromise be found? A basically voluntaristic standard for Jewish peoplehood that stands some chance of successfully holding most of us together can best be achieved by searching for a common strand that can best pass the "reality test," i.e., that is least dependent upon opinion or ideology or whim. Such a strand is—our collective memory. If most of us Jews no longer share basic assumptions about the great questions of life and faith, we at least share a past. History and literature therefore become critical in defining the basis for Jewish peoplehood. But these must be pursued passionately, with focused attention, and not merely asserted. And whatever other shreds of commonality remain with us should be protected and enhanced as well.

Thus, there must be a reintroduction of Jews to the classics of their own great literature, from the Bible down. All Jewish groups and "denominations" can teach Jewish history, no matter how much their interpretations may differ. More Jews must learn Hebrew or at least be exposed to it. We should restore the use of the classical Jewish calendar alongside the conventional secular calendar. We should continue to work for wider acceptance of the "Israel experience" (the ultimate success of which will depend on the follow-up when the young people return to their homes, and also on to what and whom they will be exposed while they are in Israel). Every Jew should be given and use a Hebrew name in addition to, if not in place of, his or her English or any other non-Hebrew name. We should create a minimum Jewish library for every Jewish home.

But ultimately, all such efforts rest upon the foundation of a genuine attempt to create mass Jewish education in Israel and the Diaspora. Nothing less than a "Marshall Plan" is needed, something on the scale, relatively, of the Manhattan Project. The "Jewish continuity" movement so far has been more in the nature of goodwill gestures, and that will not save us. A minimum Jewish education will include what we all share as Jews, such as history and literature; what should be common to all Jews, such as language and other cultural artifacts; and teaching those things which some Jews hold dear but which all Jews need to know about and respect even if they disagree.

2. Mutual recriminations among various groups accomplish nothing, and, indeed, are counterproductive. Rather, each group must undergo the process of *cheshbon ha-nefesh,* such as is now being undertaken by modern Orthodox Jews in Israel and the United States. (Wouldn't it be refreshing if every movement and organization in Jewish life would announce, before every Yom Kippur, the results of its internal stock-taking along with a list of its errors and the plans to correct them—instead of the immodest boasting of its "accomplishments?" We do believe in the Messiah. . . .)

3. A distinction must be made between two levels: the practical or political issue which affects the State of Israel, and the ideological question, which affects religion-minded Jews the world over. With regard to the latter, those who are committed to democracy (and that includes the overwhelming majority of all religious as well as non-religious Jews) must appreciate that democracy is a political system and not a metaphysical or theological construct, and that religious people do—and are entitled to—believe in higher purposes that transcend political interests or values. It is when Judaism is taken as a political system, and when democracy is treated as if it were a religion, that the conflicts become unavoidable and the systems irreconcilable. I assume, therefore, that we are being asked about the former rather than the latter.

First, it must be made clear that American democracy is not the only valid form of democracy—something most Americans are unaware of—and that other versions of democracy leave more ample room for religious expression by the society. Second, there is a large degree of commonality between democratic values and Jewish teaching. This should be researched objectively and honestly, with scholarly rectitude, and it should not sound or be apologetic. There is no need to prove that Judaism is more democratic than the American constitution; it is not necessary that every pronouncement of the ACLU or other such groups be considered critical to the existence of democracy such that Judaism must be reconciled with it. The sources for such Jewish teachings are not only Scripture and Talmud, but, even more to the point and more practically, the organization of Jewish communities in the Middle Ages in Central and Western Europe (the late Professor Irving Agus of Yeshiva University did important spadework in this area). The results of such efforts, both scholarly and popular, should be widely disseminated. Third, where they diverge, religious Jews should understand that not all Jewish doctrine is meant to be applied in all historical circumstances, and that Judaism can accommodate itself to less than ideal circumstances—as it has done successfully throughout much of its history. At the same time, other Jews should appreciate that a great deal of the polemic surrounding religion in Israel is fundamentally *cultural* rather than political, and they too must make accommodations and not expect that all Jews must assimilate to vulgar standards of American culture as the dominant political culture either in Israel or in the Jewish communities of the Diaspora.

~ 53 ~

LATVIAN JEWRY

A Lesson in Diaspora-Israel relations

Latvian Jewry suffered horribly during the Holocaust, the Latvians outdoing even the Nazis in their bestiality. Only one of the 18 major synagogues and 43 *shteiblech* and small congregations of the prewar years remains.

Survivors are trying desperately to rebuild Jewish life out of the dying embers of what once was a proud, thriving, dynamic community. In this they are supported by the SHAMIR organization, ably represented by Prof. Reuven Ferber of the Latvian University and Prof. Herman Branover of Ben-Gurion University.

Why don't they simply come to Israel?

A two-day conference on "Jews in a Changing World," held recently in the capital of Riga, pointed in the direction of an answer, raising many warning signals about Israel-Diaspora relations.

Sponsored by the Memorial Foundation for Jewish Culture and initiated by Latvia's Chief Rabbi, Nathan Barchan, this was the first post-USSR international conference of Jewish academics from the CIS and Baltic states to discuss Jewish problems in the region openly. Regional media coverage was wide.

It was impressive to hear participants, who included distinguished non-Jewish academics as well as the Latvian premier, wrestle with the dilemma of East European Jewry: cultural integration versus national identity.

One speaker, a man who appeared to be in his late 60s, asked: How can local Jews just pick up and go to Israel, abandoning the community of their fathers and forefathers? The emotion was sincere and authentic.

The answer is obvious: It is the same logic that kept Jews in Latvia (and elsewhere) in the first place.

The death in the Holocaust of 80 percent of Latvia's Jewish population is sober refutation of such misplaced sentiment. Yet somehow, the message of the rebirth of Israel has not, after al-

---

Originally published under a different title in the Jerusalem Post, *October 12, 1995.*

most 50 years of statehood, reached this very intelligent but confused man.

PARTICIPANTS CONCERNED WITH the Jewish survival of their children and grandchildren seemed to understand the importance of Jewish education.

So why not bring the youngsters to Israel, where they can thrive in a "normal" Jewish environment?

This evoked a disturbing question: What guarantee is there that my children will grow up Jewish in a country where Canaanism is on the rise and education in Judaism on the wane?

Latvian Jews have met many Israelis who inspire them. They are especially fond of Tova Herzl, Israel's ambassador in Riga. But they are frightened by Israelis who seem to be devoid of any Jewishness.

Jews in Riga are in touch with what is going on. They know about the erosion of Jewish awareness among young Israelis, about the split between "Judaism" and "Israelism," and they are spooked by the specter of deracination that emerges from the miasma of Meretz proclamations. They are fearful of America's cultural influence on Israel. "If we want a decadent American culture, we can go to America," they say.

Emotions such as these threaten to grow in importance as polarization within Israel intensifies.

Our political leaders are too preoccupied to pay attention to such matters. Moreover, they may be part of the problem. But someone, somehow, must take the lead in reversing this cultural decline and assimilation in the skewed values of mindless Americanism.

Israel and world Jewry alike owe it to themselves, as well as to the struggling remnants of once proud Jewish communities in countries only recently independent, to resurrect and revitalize the grand vision of Israel as a center of Jewish culture and spiritual inspiration.

It won't be easy—but nothing of value was ever achieved without a struggle. *Le'fum tza'ara agra,* as the Mishna taught. Or, as the saying goes: "No pain, no gain."

~ 54 ~

REFLECTIONS ON ISRAEL AT 50

Only one who was born before the 1948 declaration of the State of Israel and is old enough to remember those bitter years of the Holocaust, can *truly* appreciate the meaning of the Jewish state in its most immediate and elementary sense. For those under the age of 60 or 70, the evaluation of the State and its significance will always and of necessity be somewhat incomplete. History learned is not the same as history lived.

This does not mean that the Holocaust exhausts the importance of Israel either as a divine gift and intercession in history or as a new political entity. Nor does it mean that those born after statehood was established cannot understand or are not permitted to expound on its ideological or theological place in the hierarchy of Jewish values. It does mean that beyond all religious, political, or social views on Israel, there is a deep, visceral, gut feeling that is existential and experiential and that cannot be successfully transmitted in the idioms of speech or any ordinary communication. One cannot appreciate the renewal of life unless and until he has stared the Angel of Death in the eye or, at least, felt on his face the wind of the passing Destroyer as he was abroad in the land.

This introduction is necessary if these impressions are to be, as has been requested of me, "personal reflections." My views of Israel, then, come against a background of one who as a youngster heard over the radio the depraved ranting of Hitler announcing the *Anschluss* of Austria and the anti-Semitic, pro-Nazi sermons of Father Coughlin; who read Ford's obscene attacks against Jews; who met the first refugees from the European genocide and could not believe that the horror stories they told were possible; who recalls the *New York Post* headline, when returning from high school, announcing the number of martyrs as 6 million, and so on. I therefore grew up with a sinking feeling in the pit of my stomach that we American Jews were next on Hitler's list of extinction, that I and my parents and brother and sisters were can-

---

From Commentator, *the Yeshiva College student newspaper, in 1998.*

didates for the concentration camps and for a premature death. I even remember, with cruel clarity, the serious discussions in my family as to whether suicide should be seriously entertained if the Nazis invaded and conquered America.

For me, all the theoretical discussions about Israel pale beside this elementary fact that had we Jews had a state we might well have escaped the unspeakable tragedy of the Holocaust. That is why when, in May 1948, a few classmates from Yeshiva College and I went to work in a clandestine laboratory in upstate New York developing a rocket bullet for the young state's as yet non-existent armament industry, we felt it was the only way we could respond to the exterminations and the threats in a helpful and dignified manner. We didn't sing patriotic songs, we didn't debate theological issues, we didn't ask if our Israeli scientist supervisors were *Datiim* or Socialists; we were, all of us, Jews who might well have been one of the statistics but now could express ourselves as Jews—any kind of Jews.

This historical fact itself has religious significance. If an individual is saved from death he is required to offer a *birkhat hagomel,* and if his salvation was miraculous he must celebrate the anniversary of his deliverance thereafter as his personal "Purim." Certainly and halakhically a whole people that has emerged from the depths of despair to new hope must express thanks to the Almighty—without caviling about any necessary Messianic dimensions. We have no precise information as to what if any links exist between the *yeshuat am yisrael* we experienced with the creation of the State of Israel and the coming of *Mashiach.* I, therefore, am skeptical as to the appropriateness of the whole *at'chalta di'geulah* school and I do not recite the words *reishit tzemichat geulatenu,* in the "official" Prayer for the State of Israel. I neither confirm nor deny the Messianic nature of our redemption. That is for God to say and for Him to reveal when He will so will it. It is enough for me that this was the state founded for the broken shards of our people, and that had we only had it earlier . . .

Of course I regret the secular domination of public life in Israel. I would much prefer that its Jewish character be more pronounced—provided that could be done voluntarily. I am against "coercion" except for the most basic elements of national cohesiveness, such as a single standard for entry into Jewish peoplehood. Other than that, political-legal coercion has brought us more grief than joy.

I do not believe that nationalism—Zionism, in our case—exhausts the content of Judaism or is even the chief guarantee of Jewish continuity. I equally reject the thesis that it is "treif," that is, somehow antithetical to the values of Torah. It is enough for me that it was instrumental in establishing the state founded for the broken shards of our people, and that had we only had it earlier . . .

I am not blind to some of the uglier aspects of Israeli life which have surfaced this past half century in various sectors of the country whether in the secularist circles or, as well, in Orthodox life, including Religious Zionism with which I identify as a movement although not as a political party. I am troubled by the directions taken by various groups in Israel. But no matter—they are all my family and I will stand by them through thick and thin, and I will celebrate with them, drink a *le'chayim* to them on the "golden wedding" occasion, and reaffirm to them openly and joyously my love and my fealty and my undiminished gratitude.

Why? Because, to repeat: It is enough for me that this was the state founded for the broken shards of our people, and that had we only had it earlier . . . *Oh, if only we had had it earlier!*

~ 55 ~

THE JEWISH STATE

The Next 50 Years

I proceed on the premise that Israel should be a Jewish state and not merely a state of the Jews. This assumption is no longer self-understood. Thus, there has been much talk recently, especially by some leftist intellectuals, about radically changing the emerging collective character of the state to make it thoroughly secularist by, among other things, doing away with "Hatikva," abolishing the Law of Return, abrogating all "religious legislation," and disestablishing the official rabbinate—all this as befitting the new "post-Zionist" period.

Let us put the problem in biblical perspective. The Torah speaks of God's three covenants: with Noah, with Abraham, and with Moses. The first was the covenant with humanity at large—the universal dimension of Judaism. The second was with Abraham and his posterity. Here the Almighty promised to be the God of the Children of Abraham and vouchsafed to them their perpetuity as a people, and the Land of Israel. The third was the Torah itself—the full range of religious obligations and spiritual privileges incumbent upon Jews by virtue of their birth into the people of Israel. It is understood that each successive covenant included that which preceded it. Thus, to be a Jew in the fullest sense, one must be committed not only to the laws of the Torah but, as well, to Israel—people and land—and to all humanity, as part of the unique covenantal commitment to the Creator.

From this point of view, a Jew who lives ethically and morally, but is divorced from the Jewish community and the Land of Israel, is a good human being but a poor Jew. One who adds to this his national-ethnic loyalties as a Jew is still an incomplete Jew. And one who observes the commandments but fails to identify with his people and homeland, or is delinquent as a moral human being—is doing the unthinkable. Such a Jew, who observes the covenant of Moses but betrays his obligations under the national and the universal covenants, is living a contradiction.

This appeared in the Israeli publication, Azure, *Winter 5759/1999*

Complications, however, arise when transposing from the individual to the state and society. To put it into modern terms, a state that does not abide by the Noahide (that is, universal) covenant is not a civilized state, for that covenant implies the security of its citizens and their fundamental human rights. The Abrahamic, or national-ethnic, covenant includes such things as culture, history, traditions and the whole array of public life and discourse—all of which unify a people and make it distinct from other political-cultural entities. The Mosaic covenant addresses not only laws but the spirit as well, and because it requires will as well as conduct, it is primarily addressed to individuals. Individuals may or may not accept upon themselves this third covenant, but to insist that the collectivity do so regardless of the will of the majority of its citizens implies a degree of coercion that contradicts the fundamentally voluntaristic nature of the Mosaic covenant (based, as it is, upon freedom of the will) and is inconsistent with the democratic nature of the modern state. Note that this limitation issues not primarily from any political theory, whether that of democracy or any other, but is immanent in the nature of the Mosaic covenant, which addresses the heart and mind and will of individuals: "I have set before you life and death, blessing and curse: therefore choose life, that both you and your seed shall live" (Deuteronomy 30:19). To choose means that I must choose, out of freedom, and without any external compulsion. It is only when the great majority of the society accepts upon itself the obligations of this covenant that it applies in large measure to the state as well. Until such time, the state must refrain from imposing any transcendent or metaphysical vision upon its citizens.

Applying these criteria to the State of Israel, two consequences follow: First, that it must abide by the Abrahamic covenant, that which gives it its national character; and second, that it must not force upon its citizens the Mosaic covenant.

It is here that a good deal of analytic and sensitive disentanglement becomes critical. Where does culture end and religion begin? What is the boundary between national traditions and Halakha? What, in other words, is Abrahamic and what is Mosaic?

Of one thing I am not at all in doubt, and that is that the call by the apostles of post-Zionism is nothing more than the old Canaanite dish warmed over. Its program of dejudaization of Israel is a recipe for national disaster. A number of years ago I was invited to address a seminar of the World Union of Jewish Students in Helsinki. At the main session, a leading proponent of these ideas declared that he was not a Jew, but a member of the Hebrew nation. "You are a French national," he said to no one in particular, "and you are an English national, and you"—pointing to me—"are an American national. I am a Hebrew national." My response was more or less this: "Mr. A., in the country I come from, 'Hebrew National' is the name of a firm that manufactures kosher baloney, and while what you are proposing is baloney, I am certain it isn't kosher."

With a modicum of good will on all sides, abjuring baloney whether kosher or non-kosher, and keeping the extremes marginalized, the problem is not insoluble. The state must be culturally Jewish. True, Jewish culture is deeply bound up with religion, and the excision of all religious dimensions results in a truncated and anomalous culture. But it is possible—and has proven so for most of the state's fifty years—to develop a Jewish national character without overly interfering in the life and happiness of individual citizens. The secular majority must agree that it abides by the Abrahamic covenant, while the religious segment must declare that despite its profound commitment to the Mosaic covenant, it will not seek to impose it by law on the rest of the population. Kashrut in the army and all public institutions does not curb the freedom of or interfere with the private lives of individual Israelis, so long as the conduct of their own kitchens is outside the realm of Israeli law. The Sabbath as a day of rest for the Israeli public is a legitimate expression of the Abrahamic covenant, while insisting on imposing Mosaic-halakhic Shabbat restrictions on individuals is beyond the competence of government. The Bar-Ilan Street imbroglio in Jerusalem should not and need not become the symbol of despair in resolving the often thorny issues of locating the borderlines between the two realms. As in every society, there must be a degree of "give and take" in order to establish criteria that everyone can live with, and in order that no one be able to impose unconditional surrender on the other.

The second consequence for the State of Israel—that of refraining from imposing the Mosaic covenant—implies that if the concept of the Abrahamic covenant is accepted by Israel, the religious groups must agree to refrain from most religious legislation. It is clear to me that were it not for the legislation fought for by the Religious Zionist groups early in the state's life, Israel today would be totally deracinated and unrecognizable as a Jewish entity. They established the stream of national-religious education, along with so much else of what is now recognized as the underpinning of the Jewish character of the state. But further legislation at this juncture can only prove counterproductive. Religious Jews must be sensitive to the feelings—justified or unjustified—of large numbers of citizens and act accordingly. They must also be aware of the anomaly of numbers of their fellow Orthodox Jews who do not recognize the legitimacy of the state and yet make demands upon it.

The knottiest question of all is that of "personal status" legislation—marriage, divorce, and conversion. Here the private and the public merge, because the prospect of prohibited intermarriage among Jews is daunting. The lives and happiness of our children and their children for generations to come are at stake. Hence, while I hope that the most lenient decisions of Halakha will prevail, I am well aware of the limits placed on the interpreters of Halakha. Rabbis, unlike parliamentarians, are not free to legislate their wishes untrammeled by law and precedent. These three items, therefore, should be considered as Abrahamic rather than Mosaic, insofar as the state is concerned.

Finally, there should be no misunderstanding as to the ultimate aspiration of religious Jews. Assent to the proposition that the Mosaic covenant should not be imposed by coercion on the country does not by any means imply that religiously observant Jews do not care about other Jews, or that they despair of the acceptance by all Jews of Torah and Halakha. It does mean that all the efforts that, for the first half-century of Israel's existence, went into religious legislation must now go into education in the broadest sense, so that ultimately all Jews will return to Judaism—the *teshuvat ha-tzibbur* ("repentance of the public") for which every truly religious Jew hopes and strives. This aspiration remains one of the pillars of the Messianic redemption. But until he comes, we must make do with aspiration and inspiration, not legislation.

Chapter 10

THE HOLOCAUST

The four entries in this chapter all deal with one or another aspect of the horrendous cataclysm that afflicted our people in the twentieth century. The first deals with teaching the Holocaust and questions related to it.

The second and third are essentially ruminations, both personal and ideological, about the Holocaust. The first of the two ponders whether or not it is better to keep silent or to speak of the Holocaust, and the second—the role of the Holocaust remembrance and the need to perpetuate the story of our people through education.

Finally, on a more practical and halakhic level, I offer my opinions on the troubling question of the compensation owed to victims and survivors by the offending governments, and the proper method of distribution of such compensation.

~ 56 ~

TEACHING THE HOLOCAUST

Last year we celebrated the 30th anniversary of the liberation, marking the end of World War II. This means that a whole new generation has grown into adulthood not having known of the Holocaust from first-hand experience. For them, it is part of history. It is for this generation, and for all future generations, that the teaching of the Holocaust assumes special significance and presents new problems. "History" does have a tendency to tilt backwards into obsolescence and dissolve into irrelevance, and its most poignant lessons thus become lost to us.

Yet, in a way, I wonder if it is not too soon to relegate the Holocaust to the past. I question if we have the right to consider the Holocaust as "history."

In some subtle ways, the Holocaust seems to be open-ended, and hence not over yet. Many of the consequences of that single traumatic event in Jewish history are still being played out, and it is likely that the history of the next 20 or 50 years will have to be interpreted as reactions, even if long delayed, to the Holocaust. One may legitimately interpret the data of contemporary Jewish events as a radically different form of Holocaust, but Holocaust nonetheless. The rate of intermarriage and wholesale assimilation, despite the minor eddies and counter-currents in the direction of more intensive Jewish practice, are a gloomy indication of the truth of what I am saying. Moreover, we have not paid sufficient attention to "ZPG" (Zero Population Growth), a situation which is making the number of Jews in the world ever smaller relative to world population in general. While the rest of the world has been increasing, Jews have been decreasing. In effect, we are now confronted with the problem of a "preventive Holocaust," by which I mean, not the murder of Jews already alive, but the prevention of Jews from being born. It is less cruel to individuals, of course, but is equally destructive of the Jewish people as a whole.

Based upon an address at the National Convention of the Union of Orthodox Congregations in 1974 and published in 1976.

More directly, we cannot yet relax in considering a repetition of the genocide of 30 years ago. The events of recent years, with the ever more ominous threats of isolation and annihilation directed against Israel, and with other nations standing by as "neutrals," instinctively raises up ghosts of 30 years ago. Once again Israel is being abandoned as it faces overwhelming odds. A Holocaust that happened once can happen again. Once breached, the walls of human restraint remain weakened. The demons know their way . . . All the more reason for sending our children forewarned and forearmed—and teaching them about the Holocaust.

IT IS WITH this in mind that I address myself to the question of teaching the Holocaust. I do so not as a historian and not as a philosopher, but as an educator. We must determine how best to go about transmitting to new generations of Jews what happened to our people that almost made it impossible for Jews ever to survive on this planet.

The transmission of the teaching of the Holocaust comes in two modes: celebration and education.

By "celebration" I mean the memorializing of the martyrs of the Holocaust by means of religious devotion. Certainly this ought to include special Yizkor prayers when Yizkor is recited. In my synagogue I have also adopted a custom initiated by some Israeli synagogues, that of standing for *Av Ha-rachamim* (Father of Mercies), the memorial prayer which is recited during the Sabbath morning service. But in addition, there must by all means be a special day devoted to the Holocaust. Such a day has already been established for many years. It is the 27th day of Nissan, one week before Israel Independence Day. The day is widely observed in Israel. It is not as widely celebrated in America. (I have edited a *Tikkun*, a special booklet for services on both Holocaust Day and the Day of Independence, in the hope that it will facilitate religious observance of these days.) While it is slowly gaining currency, I unfortunately am not aware of any enthusiasm for memorializing the martyrs in this manner. Many of those people who self-righteously criticize "the rabbis" for doing nothing to remember the martyrs, themselves fail to appear at such services. Nevertheless, that must not deter us. It is to me unthinkable that religious Jews should not set aside a special day of prayer and introspection and memorialization for this purpose. It just will not do to say that this should be included in the Tisha Be'Av service. The contrast is simply too great. It is a sacrilegious diminution of the scope of the Holocaust and the suffering of its martyrs, to try to swallow them up in another, ancient observance. If Gedaliah requires a special fast, the "Fast of Gedaliah" following Rosh Hashanah, then six million Gedaliahs certainly do!

But more important than celebration is education. No effort must be spared in keeping the memory of the Holocaust alive for both Jew and non-Jew. Schools which omit the Holocaust from their curricula are guilty of an unforgivable act of moral blindness. Students are receptive to the study of the Holocaust, because they know that in it they are testing the limits of human depravity. In the universities in which I teach, a Holocaust course automatically invites high enrollment. There are Catholic universities and even high schools where special Holocaust courses are offered. But it is far from sufficient. The programs must increase many times over.

What of our Jewish schools, especially our yeshivot and day schools? Very few of them, to my knowledge, do anything at all. The most illustrious exception is the Flatbush Yeshiva in New York, where the high school department has established a separate Holocaust Documentation Center. Programs are available to others as they are being developed at the school. I am told that the Principals' Council of Torah Umesorah is busy developing such a program. Thirty years after the Holocaust certainly should be enough time to have that program in effect already. Yet other schools do nothing at all.

Yet, important as it is to teach the Holocaust to yeshiva students and Orthodox youth in general, it is even more important to do so for non-Orthodox youngsters. After all, a child raised in an Orthodox home and Orthodox synagogue is already aware, subliminally, of the possibility of Holocaust. An observant Jewish youngster who recites the daily prayers and observes the mourning and fasting of Tisha Be'Av and is taught the Midrash of the Haggadah of Passover, knows in his own bones the reality of destruction, the possibility of *churban.* He is already aware of the insecurity of the Jewish people, of the marginality of man as such, of the uncertainty of the future of the very planet, of the pervasive fragility that is part and parcel of our destiny. He is acquainted with the ubiquity and the nature of anti-Semitism. Teaching the Holocaust to such an Orthodox child, is only teaching him the latest exemplification of what he already knows from his upbringing. For the non-Orthodox child, such teaching is doubly important, because it adds a dimension of awareness that he might otherwise never attain.

WHAT ARE SOME of the elements of Holocaust teaching?

First, I would not teach the Holocaust as simply the latest illustration of anti-Semitism on the pattern of the biblical archetype, Amalek. The Holocaust must be presented as both a continuation of older anti-Semitism, and as something horribly unique.

However, this uniqueness must not focus the outrage of the students on the Nazis only. I am not interested in teaching the Holocaust as a way of condemning Germans. After a while, it becomes difficult for Jewish youngsters to acquiesce in blaming the children and grandchildren and great-grandchildren for the crimes of their ancestors. How many of us can feel personal animosity towards today's Spaniards because of Torquemada of 400 years ago? With the passage of time we have to broaden the scope of responsibility. We must teach our children that not only was one particular nation guilty of allowing itself to be caught up in murderous paranoia, but that there were two other parties that must share the guilt, though each does so in different measure. The world which witnessed such methodical sadism and kept its silence is guilty. The spectators to a crime who keep their peace, must never be allowed to attain peace. And we of the Jewish community may never feel self-righteous. We must always remember that American Jews who were adults in the period of the Holocaust will never feel completely innocent. Nor should they! That very guilt that we pass on to our children is what will galvanize them to action in time, should danger to the Jewish people ever arise again. Indeed, part of the passion and effectiveness of young Jews today on the Russian-Jewish issue is a direct result of the guilt that they impute, correctly I believe, to their parents' generation because of their inactivity and silence during World War II.

Second, I would not make the teaching of the Holocaust one unrelieved tale of horror after horror, accusation after accusation. For the Holocaust to be grasped, we may have to reduce some of its awesomeness to credible proportions, lest the lesson be lost entirely. The Holocaust may, in truth, call for one long elegy, but if future generations are to have any knowledge at all of the Holocaust, the truth may have to be diminished and diluted for instructional purposes.

Hence, instead of teaching the Holocaust in a "lachrymose" fashion, there should also be an attempt to highlight the elements of hope and creativity. For indeed, it is true that Jews managed to find hope in the very vale of hopelessness, and to discover creativity whilst in the hell of destructiveness.

The greatest instance of hope is, of course, the historic conjunction of the founding of the State of Israel and the European Holocaust. One simply cannot teach one without the other. But I would insist as an absolute that never, never must there be an attempt to make a metaphysical equation, to assert or even imply that the State is, in some measure, a compensation for the anguish of the Holocaust. Never must we be guilty of such inane and blood-chilling jingoism. I would not want to wish on the heads of Israelis, and of generations of yet unborn Israelis, that terrible onus of knowing that their State was created on the ashes of six million innocent martyrs. No such calculus of destruction and creation, no such arithmetic of historic cause and effect, may be imputed to the Creator of the world. Rather, the tie-in between the two must be taught as demonstrating a Jewish creative genius that was able to defy the Holocaust, an uncanny Jewish ability to discover hope and to build and to construct because of persecution and despite it, because of genocide and despite it.

There are many other examples of such great Jewish creativity and dignity. Certainly, the instances of resistance must never be overlooked. They are shining chapters in our history. Nor must we overlook the many cases of incredible courage of Jews in the way they went to *Kiddush Hashem* (martyrdom). Or consider this interesting fact which most people do not know: the rate of suicide in the concentration camps was startingly low. I suppose that all of us think of how we would act were we subject to such cruel circumstances. Unquestionably, when we do so, the thought of suicide as a way out flashes across the minds of each of us. Yet Jews somehow, in the camps, demonstrated a will-to-live, reflected in this low rate of suicides, that is a tribute to the stubbornness of this stiff-necked people.

Third, and very important, is the religious aspect. I am sorry to say that in most writings on the Holocaust, the role of religious Jews is sorely neglected. It is an elemental act of historic justice that we immediately redress the balance. This means that in order properly to understand the Holocaust, the extent of its horrors and the reactions of its victims, we must impart to our students a knowledge of the full, vibrant, rich, complex religious life of European Jewry. We must know how religious Jews lived—and then we will understand how they died.

This should be done not only directly in a separate course, but also imaginatively and innovatively as part of the standard curriculum. A place for teaching the Holocaust is obviously—the Akedah story, the binding of Isaac (Genesis 22). Holocaust-consciousness can be insinuated in halakhic teaching as well. I have conducted an experimental series of lectures at The Jewish Center entitled, "The Holocaust and the Halakha." I devoted four Sabbath afternoons to digesting many of the *she'elot* and *teshuvot* (responsa) that were written by rabbis in the death camps to Jews who posed halakhic questions to them.

This method of teaching accomplishes several ends simultaneously. First, it teaches the reality of the concentration camp situation without the artifice that is inevitable when an author's personality is interposed between the facts of history and the finished literary product. Second, the marvelous functioning of Halakhah in the most extreme cases of the death camps becomes a clear indication that such a system must certainly be viable for people under "normal" living circumstances. Third, it is a glowing tribute to the people of Israel that its sons and daughters can be possessed of such faith and such hope in such impossible and incredible circumstances.

THIS RAISES A tangential issue of considerable importance. The religious element has been prominent in Holocaust writing almost exclusively in the agonizing challenge that is hurled at God, attempting to pierce His silence. It may be uncomfortable to read it or, alternatively, it may afford the reader a great deal of psychological satisfaction to hear someone else put it that way. Be that as it may, I consider it an authentic Jewish religious reaction to such unprecedented suffering. These are merely new ways of rephrasing the old questions that were asked by Abraham and Moses and Jeremiah and Job all through Jewish history.

But Jewish religious experience is hardly so uncomplicated and monolithic as to permit only one response to such an overwhelmingly significant experience as deep suffering. There are, indeed, a number of legitimate Jewish reactions. One of them is the challenge by man to God, which we have mentioned. But there is another route that Jewish piety can take in the face of great grief and suffering: the reaction of piety and devotion and acceptance. This second form of religious response must not ever be despised and dismissed as mere submissiveness. In a way, by denying Jews the right to heroic gestures, this reaction-pattern commits them to more serious and more demanding heroism, to acts of incredible courage and spiritual-psychological fortitude in the face of death itself.

In going through the responsa of the Holocaust period, I chanced upon more than one such instance of Jews who believed despite all. The most memorable is that of an anonymous Jew from Oberland (Hungary) who posed a question to the late Rabbi Meisels of Chicago. They were then in Auschwitz. This must have been in 1941 or 1942. The Nazi S.S. decided that all Jewish boys under 14 who were not fit to be slave laborers were to be sent to their death. They determined this by building a scaffold, a horizontal pole attached to a vertical column, and they passed the boy under it. All those too short for their head to touch the horizontal bar were sent to special barracks, and there kept without food and water, to be sent to the crematoria that night. When the youngsters, with the instinct of the hunted, immediately recognized what was happening, the shorter ones tried to walk tiptoe past the scaffold, and when they did so they were immediately bludgeoned to death. Thus were several hundred youngsters gathered in the building, and after being counted by the S.S., they were guarded by the Kapos, the Jewish police, who were usually unscrupulous people. Parents panicked, and many of them who had some money or small jewelry on their persons or elsewhere, immediately ran to the Kapos in an attempt to bribe them to release their children. The Kapos could not do so, because if the count of the condemned Jewish boys was not the same as that which the S.S. had, the Kapos could be killed. However, they did take the bribes by capturing some other Jewish child who had heretofore been spared, and putting him into the condemned group in place of the Jewish child who was to be ransomed.

And so this Jew of Oberland came to Rabbi Meisels and said, "My only son, who is dear to me as life itself, has been taken to the barracks. I have enough to be able to give to the Kapos so as to ransom him and let him live. But I know that in order to save him, some other Jewish child must die in his place. What is the law according to the Torah: may I save my only son, or must I let him die?" Rabbi Meisels tried his best to dodge the question. He could not possibly answer him. He said to him, "My dear Jew, the Sanhedrin itself would ponder such a question deeply for weeks. Here I am in Auschwitz, without any other rabbis to consult, without books, without texts—how can I possibly give you an answer to your question?" But the Jew was persistent, and did not let go. Finally, the Jew turned to Rabbi Meisels and said to him, "If you do not answer me, it means that you are afraid to tell me the answer you really know, namely, that it is forbidden for me to do so. Therefore, I want you to know that I accept the decision of the Torah and the Halakhah fully and with joy. My son shall go to his death, but I shall not violate the law. As this is Rosh Hashanah (when the story of the *Akedah* is read in the Torah), so am I to follow in the footsteps of our Father Abraham, and this day I shall offer my child as my *Akedah*." So did he speak, and for the remainder of the day he was in a state of euphoria.

Does the memory of this kind of religious courage not deserve to be perpetuated? Should this not elicit our undying admiration, at least in the same measure as the dramatic debates with God that were characteristic of others?

This too must be memorialized when teaching the Holocaust. The Jews who stole a piece of *matzah*, knowing that if they were discovered they would be killed; the Jew who asked a rabbi in the Kovno ghetto what blessing to make when he is killed; the Jews who wanted to know if they should recite the blessing in the morning praising the Lord "who hath not made me a slave," and accepted the decision that slavery was not a matter of external status but internal resolve and awareness—these too were acts of undaunted heroism. Must we silence their faith with our rage, their confidence with our confusion? Shall we not celebrate their strength, read their *divrei Torah,* study their responsa, recount their spiritual greatness?

Having said all this, I must add that we must be careful not to transmit the Holocaust in a biased form. We must never allow the situation to develop whereby socialist schools teach the Holocaust as if only socialists were killed, and Zionist schools teach the Holocaust as if they alone bore the brunt of the whole experience, and religious schools give the impression that only religious Jews were persecuted, or only religious Jews were heroes. The works of Moshe Prager, for instance, are exceedingly important in redressing the balance about which we spoke. They are excellent in affording the student an opportunity to learn of the religious contribution and the religious dimension of the Holocaust. But never must we restrict the teaching of the Holocaust to only one group. To do so would be a falsification of the facts, and a betrayal of those who died. The Holocaust victims were not all socialists, not all secularists, not all Zionists, not all Agudists, not all Mizrachists, not all believers, and not all agnostics—they were *Kelal Yisrael,* the totality of our people.

In teaching the Holocaust, we must respond to one of its glaringly unique features. Millions of people were killed during World War II—more non-Jews than Jews. But Jews were the only ones who were killed solely because of *who* they were, not because of what they did or what they believed. Religious and atheists, Hasidim and Maskilim, observant and non-observant—all went to their deaths, and the Nazis did not care what their individual commitments were. This made the Holocaust a singular and unprecedented event: just being a Jew was a *death-warrant.*

Hence, we must teach the Holocaust so as to inculcate the students with the awareness that just being a Jew is a *life-warrant,* a summons to survive, a challenge to continue. It is a life-warrant for every Jew no matter what his opinion or ideology.

Holocaust teaching must result in a broadened and deepened *Ahavat Yisrael* (love for Israel). If nothing else, learning about the Holocaust must make the student love Jews; if for no other reason, then because no one else does. This love of Jews is not the kind of exclusive love which will alienate him from other humans. It is merely the first step towards love of mankind.

NOW, LET US turn to the next question. What are the chief values, or purposes and goals, in the teaching of the Holocaust?

For one thing, the student must emerge from all of this with a new awareness about himself and about human beings. The Holocaust was the end of innocence in a century which began with a naive belief in inevitable progress and human perfectibility. The Holocaust was the exclamation point which cruelly brought to a permanent end that ingenuous faith.

The Holocaust was a "negative" revelation, the counterpoint of Sinai. It was the great anti-Sinai apocalypse. Sinai disclosed publicly how far man could go in rising to God, and how far God was willing to go in descending to man. The Holocaust revealed, for all the world and all time, the depths to which man had sunk and the degree to which God turned away from him. Sinai revealed the mutual compatibility of man and God, and the Holocaust—their reciprocal alienation. Sinai thus became the dream of the ages, the Holocaust the nightmare. The two stretched the limits of man's capacity, each in an opposite direction.

So the first aim in Holocaust teaching is: the demonic nature of man.

It is in this connection that I always recall a memorable short story by Isaac Bashevis Singer entitled, "The Last Demon." It begins in something of the following fashion: "I am the last of the demons. Who needs demons any more now that man does their work . . ."

When we were young, in the pre-Holocaust days, how naively rationalistic we were! How troubled we were by the occasional Talmudic reference to demons. As we grew up we tried every which way to allegorize such references. But then came World War II and we learned something very terrible: the ancients were right all along. There are devils. Demons do exist. They dog our every step. But we learned one thing that perhaps they did not know as well. That is, that the demons, all of them, are visible. And they come in a special form—dressed in the body of man and speaking his language . . .

A second purpose of Holocaust teaching is: *teshuvah*, repentance. By repentance I mean, in the first instance, the classical idea of *teshuvah*, that of returning to God.

However, I should like to make it clear beyond the shadow of doubt: I do not at all recommend teaching the Holocaust in the classical mold of "on account of our sins," that the suffering of Israel was a punishment for its sins. We may say that about our exile of two thousand years ago. It was perhaps true of the destruction of the Temple. But I cannot imagine any sins so great as to deserve such enormous punishment as the Holocaust. Even if such could be imagined, it is blasphemous for us, only 30 years away from the event, to dare to utter such words. No one who survived has a right to articulate or even think such justification of unparalleled anguish. Those who might have had such a right—perished.

When theological questions are asked, students must be told that the greatest questions in the world simply have no answers. Maybe they will discover them when they grow up. Likely as not, the questions will remained suspended between heaven and earth for all eternity. We are only human, we are not divine. We cannot answer all questions. Job taught us that. What we can do is take the suffering and the grief and the anguish and the agony and try to use them to lead us a step beyond where we are now. That is what I mean by *teshuvah*. Studying what happened must not get us "hung up" on the question of "why," but propel us into responding to the question, "what then?" It must lead us to affirm our allegiance to Israel, our commitment to studying the Torah, our devotion to the Almighty.

But I also mean *teshuvah* in a second, somewhat different sense. I refer to the assumption of personal responsibility for the reconstruction and the reinvigoration of Jewish life.

Allow me to illustrate with a story that I heard personally from the individual to whom it happened. Some years ago, the faculty and student body of the Erna Michael College of Yeshiva University assembled to hear a lecture by Professor Dov Sadan of the Hebrew University. It was my privilege to introduce the guest, who has since retired, to my colleagues and students. I read a digest of his record, and was overwhelmed by the fact that this little man—so unassuming in demeanor and unprepossessing in appearance—was the author of over 40 scholarly books and hundreds of scientific articles! I stopped the introduction, turned to the guest, and asked him how it was possible for one man in so short a time to accomplish so much. When he rose to speak, he answered that question. And this is the story that he told.

Shortly after she was married, his mother became pregnant and took ill. The doctor informed her and her husband that they had a cruel choice: either to give up the child so that the mother might live, or else to allow the pregnancy to come to full term and deliver the baby, with a clear risk to the mother's survival. The mother would listen to no advice. She was stubborn: the child must live. And so when the nine months were up, the child was delivered as a healthy baby—and the mother succumbed.

Throughout his entire youth, Dov Sadan's father reminded him: "Dov, I want you to remember that your mother gave her life for you. You have got to study and achieve not only for yourself, but for her as well. Furthermore, had she given you up she might have had countless other sons and daughters. Because she preferred that you live, not only did she die, but who knows how many brothers and sisters did not come into the world because of you. Therefore, you must study and work and achieve and create and contribute not only for yourself, but for your mother and your brothers and your sisters who never came into this world!"

It is that awareness which I intend by the second form of *teshuvah*. Youngsters of this generation and the next generation and untold generations to come, must be made aware of the fact that their contribution to Jewish life must not only be for themselves, but for the six million who perished, and not only for them, but for the millions of children and grandchildren and great grandchildren that they might have had. The little handful of Jews has got to be vigorous and creative for an enormous population that might have been but never was. That is the kind of charge, of creative ferment, that Holocaust teaching must lead to.

FINALLY, WE MUST teach the Holocaust simply because it will never, never go away. It can never, must never, be forgotten.

One opinion in the Mishnah (quoted in the Passover Haggadah) is that we must mention and remember the day that we left Egypt "all the days of thy life," interpreted as meaning not only in the here-and-now, but also in the days after the Messiah comes. Apparently, there is some opinion that in the days of the Messiah, the Exodus will be surpassed by the greater redemption of the Messiah. The Prophet Zechariah tells us that Tisha Be'Av and the other three fast days will not only be obsolete after the Redemption, but they will be converted into "days of joy and gladness."

Let that be as it is. Other cataclysms can be covered by consolation, other disasters may be forgotten. But the Holocaust—never. It is an eternally ineradicable fact of Jewish history. There are wounds which will never heal. Even when the Messiah comes and we feast on the Ninth of Av, the scars of the Holocaust will be there. Forever.

In order to understand this, let us consider a classic instance in which a Jew confronted an anti-Semite. The wrestling of Jacob with an unknown and mysterious assailant, whom tradition identifies as the patron angel of Esau, is the first archetypical encounter between a Jew and a Jew-hater (Gen. 32:25–33). As a result of that battle, Jacob was wounded in his sciatic nerve. Then, when the sun rose, he was limping. That is why, the Torah tells us, in a parenthetical remark, the Children of Israel must not eat that particular sinew of an animal, "until this day."

Later, after Jacob "built himself a house," and after he "made booths for his cattle," we read that Jacob came "whole" to the city of Shechem. What does it mean that Jacob came whole or perfect? The Talmud, and a Midrash as well, quoted by Rashi, tell us that it refers to wholeness in three different areas: he was whole physically, whole financially, and whole spiritually. Rashi adds explicitly: his physical wholeness indicates that he was healed from the limp which resulted from the injury caused by the assailant on that mysterious night.

But, if the wound healed that quickly, why were Jews forbidden to eat the comparable part of the sinew of an animal in memory of Jacob's wound? Why should we be forbidden to eat "to this very day," an organ which symbolizes only a temporary wound? Must we commemorate every cold that Jacob had—every cough, every sneeze, every scratch?

I submit this answer to that question. Yes, Jacob was considered whole in his body. But he was not healed from his limp! On the contrary, Jacob remained wounded, he never healed. All his life he limped, and that limp was a perpetual reminder of his encounter with Esau's angel. That fact, that sacred scar, was a holy memento of his fateful battle and his survival. That wound in itself is a token of Jacob's perfection!

Even after Jacob made peace with Esau, even after he "built himself a house," and after he made "booths for his cattle," he was perfect by virtue of that memory, of the pain which he did not forget, of the wounds which he did not bind, of the scars which never went away.

So it is with us. The day will come when, despite everything, there will be no wars in the Middle East, hatred of Jews will disappear, Jacob and Esau will live in peace. But there shall be no perfection without the memory and the consciousness of the Holocaust. We can attain perfection only when we remember the nightmare of the Holocaust, only if we are conscious that it is an ever-running sore.

That is why we must insist upon teaching the Holocaust until *this very day*—until every day into the indefinite and endless future.

~ 57 ~

A TIME TO KEEP SILENT . . . AND A TIME TO SPEAK

It is very difficult for me to speak on this topic. I will not tell you any personal experiences of the Holocaust, for I cannot: I have none. I was a youngster living in Brooklyn when the *Shoah* occurred. Neither will I speak this evening as an historian, teacher of philosophy, or amateur of literature. I appear before you without any such scholarly or artistic pretensions. Rather, I wish to engage in some deeply felt private reflections—meditation, if you will—between me and myself: an inner dialogue, with you as courteous outsiders listening to this troubled man talking to himself.

I confess that I am beset by deep ambivalence in talking about the Holocaust, even at this late date, almost forty years after the event. I have done my share of talking and writing about the Holocaust, and yet, I am unnerved whenever I am called upon to do so.

My problem is that, having accepted to speak at this Holocaust Remembrance gathering, shall I speak at all? Can I? May I? Am I perhaps here under false pretenses?

My doubts apply only to me and others who, like me, were not *there.* Those who were need not share my hesitations. For there is a real, palpable curtain—or even a wall, a tangible obstruction—that separates those who were seared by the flames and survived, and those who merely wept; between me and those who had the *Shoah* inscribed into their flesh and psyches forever.

For those of us who did not experience the Holocaust firsthand: is it perhaps best that we keep quiet altogether? It was Ecclesiastes (3:7) who said that there is a time for everything—"A time to keep silent, and a time to speak." My dilemma is that when it comes to the Holocaust, I simultaneously feel an urge to speak and a summons to silence.

There are many good and cogent reasons for one like me to keep his peace about the Holocaust. For one thing, words—no

---

Address at Adelphi University in 1981, and thereafter published by the university.

matter how eloquent or powerful—succeed only in trivializing that which is beyond one's power to either describe or bemoan.

The Holocaust is in many ways the obverse of divinity. The Holocaust was a satanic revelation, an historic apocalyptic disclosure of the reality of evil, ugliness, darkness.

When Moses saw the burning bush, he was attracted to it by his innate curiosity. But when he understood that it was a divine revelation, "Moses hid his face, for he was afraid to look upon God" (Exodus 3: 6). What holds true for the revelation of holiness, holds equally true for the apocalyptic revelation of overarching evil, the kind that surpasses all human understanding. For, to gaze, to state, to conceptualize, to describe, to bewail, and to formulate—is, by its very nature, to limit and, therefore, to diminish.

An example: The Talmud (*Ber.* 33) tells us that in the days before the prayerbook was fixed in permanent form and reduced to a literary text, a reader was reciting the prayers in public, and was lavish in extolling God's attributes. R. Chanina turned to him sarcastically and said, "Is that all that you have to say in praise of the Lord?" What Rabbi Chanina meant to say was that man must never say more than that which tradition ordains, because when we add we thereby diminish. Augmenting words of praise is limiting the praise to our few meager adjectives. The more speech, the more insult, and therefore silence is the greatest praise.

What is true for divine compassion is true for the terrible wrath of the Deity. Anything we articulate about the suffering of the martyrs insults them, because human language is inadequate to convey the dimensions of what occurred. We trivialize such ineffable evil and suffering by mere verbalization.

So silence is recommended, lest talk become drivel, writing prattle, and symbols sacrilege.

There is a second reason for verbal restraint: silence is the most profound form of mourning and commiseration. When grief surpasses human endurance, mere verbal consolation no longer suffices. At that point, true sympathy must transcend mere words with a deep, multi-faceted, vibrant silence that says all that words can—and so much more that words cannot.

When Job was smitten with his unbearable torments, his three friends came to console him. "And when they lifted up their eyes afar off, and knew him not . . . So they sat down with him upon the ground seven days and seven nights, and none spoke a word unto him, for they saw that his grief was very great" (Job 2:12–13). If silence is the only response to the suffering of one Job, what shall we say of six million Jobs?

THERE IS A THIRD and deeply sensitive personal reason why those of us who were not present in what Elie Wiesel has called "The Kingdom of the Night" ought to hold our peace. Again, let us resort to a biblical metaphor, because when we try to speak about what happened in the Holocaust, only biblical metaphors have that sweep of terror and of grandeur and of mystery—and at times even those do not suffice.

At the destruction of the cities of Sodom and Gomorrah, as the Lord was about to "overturn" the two evil cities, angels hurried Lot and his family out, and told him, "Look not behind thee" (Gen. 19:17). Why so? Rashi, the great exegete and commentator, explains that Lot was forbidden to observe the destruction of Sodom and Gomorrah because he deserved the same fate as his countrymen, but was saved only "by the merit of Abraham", his righteous kinsman.

Lot and Sodom are, for me, metaphors for us American Jews and the Holocaust. We dare not look too intently upon the victims, even as Lot was not permitted to look back upon the perpetrators—because we too might well have been in their place!

Call it survivor's guilt or whatever you will. It is indeed mind-boggling: why was I spared in New York, while dozens of my cousins, uncles, aunts, and my aged great-grandmother were butchered in Poland? Lot at least had "the merit of Abraham." What merit did I have that my martyred kinfolk did not? Why were they murdered, why was I spared?

If I was spared by some divine design, then I find the burden unbearable, for no mortal can carry out a mission assigned at such a terrible price. It is too crushing and onerous a burden! And if my survival was sheer chance, then life and history have no meaning and make no sense to me, and all existence is a cruel joke.

"Look not behind thee." Contemplation, description and analysis of this twentieth-century diabolical paroxysm and satanic convulsion threaten the very structure of our thought and values and the very foundations of our faith and feelings. It is a philosophical atom bomb, and if we tinker with it carelessly, it threatens to destroy our entire axiological universe. Think about it too long, and you lose your equanimity—indeed your very humanity—and, like Lot's wife, you turn into a pillar of salt.

AND YET, ALTHOUGH this is a "time to keep silent," it is by the same token a "time to speak." While silence has much to commend it, if we are indeed silent, then both we and the world will forget. And forgetfulness, as the Midrash taught—and as S.Y. Agnon was fond of repeating—is the root of all evil. With all that the talk and activity about the Holocaust has often been cheapening and trivial; with all the failure of books and monuments to offer even a glimmer of solace to match the unspeakable grief; with all that our preoccupation with the Holocaust has tended to distract us from our own complicity and responsibility—the failure to speak up is far worse.

CONSIDER HOW, to this very day, with the millions of words that were written and spoken about the Holocaust, and all the art and monuments that were dedicated to the subject, still the world has failed to learn anything. And since, obviously, the world is not sensitive and subtle enough to learn from our silence, it must be shocked by our speech.

IN AMERICA—and from America the poison spreads abroad—we are treated to a "revisionist view" of the Holocaust that appears in "academic" guise declaring that the Holocaust was a hoax. The whore dresses up like a princess: the hoax theory appears in an academic "journal" accompanied by all the scholastic paraphernalia designed to impress the uncritical and the naive. It is an instance of insufferable pedantry at the service of unspeakable hypocrisy.

Yet, some benighted souls confuse the freedom of speech with academic freedom, as if the civil right of any citizen to deliver himself of any remark, no matter how stupid or false or inane, means that professors have the intellectual right to exploit their academic standing in order to propagate deliberate lies and vicious misstatements of fact.

So, let it be said here, in this hall of learning, from the podium of Adelphi University, that this is a dreadful and unpardonable error. A professor of astrophysics who denied the existence of galaxies and attributed their properties to the intervention of pixies and fairies would be booted out of the university. A professor of economics who ascribed market fluctuations to devious little gremlins would be laughed out of the classroom. A professor of psychiatry who recommended exorcism of the devil as normative therapy for neurosis would even lose his tenure.

Shall, then, professors of electrical engineering or history or chemistry be allowed to deny verifiable facts about contemporary history—in the presence of survivors who bear the scars on their bodies and souls and the numbers tattooed on their arms—with impunity as they claim the dignity of academic freedom? I grant their claim to the civic freedom of speech. But as academicians? Have we no longer any standards in the world of scholarship?

We must break our silence and speak up—loud and clear.

IN WEST GERMANY, Chancellor Helmut Schmidt plans to arm the Saudis—and announces it on Holocaust Remembrance Day itself. Without mentioning any moral debt that Germany owes to the Jews, he speaks of German's "moral commitment to Palestinians." What colossal hypocrisy!

It is hard to believe that this is 1981 and not 1984—George Orwell's *1984*—when the leader of a country that brought unparalleled devastation to the world and decimated the Jewish people not only thinks about arming the enemies of Israel (the only country that afforded the last shred of dignity to the remnants of the Holocaust), but has the temerity to describe such actions as "moral." For shame!

For thirty-five years, since Adenauer, West Germany has been trying to atone for its sins, and somehow allow itself to re-enter the community of civilized nations. Herr Schmidt has now undone it all, and for all time.

NEIGHBORING POLAND HAS now acted in a way that should elicit from us not silence, but also not formal speech—rather, peals of horrible laughter and wretched amusement. For Poland has proven that there need not be Jews in order for one to be anti-Semitic . . .

RUSSIA, WE HAVE just learned, did not permit Russian Jews to gather in a forest clearing outside Moscow to commemorate Holocaust Day. The Russians did not allow the survivors even to gather and say Kaddish for the millions who were martyred. This is the country which first pulled the shroud of obscurity over Babi Yar, not permitting a memorial plaque to mention that it was *Jews* who were so barbarically killed there. Now it repeats its offense, and even the memory of these Jews is not permitted to be preserved.

It might be in place to recall that European anti-Semitism did not begin with Germany in 1939. Hitler owed much to Russia. It was exactly 100 years ago, in May of 1881, that the Russian Minister of Interior prevailed upon the Czar to pass the infamous May Laws: one-third of all the Jews were to be killed, one-third baptized, and one third exiled. Thus was the "Jewish problem" to be solved. So Russia, which was one of the teachers of modern anti-Semitism, today will not even allow the Holocaust to be commemorated by its survivors.

At such a time, and in the face of such provocations, we dare not keep silent.

HENCE, I RETURN to my inner dialogue. My dilemma is: to speak or to keep silent. If I speak, I risk trivialization and vulgarization; if I do not, I encourage amnesia, the possibility that neither my children nor my friends, Jews or Gentiles, will ever learn anything from the Holocaust, and that the world will yet allow it to be repeated.

So cruel and paradoxical is the Holocaust that it confounds us by our very act of thinking about it. Shall we talk about it? How can we! Shall we keep silent? How dare we! We are damned if we do and damned if we don't.

Hence, we must choose to talk and study and read and analyze and remember and remind. But we must be doubly and trebly careful to choose our words with great care. We must resolve with all our hearts that:

The Holocaust must not be vulgarized into lurid entertainment for both adolescent and adult addicts of the violent and the purient.

The Holocaust must not be turned into an industry and into a form of show business. The Holocaust must not be used as a means to further private ends, even private ideological ends, so that it is invoked as an excuse, no matter how irrelevant, to propagate cherished ideas.

The Holocaust must not be diminished by abusing the terms "holocaust" or "genocide" for every object of political, social, and economic oppression. I bristle when I hear the term applied to Vietnam and El Salvador, or by the sundry American liberation movements. The term is used with such abandon that all meaning is squeezed out of it. It becomes profane, as if you are saying that the molester not only tortured his victims to death but also ran through a red light. It must not even be misused in this manner by Israeli officials when speaking of the Christian enclaves in Lebanon, who are threatened with defeat and cruel oppression, but hardly with genocide itself.

The Holocaust may be commemorated by paintings, statues and monuments, but never, never be reduced to merely statues and paintings and books and poems, as if with these objets d'art we have fulfilled our moral obligations to the martyrs.

The Holocaust must become part of education, but must not be used to distort education, especially not Jewish education. Holocaust studies must become a permanent part of the curriculum of all decent human beings, and especially of all Jews. It must! But, I am apprehensive about the proliferation of Holocaust courses when they dominate the curriculum.

Many Jewish students who otherwise have no contact with their tradition and their people have, as their main or sole exposure to 3500 years of Jewish history, only: "Holocaust studies." They learn how Jews died, but know not how they lived. They learn of the culture of the murderers, but have not the slightest notion of the culture of the victims. I am aghast because, victimized though we were for three and a half millennia, it is scandalous to teach my children and my students that our role in history was primarily that of the perpetual victims. An exclusively martyrological interpretation of Jewish history is simply all wrong.

Holocaust studies—yes! But more important, we must teach and learn how and by what lights the victims lived; what was their faith and their culture, and what were the values which sustained them throughout their struggles.

For they created one of the most vibrant cultures in the history of man—Polish Jewry.

Polish Jewry rivals Babylonian Jewry and Palestinian Jewry in the second century. Purely from a cultural point of view, it was one of the most creative communities on the face of the earth. It is therefore a well-intended but cruel joke that we play upon the East European Jewish victims when we conjure them up only in relation to the genocidal plans and acts of the Nazis, as if this exhausts their importance for human history. Shall we ignore all that they created—in religion and literature, in language and in politics, in social thought and in philosophy—and invoke their memory only by the recollection of the obscenities visited upon them in the Western world? My heart grieves for all those youngsters who flock to the "Holocaust courses" and can tell us only how many Jews of Lublin were killed in Auschwitz, and how many fell in the Warsaw ghetto uprising, but know nothing of the Lublin Yeshiva and of Warsaw Jewry's religious and literary and social and political creativity, of Yiddish and Talmud and Musar and Hasidim and labor groups and education.

Therefore, we must never teach our young people, whose primary exposure to Judaism is through Holocaust studies, that East European Jewry was simply a group of victims who died at the hands of the Nazis. This is not what the study of the Holocaust should do; it should not rob the victims of the eternity of their heritage.

- *We must* remember their lives, and also what might have become of them had they survived.
- *We must* continue to support the State of Israel, for if it had existed then, millions of the martyrs might be alive today.
- *We must* struggle against evil and bigotry and racism whenever we find them and whatever victims they claim.
- *We must* carry on their culture and their faith and their vitality—to the very end of days.

And for this—silence will not do.

SO HAVING SPOKEN, I conclude with an apology for having done so.

Better yet, I close with a prayer—the kind of prayer with which we conclude our daily prayers, on the style of "My God, keep my tongue from speaking evil, and my lips from uttering deceit":

Forgive me, O Lord, for having profaned the greatest and most horrible mystery of the history of our people with empty words from unclean lips.

Forgive me for daring to disturb the eternal and infinite and endless cry of anguish, silent and thunderous as the grave, with twitting and wayward words that barely rise above the banal and blasphemous.

Forgive me for the arrogance of attempting to find meaning in that convulsion of divine wrath which not only consumed six million lives—ten times the biblical number of Israelites who left Egypt, old and young, mothers and babies, scholars and ordinary people—but annihilated meaning itself. For the Holocaust was the "black hole" of history which, like the black hole that astronomers claim to have discovered in the galaxies, buries all within it and allows no light to escape.

Forgive me, O Lord, for thou knowest that Silence would have been worse than Speech. For while speech may not shed light, at least it can protest the darkness.

~ 58 ~

DEATH HAS NO FUTURE

The Holocaust and Jewish Education

Arbaim shanah akut be'dor. For forty years our generation struggled to understand the mystery of those fatal years of the Holocaust. Neither our speech nor our silence helped us to uncover the secrets of God or of man. Perhaps we shall have to wait another forty or another four hundred years, or perhaps we shall never be wise enough even to know how to react.

But events march on, and history does not permit us the luxury of endless contemplation. Hence, some reactions began to emerge fairly quickly. The first and enormously significant response to the Holocaust was the political one: the founding of the State of Israel. Powerlessness would never again be considered a Jewish virtue. The desperate struggles of the heroic Jewish fighters in Warsaw and elsewhere were metamorphosed into the pride of statehood and the military confidence of the Israeli Defense Forces. Today, the future of the Jewish people is unthinkable without the State of Israel.

Another response has been a holy, compulsive drive to record and testify. We do not want to forget, and we do not want the world to forget. We have resolved to keep the memory of our *Kedoshim* alive by demonstrations and by meetings such as this. And many of us have undertaken projects of sculpture and art and museums and exhibits to perpetuate the memory of the Six Million. As the years slip by and memory begins to fade, we desperately want to prevent their anguish and blood and cry from being swallowed up by the misty, gaping hole of eternal silence, banished from the annals of man by the Angel of Forgetfulness.

The efforts at remembering and reminding must continue. As long as so-called "revisionist historians" deny that the Holocaust occurred; as long as Babi Yar and Buchenwald behind the Iron Curtain contain almost no reference to Jews; as long as it is even conceivable that an American administration, which preaches

---

A Yom Hashoah address on the 40th anniversary of the Liberation on April 17, 1985 at Madison Square Garden in New York City.

more compassion for the victim than for the criminal on the domestic front, can see nothing wrong in its President honoring dead Waffen-SS while pointedly ignoring their Jewish victims in Dachau—there will be a need for Jews to remember and remind, even if we know in our hearts that the world will not long remember or want to be reminded. And let it be said here clearly and unequivocally: A courtesy call at a conveniently located concentration camp cannot compensate for the callous, obscene scandal of honoring dead Nazi killers. Surely the President's aides can arrange a visit by him to the tomb of Konrad Adenauer or some of the decent German anti-Nazis who perished at Hitler's hands for their principles.

Yet—and yet . . . these responses alone are inadequate. The problem of the Jewish people today is not the State of Israel; it will survive. The problem is not the world's conscience. I have no faith in it, though we must continue to prod and prick and provoke it. The problem of the Jewish people today is—the Jewish people. With a diminishing birth rate, an intermarriage rate exceeding 40%, Jewish illiteracy gaining ascendance daily—who says that the Holocaust is over? President Herzog of Israel estimates that we are losing 250 Jews per day! From the point of view of a massive threat to Jewish continuity, the Holocaust is open-ended.

The monster has assumed a different and more benign form, a different and bloodless shape, but its evil goal remains unchanged: a *Judenrein* world.

The Holocaust is not yet ready to be "remembered"; we are still in the midst of attempting to avoid the *final* Final Solution: a world without Jews.

In the light of this sobering, ominous reality, our responses are open to serious and deep reexamination.

I deeply sympathize with the heartfelt, sincere effort of memorial-building. But is that the Jewish way? No archaeologist has yet found a statue to the memory of R. Chanina b. Tradyon or R. Ishmael. No seeker after antiquities has yet unearthed an ancient museum to preserve the story of the victims of Masada or Betar or R. Akiva and his martyred students—or, for that matter, the victims of the Crusades or the Inquisition or Kishinev.

Our people have historically chosen different forms of memorialization. They asked for the academy of Yavneh as a substitute for and in memory of the Holy Temple. They ordained days of fasting and prayer and introspection. They devised ways of expressing *zekher le'mikdash* (Reminder of the Temple) and *zekher le'churban* (Reminder of the Destruction). They created the Talmud. In other words, they remembered the past by ensuring the future.

Museums and art have their place. In the context of an overall Jewish life, they serve as powerful instruments to recall the past for the future. But without a comprehensive wholeness, all our museums are mausoleums, our statues meaningless shards, our literature so much ephemeral gibberish.

We must seek to remember our dead, but not by being obsessed with death. We must be obsessed with life. *Lo ha-metim yehallelu Yah* (Psalm 115, "The dead praise not the Lord"). The dead cannot tell their own story. Only the living can testify to them and perpetuate them: *Va'anachnu nevarekh Yah (ibid.,* "But we will bless the Lord"). Their deaths make sense—even the sense of unspeakable and outrageous grief—only in the context of their lives. And their lives—their loves and hates, their faith and fears and culture and creativity and traditions and learning and literature and warmth and brightness and Yiddishkeit—are what we are called upon to redeem and to continue in our own lives and those of our children.

We know more or less how the Aztecs and Incas were butchered. But there is no one to mourn them today because there was no one to continue their ways and resume their story. That is bound to happen to our Six Million if we fail to ensure the continuity of our people. An extinct race has no memory. If there are no living Jews left, no one else will care about the Holocaust, and no one but a few cranky antiquarians will bother to view our art or read our literature or visit our museums.

Let me cite an example from the American-Jewish experience. There was a time when most American Jews memorialized their deceased parents by saying Kaddish for them for eleven months and on Yahrzeit and by reciting the Yizkor prayers four times a year; otherwise, their Jewishness became progressively more tenuous as they abandoned their parental lifestyles, values, and faith. What happened when these children died? For the most part, *their* children did not do for *them* what they had not done for their parents. For the most part, it was those who continued the whole rubric of Jewish life and living of their parents who also most fully cherished and reverenced their memories.

The reason for this is both profound and simple: Death has no staying power. Only life lives. Death is only past, it is over and done with. Who will remember a parent on Yizkor? Usually one who will be in *shul* as well on Hanukkah and Purim and Shabbat and even during the week. Those who somehow continue their parents' lives in their own lives will be there to note and recall their deaths. In a word: without life, death doesn't have a future.

At the Seder, a little less than two weeks ago, we ate a hard-boiled egg immediately before the meal as a sign of mourning. Jewish tradition teaches that since the first night of Passover always falls on the same night of the week as does Tisha Be'Av, the egg is a token of grief for the victims of the destruction of Jerusalem and of pogroms throughout the ages. It occurs to me that not only do we eat an egg at the Seder because no Jewish *simchah* may be conducted or complete without remembering the tragedies of Jewish history, but equally so because there can be no enduring memorial to the fallen martyrs of our people unless it lies in the context of the Seder of Jewish life. Without a child to ask the *Mah Nishtanah,* there will be no adult to sell the story of *avadim hayyinu.* Without *seder* or order; without the holiness of *kadesh* or the purity of *rechatz*—there will be no *maggid* to tell the story of Auschwitz and relate the *marror* of Buchenwald and Belzec. And so the *churban* will remain without a *zekher.* There can be no Tisha Be'Av without a Pesach. And there will be no Yom Hashoah without the rest of the Jewish calendar.

How did Jewish tradition cherish and pay homage to its heroes? We are told of the righteous King Hezekiah that upon his death he was honored greatly by the people of Judah and Jerusalem (II Chronicles 32:33), and the Talmud (*B.K.* 16b) explains that the honor that they accorded him was that *hoshivu yeshivah al kivro*—"they established a school upon his grave!"

That is what Jewish history and destiny call upon us to do now—before it is too late. The resources and energies and intellectual power of our best and brightest must be focused on making sure that there will be Jews remaining in the world lest the Holocaust prevail even while it is being denied. And that requires one thing above all else: a fierce, huge effort to expand Jewish education.

Let us resolve to build a school—a yeshiva, a day school, a Hebrew school, an elementary school, a high school, a school for adults, any genuine Jewish school—on the unmarked graves of every one of the million Jewish children done to death by the Nazi *Herrenvolk.* If not a yeshiva on every grave then, for Heaven's sake, at the very least one more Jewish child to learn how to be a Jew for the grave of every one child-martyr! A million more Jewish children learning how and what it is to be Jewish will accomplish more for the honor of the Holocaust martyrs than a million books or sculptures or buildings. Teach another million Jewish children over the globe the loveliness and meaningfulness and warmth of Jewishness, and you will have redeemed the million Jewish child-martyrs from the oblivion wished upon them by the Nazis. A million Jewish children to take place of those million who perished—that is a celebration of their lives that will not make a mockery of their deaths and that will be worthy of our most heroic efforts.

Will we have the courage to save our and our children's future from the spiritual Holocaust that threatens us? Will we have the wisdom to reorder our priorities and "establish a yeshiva over the gravesites" of our *Kedoshim*—before the hearts and minds of the majority of our children themselves turn into private little graves of the Jewish spirit?

That is the fateful question that we are obliged to answer. The future of our people lies in our hands. If we do nothing but utter a sigh and shrug our shoulders with palms extended as a sign of resignation and helplessness—then we will stand accused of being passive onlookers at this bloodless Holocaust, and our guilt will parallel that of the silent spectators of the 1930's and 1940's. But if we resolve to live on despite all, if we stand Jewishly tall and put our shoulders to the wheel and teach and instruct a new generation in the ways of Yiddishkeit, then our hands will grasp the future firmly and surely, and we shall live and the *Kedoshim* will live through us.

Etz chayyim hi la-machazikim bah. Our Torah and our Tradition are a Tree of Life, and by holding on to them we will redeem our past and honor our people by giving them a future.

~ 59 ~

HOLOCAUST COMPENSATION

from the Vantage of Jewish Law and Morality

The questions before us are of momentous, historic significance not only practically but morally. In elaborating an approach to them, I intend to foster my own moral self-understanding rather than attempt to persuade the governments on the other side. I shall endeavor to formulate a specific Jewish view in order to develop what I hope will be an authentic Jewish response to the issues before us—one based upon the classics of the Jewish tradition. In other words, I shall let the sources speak for themselves, even if such conclusions will not meet with unanimous approval, and even if I shall have hoped for different results.

Some caveats: comparisons to historic approaches and situations described and prescribed in classical texts often lead to overstating similarities and undervaluing differences. Moreover, we cannot always expect the halakhic sources to be applicable directly and without some attempt at interpretation to unprecedented situations. In such cases, we must read out of (not into) the halakhic sources the basic principles and values which motivated the detailed laws which the tradition bequeathed to us. However, if handled sensitively and honestly, such extrapolations have much to teach us, and we ignore them at our own peril. I shall try to exercise such sensitivity. If I fail, it will not be for want of trying.

There are two major issues that I shall deal with—the responsibility of governments that seized Jewish property during the Holocaust, and priorities for the proper distribution of the recovered funds to the victims and their survivors. I shall do so on the basis of biblical teachings and, more particularly, on the basis of Halakha, i.e., the Oral Law which explicates and supplements the Written Law.

The Jewish tradition can be said to distinguish between law (*dinei adam,* the laws of man) and ethics or morality (*dinei*

An address in Paris on October 17, 1999, this appeared in Tradition in Fall 2001 *shamayim,* the laws of Heaven). Law is enforceable by human courts; morality, no less obligatory, is not always actionable and is often a matter of one's conscience. However, there are times when history makes great demands on the moral conscience of nations and institutions—demands that impose mandatory action upon us, even transcending the law itself. Whether or not this is applicable in our contemporary issues remains to be seen.

LET US POSE the major question: *Are successor governments and institutions responsible to compensate victims of the Holocaust?*

The story of Elijah and Ahab (I Kings 21) is well known: Ahab, sovereign of the northern kingdom of Israel, lusts after the property of Nabot, his immediate neighbor, and he offers a generous price to buy it from him. The latter refuses, because it is his ancestral estate. Ahab falls into depression and his wife, Jezebel, takes over, promising her childish husband that *she* will obtain the estate for him. She cooks up a phony trial, where Nabot is falsely accused of blasphemy and treason and is executed—whereby Ahab seizes Nabot's lands. Incensed at this outrageous royal injustice, the prophet Elijah confronts the king and utters the immortal challenge: "Thus says the Lord, *ha-ratzachta ve'gam yarashta?!"*—"Have you murdered and also inherited?" It is morally indefensible to allow the criminal to enjoy the fruits of his crime at the expense of his victims. Elijah was not concerned with the possible criticism that a man of God should not stoop to attend to mere pecuniary matters, that a prophet should be involved only in not-for-profit issues. Money and property are an area where humans can act either justly or unjustly and it is the responsibility of men and women of rectitude and probity to support justice and condemn injustice. And to refrain from protesting is itself perfidious.[1]

This prophetic challenge is not only an expression of an intuitive sense of right and wrong, but receives formal expression as law. Thus, the Torah teaches that if one stole he must return the object to its rightful owner: "He shall restore that which he took by robbery" (Leviticus 5:21–23). The halakha is succinctly summarized by Maimonides: the thief is required to return the very item he stole; even if he had built a stolen beam into an entire building, he must destroy the building in order to return the beam. However, to make it possible for repentant thieves to make restitution without being subject to inordinate and unsustainable expenses and thus discouraged from compensating their victims, the Sages of the Talmud ordained a "decree for the penitent" allowing the thief to return only the *value* of the asset, such value determined as of the time of the crime.[2]

The application to our case is self-evident. Countries which officially and actively collaborated with the Nazis have no right to inherit the estates of the Jewish victims. Killers are not entitled to keep the property of their victims. To refuse to compensate the victims and their heirs is to compound murder with the vilest form of moral hypocrisy: *"ha-ratzachta ve'gam yarashta?!"* Legally and morally, these countries, from both a biblical and talmudic perspective, must return what was stolen from their hapless victims: "He shall restore that which he took by robbery."

It would be a mistake, however, to limit this culpability to governments which officially endorsed anti-Semitic depredations. Even those states which passively condoned the murder of Jews, which did not protest the murder and despoliation of millions of Jews, are guilty of transgressing the biblical admonition of, "Thou shalt not stand by idly while the blood of your brother is being spilled" (Lev. 19:16). Nations as well as individuals are enjoined to defend the defenseless, to succor the victims, to prevent bloodshed—certainly within their own borders.

The Halakha declares it mandatory—a *mitzva*—to prevent the pursuer (*rodef*) from achieving his nefarious goals. The bystander who fails to lift a finger to save the intended victim from the pursuer may not be formally penalized because the violation of a commandment which does not entail a positive act is not subject to judicial punishment.[3] But, as Maimonides rules, "Even though there is no flogging ordained for the transgression of such commandments, because they do not entail action, they are very serious infractions, because he who destroys but one soul . . . it is as if he had destroyed the entire world."[4] The absence of formal punishment does not imply the absence of culpability and calumny. The bystander who turned a blind eye and deaf ear to the cry of the innocent victim is a rogue, a moral leper. Most certainly he—or it, the state—cannot escape the burden of opprobrium. Cold-hearted officials, diplomats, politicians stood by and watched while our Jewish world was destroyed in Europe. Elijah would proclaim with equal eloquence, in such a case, *"Have you condoned murder and also inherited?"* It is a second degree case of what might be called, "aggravated Ahabism."

Finally, there is a third category of states that have come into possession of Jewish property even though no crimes were committed within their own borders. This includes neutral countries as well as those Allies of World War II that never succumbed to Nazism—indeed, opposed it—and that, like the United States or Great Britain, had no history of Quislings or Petains attaining formal political power. There is no fundamental blot on their records, at least insofar as our theme is concerned. Yet confiscated Jewish property—gold, diamonds, real estate, art—has somehow found its way into their treasuries. Having committed no crime, the Elijah charge is not relevant to them. Nevertheless, they are receivers of stolen goods, and the talmudic tradition considers this a serious infraction. If the owner has not despaired of retrieving his property, biblical law requires the purchaser to return the object to him without compensation, and it is up to the purchaser to sue the thief to recover his loss. However, the Sages enacted a special decree (*takkanat ha-shuk*, an "open market rule") to protect the new owner who acquired the stolen object in good faith, lest all commerce be inhibited by fear that one is innocently acquiring stolen goods.[5] This Rabbinic decree protects the innocent receiver of the stolen items by having the goods returned to the owner, and it is the owner who must then go to the trouble of instituting a suit against the thief. But this relief is not available, according to many authorities, in the case of a "notorious" thief, for then the presumption is that the buyer should have suspected the seller to have stolen the item.[6]

WE NOW TURN to the next serious question: *the proper distribution of whatever funds are made available to Jews for plundered property.*

In Jewish law, if the victims or their immediate heirs can identify their property, there is no question that it is they to whom the stolen property or its value must be returned. The principle is evident throughout the halakhic literature,[7] and every effort must be made to locate the owners.[8] Hence, such assets as art, businesses, homes, other real estate, etc., must be returned to the rightful owners or, if that would cause significant financial or social displacement, their value must be returned. But what if there is no reasonable likelihood that relatives can be identified—such as in our case where one third of our people was exterminated and it is now half a century after the Holocaust?

Here we come to an important distinction in the sources. Thus, the following statement by the Tosefta, one of the most significant legal treatises of the early years of the Common Era:

> One who steals from the public must return it to the public. Stealing from the many is more grave than stealing from an individual, for if one steals from an individual he has the opportunity to propitiate him and return the stolen item, but one who steals from the many cannot propitiate his victims and return to them what he has taken from them.[9]

The Babylonian Talmud[10] cites this source and then amplifies the principle and teaches that those who habitually steal from the general public (such as in the case of shepherds who are wont to graze their sheep in fields that belong to others, tax collectors, and revenue farmers) should restore the stolen articles to the victims if they recognize them, but if they do not—such as when public property is stolen or the victims are a large number of people—they should offer the money for *tzorkhei rabbim,* public utilities. This is defined by R. Chisda as "wells, ditches, and caves." This ruling, incorporated in the standard Code of Jewish Law,[11] is based on the notion that at least some of the anonymous victims will probably benefit from their loss as members of the larger public.[12]

Whether this principle of returning such property for use by the public is law (*dinei adam*) and hence actionable in a court of law, or morality (*dinei shamayim*), is explored by a contemporary halakhic scholar.[13] For us, it makes little difference, for there is no question of summoning independent nations to appear before a *Bet Din* sitting in Israel or France or the United States. We are armed only with the force of morality and conscience—and leave the final resolution to the Almighty: the "laws of Heaven."

In principle, then, the countries that plundered Jewish property, whose owners were, for the most part, murdered, are morally bound to make restitution to the victims or their heirs, if such can be found, or to "the community" for *tzorkhei rabbim,* the use of the public. This latter term, as we have seen, is seemingly narrowly defined as "wells, ditches, and caves," in the expectation that the victims or their heirs will benefit from such public works as part of the community.

We are then presented with two problems: first, what if there is very little likelihood that the victims or their families are present in the countries or communities in which the crimes were committed; and second, must the restitution be limited to public works such as wells, ditches, and caves?

There are commonsensical answers to both questions in halakhic literature. R. Abraham Isaac Kook, the first Chief Rabbi of what was then Palestine, discusses the first question in one of his halakhic works.[14] The public utilities which are to be the beneficiaries of the returned objects which were plundered must be located in an area where it is likely that the victims or their heirs will be in a position to benefit from them. Hence, if the Jews of the area are scattered and very few of the inhabitants remain in the original sites, the payment must be directed to those areas in which most or many of the surviving victims have repaired after the crimes were committed.

More serious and urgent is the following dilemma: what of the millions of victims who were wiped out with no heirs or family? True, the Talmud maintains that *every* Jew has relatives.[15] When the Torah (Numbers 5:8) speaks on the return of wrongfully obtained property to one who is deceased "and had no kinsman," the Talmud asks, in a tone of surprise, *"Is there, then, a Jew who has no kinsman?"* The Talmud is so emphatic that it goes on to identify the heir-less Israelite in the biblical passage as a proselyte who dies; such a one is regarded as without relatives because the previous biological relations are no longer valid, given the proposition that "a proselyte is like a newborn child."[16] But otherwise every Jew is considered as having left heirs, even if it means tracing him back to the patriarch Jacob as the common ancestor.[17]

This talmudic teaching presents us with a baffling problem. If we are to assert that every Jew must be considered to have left a relative, no matter how distant, then what of the Holocaust where entire communities—one third of our people—were wiped off the face of the planet?

Our case is so rare, so unimaginable to previous generations for whom the principle of the ubiquity of Jewish kinsmen was self-evident, that we are indeed in a position to say that in our days, tragically, history has confounded the assumption of the Talmud: vast numbers of Jews did indeed die without heirs. Or, we may put it in another way: accepting the talmudic principle as valid even for such incredible circumstances, the result is that *all* Jews, wherever they were during World War II and wherever they reside now, must be considered relatives. We are all of us survivors or relatives of survivors. If indeed all Jews can be traced to common ancestors, and are therefore related to each other, the practical effect of the remoteness of such relationships is that the claims for restitution must be made on behalf of the Jewish people as a whole. We are all *mishpacha.* It is the Jewish *people,* not individual Jewish *persons,* who have the major claim on the property taken from the Holocaust victims.

The survivors and their families have just claims to receive compensation for what was violently taken from *them.* But they have no greater claim on the property of the millions of martyrs who left no identifiable heirs. The people as such do have such creditable claim.

The second question as to the nature of the public utilities—the *tzorkhei rabbim*—is resolved in favor of a broader definition. The "wells, ditches, and caves" are only *illustrations* of public needs, and are not meant to be confining. R. Isaiah Halevi Horowitz (16th–17th century Prague) maintained that the term comprehends as well such things as donating the funds for purchasing books for a communal library, such as a the synagogue and the like—since they will be used by the public.[18] A great contemporary authority, the late R. Moshe Feinstein, holds that the funds may not be used for ordinary *tzedaka,* such as supporting individuals who are needy—presumably because this does not qualify as *tzorkhei rabbim*—but they may be used for such things as the building and repair of communal baths because they serve the public at large.

For our purpose we must focus on the theft or destruction of public property, namely, communal institutions such and synagogues, kindergartens, schools for older children and adults, Jewish clubs, etc. Certainly, if enough Jews remain in a city where such institutions once flourished, these institutions should be rebuilt with the funds made available by the authorities. But what of the hundreds or thousands of towns and villages which are now all but *Judenrein?* What of the cities where once magnificent structures were erected at enormous cost to the local Jews and philanthropists, and have then been converted into engineering schools or office buildings or governmental institutions—or stables? What of communities now composed largely of Jews who fled from faraway places, where the probability of indirect benefit to the original owners does not apply?

The very vastness of the pillage and the considerable revenue from such restitution—if indeed it ever becomes available—challenges us to exercise our most creative moral imagination.

It is only right that we consider the original, underlying purpose of such public institutions as a guide to the proper disposition of the funds. Almost all of these buildings were dedicated, one way or another, to the perpetuation of Judaism or Jewish life, mostly via education and research. That is exactly what such funds should be used for: the perpetuation of Judaism or Jewish life via Jewish education on all levels from kindergarten to high scholarship, from traditional yeshivot to Yiddishist circles, from Zionist camps to YIVO activities.

We are all in danger of a precipitous and calamitous decline of the number of Jews in the world—especially in the Diaspora but in Israel as well. We are all well acquainted with the sorry statistics. Education is not a guarantee, it is not a nostrum for all ills. But—as Churchill said of democracy, that it is a terrible form of government but the others are far worse—while education alone is inadequate, all the other proposed solutions are infinitely less effective. If we fail to take advantage of these funds for education—to perpetuate the lives of the vanished communities and not only to commemorate their deaths; and to prevent as many young Jews as we can from tumbling into the abyss of demographic implosion and spiritual rootlessness—we will be guilty of a monumental historical error, one which will be beyond the ability of any conferences, studies, or gimmicks to cure. We are honor bound use the funds of these public institutions honorably, aspiring to the same ultimate goals as they once did. We must use them to resurrect and renew Jewish life, to empower Jewish children with knowledge of their past and promise for their future, and make a creative, vibrant, flourishing Jewish community our posthumous gift to our *kedoshim*—a living memorial to their lives and aspirations, not merely commissioning silent sculptures as testaments to their annihilation.

This is not an easy task, because we will be pressured to put the bulk of our recovered resources into memorials of all kinds. Certainly, memorials must be established, and some of those already done are magnificent. But now the times call for living memorials, testaments to life, the lives and loves of the martyrs. For if there will be no Jews, two or three generations from now, to summon the memory of the *kedoshim,* who will remember them? Are we to build only for non-Jews? Are not living, breathing, proud, committed Jews a greater and more enduring memorial to the generations that perished in the Holocaust?

We are now in a position to summarize our findings which, although this study has by no means been exhaustive or comprehensive, should give us an inkling of a Jewish perspective on the question of restitution for the victims of the Holocaust.

1. It is morally repugnant to have been complicit to murder—whether directly or indirectly—and to retain the ill begotten gains. To hold on to such fruits of crime is morally outrageous. For good moral reasons, we should not be shy about pressing such claims.

2. Jewish law requires stolen goods to be returned to their lawful owners. The victims must be compensated. This holds true for countries that actively suppressed Jewish life, those that condoned the oppression, and even the nations that neither supported nor condoned violence against our people, but still came into possession of objects stolen from us. They are all honor bound to make restitution.

3. The victims or their heirs—if such are identifiable—have first claim on the returned goods or their value, provided it was their personal property that was plundered.

4. Where such identification is impossible, the restitution must be made to *Kelal Yisrael,* to the Jewish "public" or community. Because the Holocaust caused massive displacement of the survivors, hardly any Jewish community can lay claim to special treatment. East Europeans have relocated to other countries in Eastern Europe—as well as to Western Europe, to Israel, to

America, as well to South America and other countries; and the same is true for West European survivors. Because we are operating on the principle that there are victims or their heirs who exist but who cannot be identified, the restitution should be apportioned approximately according to the number of Jews—all of whom are in this sense survivors—in different geographical locations. The rule of thumb should be that restitution follows population. And we must recall that today probably half the Jews of the world are found in Israel.

5. The Jewish people are the beneficiaries of all property not reserved for the survivors and their heirs—in other words, they are the *rabbim,* the "many" or "public" whose *tzorkhim* or "needs" must be supported. The only restriction that I mentioned is that the money should not go for ordinary *tzedaka* or, for that matter, any one class of people or projects in which all other Jews cannot participate. Now, while this ruling is completely consistent with the talmudic example of "wells, ditches, and caves"—items from which all may benefit—we must still ask if providing for ailing or impoverished *survivors* violates this principle, or upholds it.

6. Finally, we treated as a separate matter the question of compensation for Jewish communal institutions that were destroyed. I suggested that the funds be used to perpetuate the very purpose that inspired their founding, especially Jewish schools, as the *real* and most enduring tributes to the martyrs—the development of Jewish minds and hearts and personalities, not just mute monuments. Jewish education—of all kinds and on all levels—is that which can revive and re-empower the engines of Jewish creativity as we enter the seventh decade of the eighth century of the sixth milennium.

What is demanded of us at this critical time is wisdom and courage and mutual respect and the avoidance of bitter polemics. Above all, both history and destiny summon us to exercise our wisdom. For, as Scripture teaches us, "this—the Torah—is (the source of) your wisdom and understanding in the sight of the peoples (of the world) . . . who shall say, 'Surely this great nation is a wise and understanding people' " (Deut. 4:6).

May we prove worthy of that encomium.

Notes

1. Interestingly, not only the concept but even the very phrase—*ha-ratzachta ve'gam yarashta*—is echoed throughout the ages as a categorical rejection of the retention of ill-begotten gains. See *Midrash Pirkei de-Rabbi Eliezer, Horev 21,* which reads back the almost identical dialogue into the biblical narrative of Cain and Abel. And much later, one of the most prolific decisors of the 14th–15th century, Rabbi Simeon ben Tzemach Duran of Majorca and Algiers (1361–1444) invokes the immortal words of Elijah in ruling on behalf of a woman abused by her husband in a divorce case (*Shut Tashbetz, II 8*). This prophetic utterance is suffused with a sense of moral rectitude and revulsion at an obvious injustice. Its power has not diminished with time.

2. Rambam, *Hilkhot Gezela* 1:5, 2:2.

3. Rambam, *Hil. Rotzeiach* 1:15.

4. Op. Cit., 1:16.

5. *Bava Kamma* 115a.

6. On this subject in general, see Rema to *Shulchan Arukh Chosen Mishpat 356, 360, et passim,* and *Arokh ha-Shulchan* ad loc.

7. Meiri, *Chibbur ha-Teshuva* 1:11; *Shulchan Arukh ha-Rav, Choshen Mishpat,* 366:2.

8. *Shut Radvaz* III 504.

9. Tosefta (ed. Lieberman) *Bava Kamma* chapter 10.

10. *Bava Kamma* 94b.

11. *Shulchan Arukh Choshen Mishpat,* 366:2.

12. See *Arokh ha-Shulchan,* ibid.

13. R. Yaakov Yeshaya Blau, *Pit'chei Choshen,* 4:18, n.3.

14. *Shut Orach Mishpat, Choshen Mishpat* 18.

15. *Sanhedrin* 68b.

16. *Yevamot* 48b.

17. Rashi to *Bava Kamma* 109a, s.v. *ve'khi yesh.*

18. As cited in R. Israel Meir Kagan's *Ahavat Chessed.*

EPILOGUE: PAST, PRESENT, AND FUTURE

I conclude this work with a (partially truncated) talk I gave to the annual dinner of RIETS (Rabbi Isaac Elchanan Theological Seminary) on June 11, 2001 in honor of my imminent retirement as President and Rosh HaYeshiva.

~ 60 ~

PAST, PRESENT, AND FUTURE

My remarks will concern the past, the present, and the future. Let me begin with the past.

I conclude this year not only 25 years as president of YU-RIETS, but also 50 years of *avodat ha-kodesh,* of sacred service to the Jewish community, especially the Torah community. The first quarter century I spent in the rabbinate, the second in the leadership of Yeshiva.

Because I believe that to live is to learn, and that when you stop learning you have effectively stopped living, I wish to summarize for myself certain lessons that I learned from my combined experiences. Perhaps they may prove of relevance to others, even if they sound banal and ordinary. Even cliches may contain kernels of truth. So I share with you some hard-earned lessons of these past 50 years.

I learned that all idols have clay feet, and that every human being, no matter how low on the ladder of success, possesses sparks of greatness; that some of the mightiest have fatal weaknesses, and the weakest hidden sources of surprising strength; that almost every closet contains a skeleton, and even the hardest of hearts a grain of goodness, a molecule of compassion; that the smart are not always wise, and the wise not always smart; that no one knows everything, but everyone knows something worth knowing; that the rich are often vulnerable, and the poor often resolute; that the pious can be tempted, and the sinners tempered. I learned of the secret follies of the sophisticated, and the flashes of insight of ordinary folk.

What did all this knowledge bring me? It taught me that I must judge people with understanding and compassion; that foolishness and weakness and ignorance and spite and envy are, at bottom, part of our human endowment, and that we must all struggle to restrain them; that some are more successful in this encounter than others, but no one ever achieves complete and permanent victory, for the battle goes on endlessly in the soul of man. And also that every human being has the capacity for decency and goodness and compassion and friendship and love. Therefore, I must be tolerant and respectful and civil—even towards those with whom I profoundly disagree. In a word, I had to relearn what I learned but did not understand in my youth, namely, that "The Torah's ways are the ways of pleasantness and its paths are the paths of peace." And so must be our ways and paths.

In my work for Yeshiva, I benefited greatly from the decency and generosity of spirit of countless individuals. I also suffered public insults, unfair and derogatory criticism—on behalf of you, the schools and community I love and champion—from Right and from Left. (I consider myself an equal opportunity target!) Because of the virtue of moderation and tolerance—"the ways of pleasantness"—that I learned these 50 years, I am moved to forgive those who would never forgive me. I would suffer the slings and arrows again gladly on behalf of this cause and my people, ready to be *mekabbel yisurim be'ahavah*—to embrace suffering with love—because one never tires of defending his or her home—*be'ahavah*, with love.

I TURN NOW to the present. I cannot impress upon you the importance of what RIETS is doing. Even if you think you know—even if I think *I* know—we do not know enough, and we should know more.

Let me share with you a few reports by outside observers. The first comes from a letter from an alumnus, a distinguished lawyer in Jerusalem:

> A coworker of mine happened to be speaking with Rav___, the rosh yeshiva of [a yeshiva beyond the Green Line], who told him: "Whenever I travel on an airplane and I see someone carrying a briefcase with a laptop computer and a *Gemara*, I know this is a YU graduate." Rav___ said he watches these men with envy: they spend part of the trip working on computers, part of the trip reading business reports, and part of the trip learning *Gemara*. Rav___ said he was envious that neither his yeshiva nor any other yeshiva in Israel can produce this type of individual.

The second testimony is something I received in the mail last week: a handwritten letter on two scraps of paper by a rabbi (whom I do not know) who had just returned from a lengthy stay at Methodist Hospital in New York, where he was attended by physicians with YU backgrounds. He was astounded by their human touch and sensitivity—and professional competence—as well as by the readiness of these physicians and other YU alumni on staff to engage him in *divrei Torah*. He concludes his brief note as follows: "Thanks to YU, Methodist Hospital is 3/4 of a *Beis Medrash* . . ."

The final item comes from a series of articles in the *London Daily Telegraph*, April 10, 2001. The writer is a highly intelligent and well read non-Jewish journalist who was intrigued by the Jews and was searching for their "secret." He visited with us a few months ago. He writes:

> Nobody will ever begin to understand the Jews until they have visited a yeshiva—a school for the study of the Talmud—and seen hundreds of young men engaged in a passionate discussion of its text.
>
> It was nine in the evening when I arrived at the Yeshiva University in New York. A buzz of furious sound was coming from one of its libraries. Here, in a largish room, were 400 young men, sitting in pairs across desks rather like chess players and surrounded by piles of hefty tomes, arguing heatedly. It could scarely have been more different from the obligatory silence of the Bodleian. They were all studying the Talmud, line by line, and this was no exercise in dry scholarship. As I soon realized, I was in the presence of the fissile core of Judaism . . .
>
> I have never, in any university or school, seen such intellectual intensity, such absorption, such total fascination. All these young men were in that library entirely voluntarily. They gained no extra credits for being there. All of them had already done either a full day of study or endured a long and bruising session on Wall Street. One of the people I talked to was a merchant banker, another a derivatives trader at Goldman Sachs.

So cherish this great, historic institution. You will need it for your children and grandchildren. There's nothing quite like it anyplace else in the world. Give it your love. Give it your support. It is worthy of your best efforts.

Let me now turn to the future.

WE MUST resolutely reaffirm the mutually beneficial relationship between the University and RIETS. Legally, the two schools are separate corporate bodies, and so they are indeed. Nevertheless, the spiritual bond between them continues as it should. We often say that "RIETS is the heart of Yeshiva." It deserves reiteration. The heart is an organ that can be detached from the body; it can survive an operation whereby the heart is treated outside the body. But who wants to spend the rest of his mortal existence in such a precarious and unnatural state? So we must make every effort to enhance good relationships. The heart must always be integrated with the body.

Yeshiva and RIETS will soon be choosing the future leadership of our combined institution. I have been, and will be, addressing the appropriate official bodies on this matter in detail. But I feel it is important for me to say this now, in public, to the Yeshiva family at large.

When Moses prepared to step down from his leadership role, he prayed, "Let the Lord, the God of the spirits of all flesh, appoint a man over the community." Moses wanted to be succeeded by someone very much like himself, "a man for all seasons," one blessed with diverse talents—*ha-ruchot,* "spirits," in the plural. God's answer was clear: "Take Joshua the son of Nun, a man who possesses *ruach*"—"spirit," in the singular. It is not necessary for a leader to have all "spirits," all talents, all powers and potencies. It is enough if he has *ruach,* spirit—courage, passion, inspiration, resolve, determination. Not everyone can or need be a Moses. And note: neither Moses nor God asks for more than one person to fill Moses' enormous shoes. There is no talk of a division of labor, one to serve as general and the other as *rosh yeshiva.* Each considered only one person—*ish.* And *ruach,* spirit, "fire in the belly," is a more important token of future success as a leader than *ruchot,* a bundle of talents full blown.

I firmly believe that one person should serve in both presidencies. The single presidency will guarantee the smooth functioning of the entire institution. You cannot separate Yeshiva from University without injuring Yeshiva University. Divide them, and you will have institutionalized a fundamental division between RIETS and YU and, even more significantly, between Torah and Madda. Yeshiva will not be able to overcome this schizoid existence and still remain true to its sacred mission.

Moreover, a single presidency is a *symbol* of the ultimate synergy between Torah and Madda. Let me offer an example from my own experience. At the beginning of my tenure as president, some 23 or 24 years ago in the midst of our financial crisis, I was told that the beautiful dome of our Main Building, now known as David H. Zysman Hall, was leaking and in danger of collapse. It could be repaired, but the cost would be prohibitive. I was advised: it is more prudent to get rid of the dome altogether. It was altogether logical: the repair costs far more than we can afford, hence it is best to be done with it and remove it. Yet I resisted because this building is not only a landmark—it is vital to the mental image of Yeshiva, and the dome is more than a logo; it is its crown, the symbol of our home. Without it, our symbol fails; our reputation, like our edifice, is decapitated.

If that is true for a mute piece of architecture, how much more so for the living leadership of this, our great home. The president, as a symbol, should be a PhD and a *lamdan*. He should have an advanced academic degree and be a rav, even though not necessarily a pulpit Rabbi. You are probably aware that NYU recently elected Dr. John Sexton as its new president. Wouldn't it be nice if we upstaged NYU by having as our president not a *sexton* but a *rabbi?* . . .

Finally, let me leave you with a plea to preserve our unique vision.

Orthodoxy today is divided roughly into two camps. We need and must cherish both, for who can tell which will better survive and thrive in the long trajectory of history? Therefore we must respect and cooperate with each other. Never must we look down upon our *haredi* brethren. They have amongst them people of exemplary devotion and sacrifice, of great scholarship, of humane outlook and love of Torah. Whether or not they reciprocate, we must value them—at the same time that we disagree. The *haredim* are more inwardly inclined, they reject advanced secular studies except for vocational (*parnasah*) reasons, they are skeptical of the State of Israel although devoted to Eretz Israel, etc. Our vision, rooted in Torah, is different, although what we share in common is far greater than the differences between us. That vision includes: Torah Umadda, maximum openness towards all Jews within the confines of Halakhah, a positive attitude towards the State of Israel, and universal concerns. At root, the differences are as much psychological as philosophical.

We read this coming Shabbat of the 12 princes whom Moses sent to spy out the Land of Canaan—the land they were preparing to conquer and settle. Moses' instructions to them were, "See what kind of country it is. Are the people strong or weak, few or many? . . . Are the towns they live in open or fortified?" And so on. The spies returned with two reports. The majority of 10 was discouraging: it is rich country, fertile, flowing with milk and honey, but the giants who populate the land dwell "in very strong fortresses." Caleb and Joshua came back with far more encouragement. "We can rise up against them, possess the land, and we shall overcome them." The rebuttal of the majority was firm: "we cannot rise up," they are too strong. The conflict was joined, the people sided with the majority, and the result was utter chaos, disaster. The refusal of the people to trust the Almighty turned the entire incident into an historic tragedy.

But there are some troubling questions in this account. For one, weren't the 10 telling the truth as they saw it? Isn't that what they were commissioned to do? And second, what lay at the root of the disagreement—was it mere opinion about strategy, or was something more involved?

I believe that there were serious and fundamental differences in approach and in interpretation. And it revolved around the understanding of what Moses meant when he said "if the cities are open or fortified." The majority considered that open cities were conquerable, but fortresses were not. But that was not what Moses meant! As Rashi, quoting the Midrash, explains: "Moses gave them a sign—if they live in open cities, they are powerful, for they are confident of their strength; but if they live in fortresses, they are weak."

We at YU and RIETS hold that openness is a sign of courage and confidence, and that a fortress psychology issues from fear and frailty. I have no complaints against those who prefer the protection of fortresses. And I have no sympathy for those who would leave us totally exposed and defenseless against the onslaught of a materialistic and hedonistic society. But we feel confident and, despite the risks—and who has no risks?—we will prevail and help keep Torah and the Torah tradition alive without artificial walls. Our Yeshiva has pioneered an educational system founded on confidence and strength, one that does not rely on ghetto walls—coerced or voluntary—to sustain us. We can meet modernity head on, critically but openly, and "we shall prevail."

I plead with you: do not be discouraged by the gloomy prognosticators, even those within our own ranks, who tell us that our cause is doomed. Do not be demoralized by hand-wringing peddlers of pessimism. If others tell us that "we cannot go up [to the land] for they are stronger than us, let us respond, "we can rise up against them and we shall overcome them." We are sufficiently bold and self-assured to say that we stand for Torah Umadda not only for vocational purposes but for an engagement with the powerful culture of our times on its highest levels—scientific, humanistic, sociological, literary. When our great and revered teacher, the Rav, went to study at the University of Berlin at the behest of his parents, he did so not for *parnasah,* to study accounting or marketing or even medicine or law—and certainly not to dodge the Russian draft. He went to encounter Kant and Cohen and Einstein. We intend to learn from him. We are no less human for our devotion to Torah; and we are no less Jewish for our commitment to worldly wisdom. That is what we are all about. Be proud of it, encourage it, publicize it, love it. We shall overcome all obstacles—and prevail.

I CAME HERE as a student 56 years ago, and I have been president and *Rosh ha-Yeshiva* of RIETS for 25 years. Now, as I near my own change of status, I offer a *mizmor le'todah,* a psalm of thanksgiving, to all those who made my life fuller—if not always easier—but richer, more meaningful, more helpful, more focused, more rewarding.

I learned much from my colleagues, the *roshei yeshiva,* whose commitment and erudition never fail to astound me; and "from my students above all." Many of them are stars; all of them are serious and committed. They are magnificent, the very promise of our future. I have confidence in them; they will rise up, and they and our alumni will help usher in a renaissance of Jewish life and learning in their generation.

I thank you, our Board members and supporters, for the unstinting generosity which made it possible for RIETS to become the powerful and enlightened center of *harbatzat ha-torah* that it is for well over a century.

I thank my colleagues in administration—vice presidents, deans, directors, staff, all—for their professional competence, for their sacrifice of time and peace of mind, for their personal loyalty and genuine friendship. I thank you for doing what is often a thankless job.

All of you, and many others who are not here, have given me the opportunity to serve the Almighty and *am Yisrael* in ways and to an extent I never imagined in my youth. You have allowed me to dedicate whatever meager talents I possess to the noblest of all causes: the advancement of Torah, without which our people have no future. And without Jews, the world would be a grim place indeed—more dangerous and less interesting.

Above all, I am deeply indebted to my beloved family—my four children, who together have attended eight of our schools; my four children-in-law, who likewise have attended eight of our schools, from high school through *semikhah*; my brother, Rabbi Maurice Lamm—a *musmakh* and Yeshiva College alumnus, and my two sisters—one here, one in Israel—who went through two of our schools; and my grandchildren, one now in Stern College, one coming into MSTA, and one slated for Stern College this coming semester. They are dearer to me than life itself. So my family has benefited enormously from Yeshiva, and Yeshiva from them. I am proud of them, more than they may be of me.

The purpose of RIETS is to increase the sacred knowledge of Torah, and the purpose of the University is likewise to increase knowledge—of all things, all branches of wisdom. The Sages taught us that knowledge is not an end in itself: "The purpose of wisdom is repentance and good deeds" (*Ber.* 17). To put it another way, wisdom—of Torah or other disciplines—must lead to noble character.

So I conclude with a brief description of the Jewish ideal of character. A *baal middot,* a person of character, is essentially one who is modest and retiring without false humility; one who aspires to enlightment without seeking the limelight; one who loves and pursues peace, thus never fomenting dissension unnecessarily, never speaking ill of others; one who is utterly loyal, a true friend, whose character is elegant and charming; and, above all, who—as Ramban expands upon the commandment to love one's neighbor as one's self—

> One must love one's fellow in all matters as he loves himself, [desiring] all good things [for him], loving him in all matters, desiring to obtain for his beloved friend wealth and goods and glory and knowledge and wisdom—and not only that his friend be equal to him, but always wishing in his heart that the friend exceed him in all good things.

I have had and do have the exquisite blessing of learning from such a friend, benefiting from her for over 47 years in love and devotion—the wonderful, gracious, giving mother of my children and the grandmother of our fabulous grandchildren. As the great R. Akiva said of his wife in talking to his students, "*Sheli ve'shelakhem shelah hu*—both what I have [achieved] and what you have [achieved] is thanks to her."

And I thank all of you. May the Master of the Universe grant you and your families many happy years of health and vigor, love of God, of Torah, of Israel, and of all humans; and may the final redemption arrive "during your lifetime and during your days, and during the lifetime of all the House of Israel, speedily and soon."